SPAIN UNMOORED

NEW ANTHROPOLOGIES OF EUROPE
*Michael Herzfeld, Melissa L. Caldwell, and
Deborah Reed-Danahay, editors*

PUBLIC CULTURES OF THE MIDDLE EAST AND NORTH AFRICA
*Paul A. Silverstein, Susan Slyomovics, and
Ted Swedenburg, editors*

SPAIN UNMOORED

Migration, Conversion, and the *Politics of Islam*

MIKAELA H. ROGOZEN-SOLTAR

INDIANA UNIVERSITY PRESS

Bloomington & Indianapolis

This book is a publication of

Indiana University Press
Office of Scholarly Publishing
Herman B Wells Library 350
1320 East 10th Street
Bloomington, Indiana 47405 USA

iupress.indiana.edu

Manufactured in the United States of
America

Cataloging information is available from
the Library of Congress.

ISBN 978-0-253-02474-9 (cloth)
ISBN 978-0-253-02489-3 (paperback)
ISBN 978-0-253-02506-7 (ebook)

1 2 3 4 5 22 21 20 19 18 17

For Arthur, Isabel, Manny, and Frances;
the last of whom earned a PhD in her sixties,
decades after being told that women did not do such things,
and whose memory inspired me as I trudged through the snow
in Ann Arbor and the sunshine in Spain.

CONTENTS

ACKNOWLEDGMENTS

WRITING a book takes a long time. I began thinking about Islam and migration in Spain as an undergraduate and finished this project as a faculty member. Many generous people helped me along the way.

Thanks cannot express my debt to the people who opened their homes and lives to me in Granada. I was humbled to share in the joyous and painful, benevolent and disagreeable, strong and vulnerable sides of their lives. While they are named pseudonymously here, I hope they will see their experiences and beliefs represented. They made this book.

At Indiana University Press, I am grateful to Rebecca Tolen for bringing this project on board, and to Gary Dunham and Janice Frisch for guidance through the later stages of publication. Thanks to Michael Herzfeld, Melissa L. Caldwell, and Deborah Reed-Danahay, and to Paul Silverstein, Susan Slyomovics, and Ted Swedenburg for including my book in the New Anthropologies of Europe series and the Public Cultures of the Middle East and North Africa series, respectively.

Research is expensive and cumbersome, and I thank the institutions that made this project financially and logistically possible: the National Science Foundation Graduate Research Fellowship Program; the U.S. Department of Education FLAS Fellowship program; the Department of Anthropology, the Rackham Graduate School, and the Center for Middle Eastern and North African Studies at the University of Michigan; the Council on Middle East Studies and the Department of Anthropology at Yale University; the Fox Center for Humanistic Inquiry at Emory

University; the *Universidad Autónoma de Madrid*; and the *Universidad de Granada*. In Spain, I am especially grateful to Margit Sperling and Liliana Suárez for their good humor and hospitality.

A long time ago, Arjun Guneratne inspired me to become an anthropology major, and Dianna Shandy suggested one day that I ditch my law school plans for something that had never crossed my mind: a PhD. Thank you! At the University of Michigan, I was buoyed by the unwavering support of committee members who believed in my project, and whose astute suggestions made it infinitely better. Deepest thanks to Andrew Shryock, Marcia Inhorn, Miriam Ticktin, Alaina Lemon, and Hussein Fancy for your wisdom, guidance, and enthusiasm in grad school and beyond.

Communities of friends and intellectual co-conspirators have made researching and writing this book more of a joy and less of a slog. Thanks to Kelly Fayard, Matt Kroot, Robin Nelson, Lauryn Parks, Drew Rodríguez, and Jessica Smith in Ann Arbor; to Andrew Braver, Rose Keimig, D'arcy Saum, Bonnie Rose Schulman, and Amy Zhang in New Haven; and to Steve Black in Decatur. The Anthropology Department at the University of Nevada Reno has been a wonderful place to land, and I am grateful to my supportive colleagues there, especially Debbie Boehm, Sarah Cowie, Jenanne Ferguson, Geoff Smith, Erin Stiles, and Carolyn White, as well as colleagues at the Gender, Race, and Identity Program. Writing "Meet-and-Scolds" over coffee with Meredith Oda helped me get this book out the door, and with more coffee than scolding.

No writer can succeed without a cadre of willing readers. Naor Ben-Yehoyada, Lizzy Falconi, Katherine Fusco, Amy Pason, Jessica Robbins-Ruszkowski, and Jim Webber read select chapters and gave excellent feedback. Over the years, John Bowen, Susan Coutin, Katherine Ewing, Mayanthi Fernando, Engseng Ho, Esra Özyürek, and Leti Volpp all provided helpful comments on conference papers and article drafts that turned into book sections. Thanks to Eric Calderwood at the University of Michigan and Maribel Fierro at the *Consejo Superior de Investigaciones Científicas* in Madrid for organizing rich symposia in which I was able to test-drive some ideas for this book. Cheers to Richard Nance for helping me choose a title.

Several brave and patient souls read the entire manuscript. Many thanks to Jonathan Shannon and Paul Silverstein for generous feedback that greatly improved the book. Without the awesome Kathryn Graber and Emily McKee, this book would not exist. Thanks for reading everything from the nascent scraps of ideas to the final chapters with a blend of kindness and fearsome intelligence. Our writing group meetings are always a reminder that I love anthropology, and that writing is even more rewarding when publications are shared victories. Without Emily Wentzell's (often comically musical) encouragement, I would have given up on this project numerous times; without her friendship, graduate school and postdoctoral work would have been far less fun; and without her editorial wisdom and singular ability to make me cut words, this book could easily have run ten thousand pages and made little to no sense.

Finally, Anna Armentrout and Eve Rutzick, thanks for making it seem cool to be smart since we were little kids. Johanna, thanks for always cheerleading me. Mom and Dad, thanks for teaching me to care about the world, for providing a cozy place to write in the woods, and for being unfailingly supportive. This book is for the migrants in my family: Ben and Henna, Barnett and Esther, Pop and Sarah, and Grandma B., who came to America, and whose lives and stories helped inspire my interest in migration and minority religions.

PREFACE

Between Convivencia *and* Malafollá: *Coexistence or Exclusion?*

LIKE many shy anthropologists, the first thing I did when I moved to Granada, Spain, in the summer of 2007 was sign up for refresher language classes despite already speaking Spanish. I found the weekly schedule of classes comforting as I slowly began to enter the world of full-time field-work, researching Islam and migration in the southern Spanish region called Andalusia. Luckily, while I did not initially envision it as research, Spanish class became a valuable field site. Nuria, the instructor of my conversation class, took it upon herself to teach her students not only local colloquialisms and norms of Andalusian language use, but also her take on the "character" of *Granadinos*, the inhabitants of the city. She told endless stories about her family, neighbors, and coworkers, emphasizing what she saw as "typical" or "representative" illustrations of Andalusian regional identity in general, and of *Granadino* culture in particular. She wanted us to learn to speak like Spain's southerners, and to understand them. It was through Nuria's discussions of "Andalusianness" that I first learned about the concept of the *Granadino malafollá* (rudeness, or a rude person who is inhospitable to others, especially to outsiders).

One day, Nuria told the following story. Arriving in class huffing and puffing with annoyance, she declared that she was "over" going to her neighborhood grocery store, and that we would not believe what had just happened there. While in line to pay, Nuria had overheard the woman behind her say to a companion, "Today *la mora* is coming to clean my house." *La mora* (literally, the Moor) referred to the woman's Moroccan or

Muslim housekeeper. It is the feminine version of *moro*, a term often used pejoratively to refer to Muslims, especially Moroccan migrants. Nuria, who prided herself on being stubborn and outspoken, had whirled around to tell the woman that she was offended by her manner of speaking about Muslim migrants. Rather than referring to her housekeeper with the racially charged term "*la mora*," why not use her actual name or job title? Nuria told the woman that she ought to be more respectful. Now in class, she explained that while she could put up with—and even expected—some level of public incivility in Granada, this kind of unapologetic racism was dehumanizing, and beyond the pale. Reiterating her disgust with this woman's failure to respect diversity, she concluded, throwing her hands in the air to signal defeat and incredulity, "I mean, what a *malafollá*!"

One year prior, while conducting preliminary fieldwork, I had already been introduced to questions of multiculturalism in Granada through a different word: *convivencia* (literally, living together). The evening I arrived in town in 2006, I collapsed with exhaustion onto the couch in the apartment I was to share for the summer with a local schoolteacher, a small-business owner, and an Argentinian shop worker. Jet-lagged but excited, I tried to stay awake as they introduced themselves. Before I had a chance to tell them that I was in Granada to study historical memories of Islamic Spain and the contemporary place of Muslims in the city, my new housemates broached my research topic themselves as they began to tell me about Granada. They told me that I would love living there because it was a very international city and always had been. The teacher asked me if I knew much about local history. When I said, "Not enough," he explained that Andalusia was the longest-held region of Islamic Iberia, and that Granada especially had been home to "*convivencia*." *Convivencia* referred to the peaceful, harmonious interaction of "*las tres culturas de Granada*"— "the three cultures of Granada": Muslims, Jews, and Christians—who all lived together and mutually influenced one another, he continued, until the Catholic Kings completed the "reconquest" of Muslim-ruled Spain and expelled the Jews and Muslims who would not convert, or killed them. The business owner joined in, adding that *convivencia* had left a lasting mark on the south, making it different from the rest of Spain. Granada, she said, was a place of multiculturalism, and even native-born, Catholic Andalusians were "probably a little Jewish," or "potentially Muslim."

Lowering her voice to a titillated whisper and leaning toward me, she confessed proudly, "I'm pretty sure there are Jewish roots in my family." Over the course of my fieldwork, as I met new acquaintances on a daily basis, many people echoed my housemates, insisting that I would love living in Granada because it was a city formed by the interaction of "the three cultures" and was imbued with a certain exotic magic as a result of this historical *convivencia*.

What exactly do *convivencia* and *malafollá* mean in Granada? These are slippery terms *Granadinos* use frequently both to describe themselves and to reference their reputation within Spain and the world at large. Each indexes ideas about Granada's Muslim history, about the city's growing Muslim minority of migrants and converts to Islam, and about broader regional connections to Europe and North Africa. Both are ambivalent terms that people use angrily, affectionately, proudly, and sheepishly. My goal here is not to weigh in on the vexed historiography of *convivencia* or the precise linguistic heritage of the word *malafollá*. Instead, I want to productively juxtapose *convivencia* with *malafollá* in my *Granadino* research participants' discussions of multiculturalism and city identity to shed light on contemporary debates about religious and cultural pluralism in a city undergoing rapid change. The arrival of southern Spain's growing Muslim minority has coincided with the country's relatively recent transition to democracy after nearly four decades of dictatorship. This has pushed the question of multiculturalism to the center of broader deliberations about the cultivation of democratic politics and citizenship in Spain.

Generally speaking, in Granada *convivencia* refers to the supposedly convivial coexistence of medieval Jews, Muslims, and Christians under Muslim rule in Granada's distant past. But it also appears in residents' claims that the city today is home to harmonious coexistence among diverse residents, ensured by welcoming and civilized attitudes thought to stem from the city's historical experiences with religious and cultural pluralism. Although the idea of medieval *convivencia* is often associated with Spain in general, as residents of the longest-held Muslim kingdom of medieval Spain, *Granadinos* claim ownership over the concept, asserting their city as the birthplace of successful multiculturalism. People use the word to refer specifically to questions of religious and cultural pluralism in the context of migration and conversion to Islam today, as well as to broader discussions of city planning, the challenges of sharing urban space, and the need for Granada to develop a cosmopolitan, sophisticated, and civilized public sphere to consolidate the city's place in democratic Spain and Europe.

Malafollá, in contrast, is usually applied to individuals and groups who are grumpy, unnecessarily rude to the general public, and unhelpful to outsiders. It is a common label for *Granadinos* who engage regularly with the public and have a reputation for being unfriendly in this capacity, such as bus drivers, public employees, and restaurant servers. People also regularly apply it to any *Granadino* who is rude, sarcastic, or flippant to those outside his or her family or social network, especially to outsiders such as migrants and other minorities, but also tourists and study-abroad students. Within Spain, especially the south, *Granadinos* are (in)famous for "their *malafollá*;" the word is best known as part of the longer phrase, pronounced in Andalusian dialect, "*la malafollá de Graná*" (Granada's *malafollá*), which links the very definition of *malafollá* to Granada itself, inscribing rudeness and inhospitality in the essence of the city. The etymology of the term is a local source of crude humor because it sounds like a combination of *mala* (bad) and *follá*, which may come from the verb *follar* (to fuck). Though this is questionable, most people I have spoken with about the term assume it means both to be a participant in and the result of bad sex. Some, especially the young, take this at face value and find it hilarious, while others see in this etymology a broader condemnation of *Granadinos* as products of unfortunate sexual unions, presumably among the city's multicultural and multireligious ancestors.

Convivencia and *malafollá* structure ambivalent and anxiety-ridden discussions about how best to move forward with managing an increasingly plural urban society in Granada. For many people, the city's future seems to lie in finding the best way to cultivate a relationship with its diverse past. The search for Muslim and migrant space in the city is shaped by *Granadinos*' discourses of *convivencia* and *malafollá*, which are each in turn informed by Granada's long history of entanglement with Islam, religious conversion, and trans-Mediterranean population mobility. My research participants' persistent use of these terms to describe the city's residents, its ethos, and its reputation reveals their understandings of Granada as a Mediterranean zone of encounter. The conflicting meanings of *convivencia* and *malafollá*, one asserting an innate openness, the other insisting on a characteristic inhospitality, point to the constant interaction of inclusion and exclusion of Islam in Granada. These terms also hint at the linkages of local ambivalence about Islam to multiple scales of belonging that span the city itself, the region of Andalusia, the Spanish state, and the porous but increasingly policed borders between North Africa and Mediterranean Europe.

The words *convivencia* and *malafollá* popped up constantly in conversation, as common ways to refer to the city's history, its people, and a variety of kinds of social situations. At first I saw their ubiquity as an entertaining quirk, but I soon learned to take their prevalence seriously. I realized that by using *convivencia* and *malafollá* as shorthand for their own behavior and for the city itself, *Granadinos* were defining their city in terms of how its residents related to outsiders and more generally managed social difference. If *convivencia* casts contemporary Granada as a site of successful multiculturalism rooted in a history of peaceful pluralism, *malafollá* offers a competing vision of Granada as an exclusionary, inhospitable society resulting from a history of unholy unions and cross-cultural interactions gone awry. Why, I often wondered, would a city define its ethos and character so specifically in terms of its engagement with cultural and religious diversity, and why in such contrasting ways? This book is an attempt to answer that question.

SPAIN UNMOORED

Introduction

---------- ❖ ----------

ANDALUSIAN ENCOUNTERS
AND THE POLITICS OF ISLAM

THE FIGHT

"This part of Granada feels like home, like Morocco," said Mairame, a Moroccan migrant to Spain. We were drinking tea together on the patio of a teahouse in the Andalusian city of Granada. Our table faced a large public square in the *Albayzín*, the city's medieval, Moorish quarter, which dates back to Spain's eight-hundred-year Muslim period (711–1492). Today, the *Albayzín* is home to a "little Morocco" of sorts. Moroccan-themed, tourist-oriented shops selling falafel, belly dancing outfits, Moroccan tea, and goatskin lamps line the neighborhood's narrow streets, which curve uphill toward the Sierra Nevada mountain range and the famous Alhambra, a Moorish-built palace that looms over the city. Tucked in among the *Albayzín*'s souvenir shops, many owned by Spanish and European converts to Islam and run by Moroccan and Middle Eastern migrant employees, are a few establishments oriented less toward tourists and more toward the growing Muslim population in the area. There is a halal butcher shop, a calling center where migrants can phone family abroad, and a modest mosque located in a semirestored building with a Moorish façade. Mairame told me that the *Albayzín* made her feel comfortable in Spain because of its familiar, Moroccan-style architecture and its vibrant Muslim community. Watching global tourists perusing the shops, we overheard a man comment excitedly in American English to his female companion, "It's like we're really in Morocco. Like we're actually in an *Arab country*, except we're in Spain!"

A sudden crash distracted us, as five men, yelling and throwing punches, tumbled out the front door of a nearby Moroccan restaurant, knocking over a table and the restaurant's menu board. Tourists, diners, and shop workers gasped collectively at what appeared to be a brawl unfolding between two Moroccan waiters and three Spaniards. "You stupid Moors! Get out of here! This isn't your country! Go home!" one of the Spaniards cried out in an accent that immediately identified him as a local Andalusian. "Whatever, I speak better Spanish than *you* do," one of the Moroccans retorted, mocking his opponent's stigmatized Andalusian accent.

For the next five or ten minutes, the fighting escalated as Mairame and I sat staring in shock. The group of Spanish young men grew, and migrant Muslim shop workers poured out of their stores to intervene. Eventually, a police car arrived. Several officers broke up the fight and separated the brawling parties and their onlookers. Most of the bystanders were young Moroccan men, along with several men from Syria and Pakistan; the few Moroccan women who worked in falafel shops and teahouses remained inside. Though I knew many European convert Muslims who lived and worked nearby, I did not see any at the scene, which instead pitted migrant Muslims against presumably non-Muslim Andalusians. Each side yelled at the police officers, arguing that the other group had started the conflict. A young Moroccan on the verge of tears pointed accusatorily at the Spaniards. But as he began to yell, a police officer brushed him aside and he tripped backward on the uneven cobblestones, landing on the ground. Some of the other Moroccan men retreated to the back of the crowd and became quiet at the sight of the police. Later I would learn that these men were undocumented migrants, who avoid the police at all costs for fear of deportation or extended incarceration in one of Spain's notorious Temporary Immigrant Residential Centers (*Centros de Estancia Temporal de Inmigrantes* [CETIs]).

Two police officers corralled a spiky-haired Spaniard, dragging him to the opposite corner of the square, where he stood pumping his fist in the direction of the crowd and yelling tirelessly as if on loop, "*Moro! Maricón! Moro! Maricón!*" (Moor! Faggot! Moor! Faggot!) Finally, the police ushered him away down the street, chuckling in a manner more bemused than punitive, and the remaining Spanish contingent followed them. The group of Moroccan and Middle Eastern men went back to the doorways of their respective businesses, where they resumed smiling at tourists and other shoppers, who returned to inspecting imported goatskin lamps and hookah pipes. The whole episode lasted no more than twenty minutes.

How did the *Albayzín* neighborhood transition so quickly that afternoon from a place where Mairame, a Moroccan migrant, felt "at home" in Spain to a site of religious discrimination and ethnoracial violence? Celebration of Islam and racialized religious tensions are intertwined parts of daily social life in Granada, a city where Muslim-themed tourism, Islamic cultural institutions, and locals' conversions to Islam coexist with anti-Muslim graffiti, opposition to mosques, and marginalization of Muslims, especially Moroccan migrants. The incident described here illustrates how anti-Muslim sentiment can erupt into outright physical violence and policing in the city, even in purportedly "safe" places like the *Albayzín*, with its established Muslim community and its public championing of Spain's Muslim past for tourist audiences. This fight was characteristic of Granada's ambivalence about Islam and points toward the central themes of this book: the coexistence of both convert and migrant Muslims in Spain and the differences between them; the tension between Islamophobic antipathy toward Muslims and Islamophilic celebration of Granada's Moorish legacy; and historically rooted anxiety about what Islam in Granada means for the Andalusian region's place at the margins between Europe and North Africa.

This book is an ethnography of social encounters between Muslim migrants, European converts to Islam, and Catholic and secular Spaniards.[1] In the chapters that follow, I trace how residents of Granada differently mobilize historical narratives about Andalusia's Muslim past to navigate renewed ethnic and religious pluralism in the city today. Non-Muslims are highly ambivalent about Granada's Muslim history, both celebrating it as formative to city and regional identities and ruing it as an embarrassing and tragic Muslim occupation. Many Muslims, meanwhile, see their arrival in Granada as a diasporic homecoming, claiming territorial rootedness in the city based on its Moorish past. As a result, Muslims are both included and excluded in social and political life in Granada. But inclusion and exclusion happen in divergent ways for converts and migrants, who are differently incorporated as minority subjects in Spain, resulting in a hierarchical, unequal multiculturalism. I explore the emergence of this unequal multiculturalism in the city of Granada, focusing on its gendered, racial, and political dimensions. In the process, I demonstrate the impact of complex Mediterranean historical entanglements on debates about multiculturalism in southern Europe today. Ultimately, this ethnography reveals how Europe's Muslim past continues to influence its present, questioning common political narratives of Europe's cohesion as a Christian-turned-secular cultural space, as well as equally monolithic, rosy narratives that herald Spanish *convivencia* (interfaith harmony) as the answer to Europe's multicultural challenges.

GRANADA: SPAIN'S "MOST MUSLIM CITY"

Perhaps no other city symbolizes Spain's history of religious pluralism as poignantly as Granada, where historical and contemporary interreligious encounters are marked conspicuously in the city's architectural styles, urban layout, and social interactions. Granada was the longest-held Muslim territory of *al-Andalus* (medieval Muslim Spain), and its urban landscape is shaped by monuments to city, regional, national, and international religious and cultural histories of coexistence and violence. The three main sections of the original city reflect the social borders established in the eighth through the fifteenth centuries. Above the city's main street lies the Moorish-built *Albayzín* hillside quarter and its pinnacle, the Alhambra palace, which draws millions of tourists annually (González Alcantud 2011). Sloping downhill on the other side of the Alhambra is the *Realejo*, medieval Granada's Jewish quarter. Below these hillside neighborhoods lies the historic center of the Catholic city, mostly built since the close of the fifteenth century when Muslim Granada was captured as part of the newly emerging Catholic Spanish nation-state. At the node where these three neighborhoods meet, a small public square houses an imposing statue of Queen Isabel ("the Catholic") on a throne, with Columbus before her on bent knee, evoking the Catholicization of Spain and the New World at once. Next door sits the enormous cathedral, commissioned after Granada's 1492 surrender to celebrate the consolidation of Catholicism.

Lying outside these central neighborhoods are the modern expansions of the city, including middle-class neighborhoods and industrial outskirts that house lower-income residents.

To highlight the spatialization of minority inclusion and exclusion in this heterogeneous urban context, this book provides an ethnographic account of the zones of encounter between a wide array of urban players in the unfolding story of Islam in Granada. The story I tell moves across the city, from the *Albayzín*, with its famous cultivation of Muslim heritage, to peripherally located, disenfranchised migrant neighborhoods. Along with their embrace of Islam as a religion, converts have adopted the once-dilapidated Moorish quarter as a space for residence and business; many have restored Moorish-built homes in the upper hills of the *Albayzín*, where they also have a prominent mosque, and converts own many of the shops in the new Islamic-themed, tourist-oriented downhill area known as the "lower *Albayzín*," where the fight broke out. Moroccans tend to live in more marginal areas, in the large neighborhoods of urban sprawl that surround the city and have traditionally been home to Granada's Roma and working-class families. A small minority are employed in the lower *Albayzín*, but only a handful are business owners and few can afford to live in the increasingly gentrified neighborhood. The distance from the city center to the outlying neighborhoods like the *Polígono*, where many Muslim migrants live, is short—some areas are thirty minutes by bus— yet most *Granadinos* who live closer to the city center never set foot there.

Following Morgan Liu and other urban ethnographers, I have pursued the significant links between the physical and social urban landscapes of Granada. Just as it moves across neighborhoods, this ethnography moves across social boundaries, recognizing that "large social distances can be spanned within small geometric distances in an urban landscape" (Liu 2012, 4). When the winding cobblestone streets of the *Albayzín* give way to the giant boulevards of the city center, lined with modernist sculptures, and these in turn lead to the postindustrial outskirts of plain pavement and rows of low-income cement housing, each transition in the built environment heralds social divisions as well. Granada's intersecting neighborhoods, whose architecture recalls a history of fraught relationships across religious and cultural divides, help create complex patterns of empathy and antagonism among social actors in the city today. As a result, this is not a traditional ethnography of a clear-cut group or community, nor a comparative case study of separate groups.[2] My focus is on the social encounters between and among overlapping and diverse communities of Catholic and secular Andalusians, Muslim migrants, and converts to Islam. I am interested in what happens in the spaces where these people are drawn together, in the conflicts that sometimes divide them, in the aspects of their lives that are unwelcome in shared spaces of encounter, and in the hierarchically configured political and social processes that shape their encounters and separations. Next, I introduce these communities and their interactions with one another.

Spain's "New" Muslims

My research participants tend to frame contemporary Islam in Granada as part of a long history beginning with medieval Muslim Iberia, refusing to see Islam in the city as new. Yet the recent reemergence of a sizable, visible community of living, breathing Muslim converts and migrants after centuries of hegemonic Catholicism bears explanation. The difficulty of approximating undocumented migration patterns and the lack of a category for religious affiliation in the Spanish census make population estimates for Muslims in Spain vary widely. Recent data indicate that 10.7 percent of Spain's population is migrant (MESS 2015) and 3.6 percent of the population is Muslim (approximately 1.7 million people) (UCIDE 2012). According to the same study, nearly half the Muslims in Spain are of Moroccan origin, slightly over five hundred thousand Muslims have Spanish citizenship, and twenty-one thousand are Spanish-born converts. These numbers do not include undocumented Muslim migrants and may not include non-Spanish Europeans in the calculation of converts; accounting for these groups would likely swell the numbers considerably. Overall, Andalusia is home to the second-highest regional population of Muslims in Spain, after Catalonia (UCIDE 2012). In the city of Granada, somewhere between five thousand and twenty-five thousand people, or between 2 and 10 percent of the city's population, are Muslim (INE 2008). Most are migrants, and only between five hundred and two thousand are converts to Islam (D. Coleman 2008). Because of the difficulty of relying on statistics, I am less concerned with population size and more interested in emphasizing the diversity of Spain's Muslim and migrant communities, as well as the fact that the reemergence of a Muslim minority in Granada has been shaped by broader developments in Spanish political and economic history.

The so-called return of Muslims to Granada in the twentieth century is best understood as a two-part process beginning in the late 1970s and early 1980s with Spain's transition to democracy after the fascist dictatorship of General Francisco Franco (1936–1975) and his enforced national Catholicism. In the ensuing climate of social experimentation, a broad movement of Spaniards and other Europeans in Spain converted to Islam. Many became followers of Sheikh Abdulqadir, a Scottish-born convert to Islam with a global Sufi following in Europe, North America, southern Africa, and Latin America, known as the *Murabitun*. Taking their name from the *Almoravids*, whose dynasty in the eleventh and twelfth centuries spanned parts of the Maghreb and Iberia, the Murabitun movement coalesced in Andalusia in the 1980s. It has been alternately characterized by anthropologists as an anticapitalist movement that unites a political-economic critique of European enlightenment values with public religiosity (Bubandt 2009), by bloggers as a group of anti-Semitic conspiracy theorists (e.g., VNN Forums 2007), and by others as the "moderate" branch of Islam most accepted by the Spanish state (Leman et al. 2010). In fact, the converts I came to know in Granada were a heterogeneous group of people with varying degrees of knowledge about and interest in the global Murabitun movement. Many of the convert Muslims in Granada today, particularly younger and more recent converts, do not identify as Murabitun, although many frequent Granada's Murabitun-founded mosque and were initially educated about Islam by older Murabitun converts.

Converts' processes of becoming Muslim, their religious convictions, and their political leanings varied. Those I worked with cited diverse reasons for their initial interest in Islam, including philosophical critiques of Western European politics and enlightenment values; aesthetic interests in Sufi practices that blossomed into belief in Islamic theology; the influence of learning about Islam through platonic and romantic relationships with Muslims; personal traumas that prompted reevaluations of spirituality; and experiencing a call to Islam after spending time in the Moorish ambience of Granada's medieval quarter. Older converts recalled their conversions in the late 1970s and early 1980s as natural progressions from their participation in counterculture movements. Many of these converts narrated their conversion processes in terms of a desire to reclaim a non-Catholic Andalusian tradition in the wake of Franco's demise, or as part of a search for alternative lifestyles in the face of disillusionment with 1960s radical politics.

I do not consider these to be "real" political or sociological explanations to which one can reduce (or that can supplant) converts' religious interest in Islam. A search for such explanations may unintentionally imply a kind of reluctance to take seriously converts' religiosity. While some researchers have focused on the political and social conditions that make conversion possible or appealing in Europe (e.g., Roy 2010), I am more interested in the social processes and personal and political outcomes of conversion. I mention these explanatory narratives here simply to help illustrate the heterogeneity of converts' paths to Islam in Granada.

Converts' socioeconomic positioning in Granada was diverse as well. Some older converts were wealthy, well-established professionals—doctors, lawyers, and business leaders—who owned prized "heritage" properties in the historic Moorish quarter. Others were restaurant and café owners, artists, and tourism entrepreneurs. Younger or more recently converted European Muslims often came from middle- and working-class families with fewer economic resources. Convert Muslims in Granada engage in a strong economic support network, often organized through converts' preferred mosque. Less well-off converts were often taken care of by other converts, not through direct financial donations but through hand-me-down clothing and daily dinner invitations. Converts also employed one another frequently as salespeople in shops and as front office staff in businesses. These practices helped create financial security within the convert community, as well as building social ties among converts from different backgrounds.

The second prominent group of Muslims to arrive in Granada in the twentieth century has been Muslim migrants, primarily from Morocco but also from the Middle East and sub-Saharan Africa, with growing Syrian, Pakistani, Nigerian, and Senegalese communities. In particular, Granada is becoming a key node in the global Senegalese diaspora (Buggenhagen 2012). These Muslims are part of a broader wave of global migration to Spain over the last decades (Arango 2000; Leinaweaver 2013). I use the term *migrant* to refer to residents of Granada born elsewhere, as well as their children. These children are often treated as foreigners despite being born in Spain and sometimes having Spanish citizenship, a phenomenon that illustrates the way racial designations mediate how citizenship works in practice in southern Europe (Fikes 2009). I use *migrant* instead of or alongside *immigrant* to reflect the fact that mobility is often more multidirectional and ongoing than the term *immigrant* implies, with its connotations of unidirectional movement and then settlement in a fixed place (Boehm 2012, 2016). I use *migrant* rather than the common *transmigrant* (Glick Schiller et al. 1995) to emphasize how my North African interlocutors' discourses of mobility and belonging in Spain trouble normative claims about the border between Spain and North Africa, questioning whether they have really crossed borders transnationally.

The 1980s transition to democracy and Spain's full entrance into the European economy fueled dramatic economic growth, and the number of Moroccans and migrants from other Muslim-majority countries arriving in Spain rose considerably into the 1990s through the mid-2000s. Spain became for a time the Western European country with the fastest-growing migrant population (Arango 2000; Cornelius 2004). Public and political reaction to migration, along with Muslim migrants' rights activism and civic participation, coincided with the first decade of institutionalized democracy in Spain, immediately marking migration and religious diversity as key political issues of the new democratic state (Guia 2014). While many Moroccans in Spain have settled in urban, industrial sections of Madrid and Barcelona, smaller cities and agricultural areas of Andalusia and the adjacent eastern region of Extremadura are increasingly also home to many Moroccan migrants (García Sánchez 2014).

Within Andalusia, Granada has had its own particular trajectory of migration from Morocco. In newly democratic Andalusia in the early 1990s, the Moroccan presence was mainly restricted to male seasonal agricultural migrants and young men (and some women) who came to study at the University of Granada, particularly in the School of Pharmacy, which maintains accords for the admission of Moroccan students. Following a general pattern of the feminization of Moroccan emigration since the mid-1990s (Ramírez 2004), many migrants in Granada today are women. The contemporary Moroccan population is larger and more diverse, as

Moroccans have stepped into a wide array of positions in the labor market, filling a void left by Andalusians newly experiencing upward mobility during the economic boom of the early 2000s (Calavita 2005).

As with other Spanish cities, Granada's Moroccan population reflects the ethnic, religious, and socioeconomic diversity of Morocco, though more Moroccans I worked with identified as Arab than Amazigh (North African Indigenous People). Most Moroccans in Granada are from urban areas in central or northern Morocco (Dietz 2004), with fewer from small towns in the Rif Mountains. My research participants were primarily from northern Morocco, which has stronger historical and economic ties to Spain than the rest of Morocco, due to Spanish colonialism. Some Moroccans came to Spain because of proximity, and some chose Spain because of linguistic ease. Having grown up in northern Morocco, some spoke Spanish well, either because they came from well-to-do families that sent them to Arabic-Spanish bilingual schools or because they had picked up Spanish through participation in the northern Moroccan tourism economy that caters heavily to Spanish visitors. Migrants left Morocco and other countries primarily for economic reasons, looking for better work and educational opportunities for themselves and their children. A few from sub-Saharan Africa had refugee status due to political violence at home.

Most migrants I knew came to Spain as seasonal labor migrants. Men often worked in agriculture, especially olive and strawberry harvests, during part of the year, and spent the remaining months in the construction sector. A handful had jobs in professional fields, as pharmacists, bookstore owners, and IT specialists. About half of the migrant women in my study worked outside the home, usually as housekeepers or live-in domestic workers. Muslim migrant men and women were also in Granada as students and small-business owners. Many were women emigrating to reunite with family members, or on their own, while some were the first and only members of their families to emigrate, hoping to send remittances to extended families in Morocco. Others had family networks spread across North Africa and Mediterranean Europe as part of the well-established Moroccan diaspora in Europe, especially in France (Silverstein 2004) and Italy (Salih 2003). Most resided in Spain with legal residence, but a significant minority experienced undocumented status at some point during my fieldwork, usually either because legal requirements for residency changed, resulting in a loss of legal status, or when they were not able to renew residence permits because of unemployment and financial limitations or missing documents, common predicaments for migrants across Europe (Ticktin 2011).

While many of Granada's convert Muslims were members of the Murabitun Sufi movement, migrant Muslims from Morocco and elsewhere were far less likely to practice Sufism (despite Sufism's long-standing and widespread history in Morocco). Across convert and migrant communities I worked with, religious practice varied widely. Converts and migrants are both communities expected in public discourse to be especially devout. Non-Muslims in Granada often told me that their Muslim neighbors were very religious, referring either to a kind of "zeal of the convert" narrative or to the idea that migrants cope with new lives in non-Muslim-majority societies by clinging more closely to religious tradition. In fact, over the years I have observed a huge range of religious belief and practice. Some converts were indeed initially very keen on observing all religious obligations and then later relaxed certain practices, but others took on practices like prayer, fasting, and celebrating holidays and other rituals slowly and gradually, moving from a relatively secularized position to a more devout practice years after conversion. Similarly, some Muslim migrants described a gradual move away from regular prayer or decreased mosque attendance, finding it harder to stick with religious practice in the absence of their families after migrating. Some relished the opportunity to adopt secular practices that would have brought critique back in their natal homes. But others missed the familiarity of a Muslim-majority country and became more interested in pious practice as they began to organize their social lives more around mosques and Islamic institutions where they could meet fellow migrants. In other words, conversion and migration do not predict particularly pious sensibilities (or a lack thereof) among Muslims in Granada. Instead, they are experiences that create new social contexts and personal circumstances that can prompt conscious considerations of the role of religion in people's lives and can lead to changes in any number of directions.

Regardless of the extent to which they considered themselves "practicing" or the diverse ways they expressed their piety, Muslims in Granada largely created social lives that revolved around their religious communities. Even Muslims who considered themselves secular or non-practicing frequented mosques, Islamic cultural institutions, and Muslim nonprofit associations as primary places of community formation. They also socialized in teahouses near their places of worship and in the homes of fellow Muslims.

Although Spain is now home to migrant communities from around the world and to a visible community of convert Muslims, *Granadinos* by and large associate both Islam and migration with Moroccans, who have become socially synonymous with both the categories *migrant* and *Muslim* in Spain (López García 2006). Moroccans are often referred to casually as *moros*. Technically, this is the Spanish term for the historical Moors, but Spaniards use *moro* to refer to Moroccans, and occasionally to all migrants or all Muslims. (African Muslims are also sometimes referred to as *Africanos* or *Negros*). *Moro* is used pejoratively to purposely insult, as in the fight described earlier, in which an angry Spaniard yelled "*Moro!* Faggot!" at his Moroccan opponents. Non-Muslims also use the term more casually, in purportedly neutral, referential fashion to speak about Muslims or Moroccans, though my Muslim research participants find this referential usage equally offensive. Because of its negative connotations, occasionally people use *moro* to insult non-migrant non-Muslims. For instance, Andalusian women sometimes refer to chauvinist men or abusive husbands with the adjective *moro*, highlighting local ideologies about Islam as a religion marked by abnormal gender relations. The slippery referential content of *moro* aids in the conflations of historical Moors with present-day Muslims and of Muslims with migrants. It also contributes to the social construction of Muslims as an amorphous, undifferentiated mass.

The non-Muslim and non-migrant majority receiving Granada's new Muslim residents is as heterogeneous as the Muslim population. It includes devout and nonpracticing Catholics, staunchly secular people, wealthy businesspeople and landowners, middle-class Andalusians, the unemployed, Spanish Roma, European expatriates, global tourists, college-age study-abroad students, and migrants from around the world, all of whom exhibit varied attitudes toward Islam and multiculturalism. As many residents have commented to me over the past decade, Granada is known not only as Spain's "most Muslim city" but also as one of its most international cities in general, with a tradition of drawing in bohemian and counterculture collectives. But the city has also long been home to conservative and right-leaning, landowning classes and has a longtime conservative mayor, in stark contrast to the heavily left-leaning, historically impoverished population of the surrounding province of Granada and rural Andalusia at large. The category of people I call, following my research participants, *Granadinos*, is not a static, uniform category but rather encompasses the city's diverse residents. While they sometimes saw non-Muslims as an undifferentiated (and threatening) mass, Muslims occasionally recognized this heterogeneity in their complex and contextual identifications with or against various non-Muslims.

Triangulated Encounters: Islam, Christianity, and Secularism

Debates about Islam in Granada are not reducible to a conflict between supposedly secular Europeans and religious Muslims. Social encounters across religious, ethnic, and cultural boundaries in Granada reflect a convergence of contestations over religion and migration. This convergence stems from historically informed, complex interactions between Islam, Christianity, and secularism on the religious front, and between Andalusians' own history of labor emigration and new Muslim migration to the region on the migration front. Further, residents experience these encounters in the context of ongoing questions about Andalusia's and Spain's membership and marginality in Europe. Andalusia has long been cast by Spaniards and outside observers as non-European both because of its recent history of mass emigration to northern Europe and because of regional religious difference, first in the form of Muslim influence and later due to Catholicism's prominence. This history of marginality within Europe helped solidify questions about religious difference and population mobility as sensitive topics for Andalusian regional identity.

On the one hand, many Muslims resented what they saw as Catholicism's enormous influence in shaping Andalusian public life. In this sense, they shared a critique of local Catholicism that I also encountered among self-declared secular *Granadinos*. Many complained about Catholic triumphalism, especially during public religious events like Andalusia's famous Holy Week processions leading up to Easter, which my Moroccan Arabic teacher described to me in the following way. Our class's spring break was taken during the Holy Week holiday, during which public procession participants dress in costumes derived from the clothing of Inquisitorial penitents. The teacher announced it by saying, "We'll take next week off while the Spaniards are celebrating the Inquisition." Others pointed to the material mark of Catholicism in the city's built landscape, noting crosses in public places, the common practice of saying *"Jesús"* when someone sneezes, ubiquitous street names like *Matamoros* (Moor slayer), and a plethora of colloquial phrases that implicitly align Catholicism with normalcy, health, and goodness. These include *"No estoy muy Católica hoy"* (I'm not very Catholic today) to say "I'm sick"; *"No hay moros en la costa"* (There are no Moors on the shore) to say "The coast is clear"; or *"Habían moros y cristianos"* (There were Moors and Christians) to say "There was a scuffle," as in reporting a bar fight between neighbors. These linguistic and material markers created something of an unintentional "ambient" Catholicism in the city (e.g., Engelke 2012), which, if barely noticed by many non-Muslims, bothered many of my Muslim interlocutors immensely.

On the other hand, Andalusia has itself been historically constructed as flamboyantly Catholic and therefore insufficiently modern and secular. The role of the Catholic Church in public life is subject to constant, often heated debate in Spain, and some of my nonreligious research participants worried that Spain would never be secular enough to be fully European, not just because of the Muslim legacy of *al-Andalus* or the growing Muslim community today, but also because of Spain's history of national Catholicism and reputation for public religious display, especially in Andalusia. These anxieties mirror long-standing scholarly depictions of Spain as outside Europe due to pathological religious fervor and supposed Catholic obsession with penitence and pain, especially among Andalusians. Given that dominant narratives of Europe and modernity often rest on claims of secularism and/or Protestant Christianity (Asad 2003; Fernando 2014; Keane 2007), efforts to more securely place Andalusia and Spain within Europe engender concerns about not only Islam but also Catholicism.

Thus, while Muslims sometimes joined secular people in critiquing Catholicism, these antagonisms between devout Catholics and secularists also contributed to Muslims' occasional sense of affinity with Catholics. During moments of highly publicized secular critiques of religion, some Muslims were prompted to consider Catholics as allies in the defense of religiosity. When an atheist organization ran advertisements on the sides of city buses denouncing belief in God with the slogan "God does not exist. Enjoy your life," one Moroccan woman told me how offended she was, and how she had talked about it with her Catholic neighbors. In other conversations, these same neighbors figured as exclusionary Catholics she feared would discriminate against her Muslim family. But in this moment, she was grateful for their shared belief in God and in the role of religion in shaping decisions about how to live life. She saw them as religious allies within an increasingly non- and even antireligious Spanish populace. Such moments of affinity came from Catholics as well. At a migrant social services nongovernmental organization (NGO) where I volunteered, secular staff often expressed a desire to nudge Muslim migrant clients away from religiously informed practices and life decisions, while Catholic nuns volunteering at the same organization actually started a separate nonprofit association on the side to facilitate religious activities. The main instigator of this group at one point asked me for advice about how to start an NGO, saying she hoped to make sure migrants had a space for attending to "the spiritual" amid all the practically oriented job skills training, language classes, and legal support that dominated migrant social services offices (cf. García-Cano Torrico 2004). Andalusian conversations about religious pluralism must be understood, then, not as a case of Islam's interaction with a singular, secular European mainstream but rather in terms of complex triangulations between heterogeneous secular, Catholic, and Muslim actors.[3]

In a similar sense, the incorporation of new migrants to Spain must be understood in relation to Andalusians' own long history of mass emigration. Along with perceptions of Andalusians' overly fervent Catholicism, regional labor emigration has long been a marker of marginality (Rogozen-Soltar 2012a). Today, former emigrants who left Andalusia under Franco are increasingly returning to Spain, prompting proclamations of modernity and Europeanness that cast receiving, rather than sending, migrants as central to Andalusian progress. At the same time, Spain's ongoing economic crisis has resulted in unemployment rates for Andalusia's youth that hover around 62 percent (ABC [Sevilla] 2014), spurring a new wave of economic-driven youth emigration from the region. As a result, Andalusians sometimes posit regional labor emigration as a basis for solidarity with migrants in a discourse akin to seeing regional

Moorish history as a basis for including Muslim newcomers. Much like Islamic history, Andalusian experiences with emigration become a slippery resource that residents use to signify both new migrants' sameness and difference in Granada, even as its valences continually change over time (Rogozen-Soltar 2016).

CONVERSION, MIGRATION, AND UNEQUAL MULTICULTURALISM

Southern Spain is a unique sociohistorical context for the study of Islam in Europe because the Muslim population includes both migrants and a strong convert movement. Andalusia provides an opportunity to ask how Muslim migration and conversion influence and parallel one another, as well as how the individual complexities of each phenomenon are illuminated by exploring the differences between them. To do so, this book joins Muslim migration and conversion to Islam in Europe within one analytic frame. Although they often co-occur, scholarship on conversion and migration tends to be separate, or to focus primarily on one or the other.[4] I focus on the convergence of migration and conversion as transformative social phenomena, investigating migrants' and converts' shared efforts to carve out social space for Islam in Granada, their various engagements in the larger project of memorializing and politicizing the history of Muslim Spain, and their debates about Islam, politics, and minority representation. Studying Muslim migration has become the dominant paradigm for discussing Islam in Europe, where scholars have focused on current migrants or on the children and grandchildren of twentieth-century Muslim guest workers. Yet converts in Granada, though considerably outnumbered by migrants, are some of the city's most vocal Muslims. To grasp the unfolding story of Islam in Granada, I consider how debates about Islam in the city are shaped by the arrival of foreign-born, migrant Muslims, but also by deep-seated local interest in Islam as something potentially inherent to the host society's social fabric and regional identity, epitomized in conversions to Islam.

Conceptualizing conversion and migration in Spain together also provides new ways of approaching core concepts in the anthropological study of both processes, including mobility, borders, and social transformation. Both migration and conversion are social processes that highlight where boundaries are, how they are produced, and when they may be transgressed. Transnational migrants cross political-legal borders separating modern nation-states, and converts traverse religious and cultural boundaries that organize social life. Studying these processes together is a productive way of thinking through how borders and boundaries work and how mobility across political and social boundaries takes place, as well as the connections between official political borders and social boundaries in everyday life (Pelkmans 2010).

A central preoccupation of both migration studies and conversion literature has been the extent to which people involved in such processes change. In migration and diaspora studies, scholars debate the nature of hybridity, often comparing migrants' or diasporic peoples' supposedly hybrid identities (imagined as the result of experiencing cultural shifts or living between multiple cultural influences) to the presumably stable identities of non-migrant groups (e.g., Cagal 1997; Gilroy 1995). In a different but parallel conversation, scholars of conversion dispute the extent to which religious converts retain elements of their prior pieties or cosmologies, debating the roles of continuity, syncretism, and radical rupture in religious conversion (Chua 2012; Comaroff and Comaroff 1991; Engelke 2004; Robbins 2011).

I suggest that *both* hybridity and stability characterize *both* migrants and non-migrants as well as Muslims and non-Muslims in Granada. In other words, stasis and change, or rootedness and instability, are not the polar opposites they may seem to be, and they do not map neatly onto kinds of social groups. The concept of hybridity may lead analysts to imagine that mobile people (e.g., those who cross borders, be they political, geographic, or religious) have a fundamentally different process of identity formation and qualitatively different ways of forming attachments to places and social groups than those who stay put. Yet in Granada, it is not only Muslim migrants or converts who experience so-called hybridity. Members of Granada's non-Muslim, non-migrant majority engage in long-term debates about the degree of their own regional Muslimness. This leads to boundary crossing in the form of religious conversion, and to serious self-examination and feelings of unbelonging in Spain among even non-Muslim Andalusians, as members of a region sometimes marginalized due to an imagined Moorish stain. Catholic and secular *Granadinos* thus experience shifts in allegiance, identification, and self-presentation in relation to ideas of Europe and of Islam nearly as much as converts and migrants.

By the same token, Andalusian-born Catholics and secular people are not the only residents of Granada who claim territorial rootedness and political belonging in the city. Muslim migrants claim belonging in Granada based on their own ancestry and the city's Muslim heritage. Spanish converts claim rootedness as Spaniards or Europeans and as Muslims, blurring the assumed boundaries between these categories. By examining conversion and migration together, my aim is to push past the tendency to analyze host societies as mere context for migration, and instead to see non-migrant Andalusians and foreign-born Muslims as co-producing one another's subjectivities and social positions.

Placing conversion and migration into one frame also brings into focus the wide diversity of Islam in Europe, including the possibilities for solidarity among co-religionists of different ethnic, national, and class backgrounds as well as the tensions that arise between Muslims with different experiences of inclusion and exclusion in Europe. Converts and migrants are not uniformly discriminated against by anti-Muslim sectors, nor are they able to harness celebratory discourses about Islam to protect and empower their communities in equal measure.

Paul Silverstein argues that racialization, defined as "the processes through which any diacritic of social personhood—including class, ethnicity, generation, kinship/affinity, and positions within fields of power—comes to be essentialized, naturalized, and/or biologized," has become "an inescapable social fact" for Muslim migrants in Europe (2005, 364). In Granada, class difference, perceived foreignness, and historical memories of the Moorish past conspire to racialize Muslims through locally particular understandings of difference that incorporate migrants and converts in distinct ways. Moroccans are more visible as racial, religious, and national outsiders, readily slotted into the dangerous *moro* category. Their physical appearance, accented Spanish, and structural marginalization in the labor market all mark them in more permanent and publicly inescapable ways. Moroccans are also stigmatized as migrants; the fact of mobility itself is constructed as a marker of otherness and a priori marginality, as it is in much of Europe (Lemon 2000; Suárez-Navaz 2004). Migrants are at once more vulnerable to housing and labor discrimination and acts of hostility or violence, and less able to access local networks of support, police, or legal aid in response to these problems.

In contrast, converts were far less likely to experience financial hardship, housing shortages, or legal problems as a result of discrimination. When stereotypes about converts did arise among my non-Muslim interlocutors, they often portrayed converts as sinister traitors or gullible fools, duped into a New Age cult. Without the social markers that allow easy identification of migrant Muslims, converts may be envisioned by some Europeans as a kind of extra-dangerous invisible "sleeper cell" that can plot Muslim takeover all the more easily, as Esra Özyürek has found in Germany (2009). In Granada, this ability to pass unnoticed surely contributes to fearful imaginaries of converts as enemies within. But in a practical sense, it also allows some converts to avoid being recognized as Muslims on a daily basis, to choose when they wish to take on the responsibility of minority status and when they need, as one convert woman put it when explaining her choice to occasionally run errands sans headscarf, "a break" from being seen as anything but Spanish citizens or northern European expatriates. Moroccans, of course, cannot easily take a break from being seen as different, even by removing a headscarf.

Muslims' racialization is thus clearly crosscut by national differences, and it is also a distinctly gendered phenomenon. Most convert men are virtually undetectable as Muslims in routine public interactions, and most convert women wore a style of headscarf that resembles trendy scarves worn by "hippies" rather than obviously Muslim garments. Moroccan women's hijabs usually covered their hair, upper forehead, ears, and neck with two layers of close-fitting material. Many convert women wore a loosely wrapped, turban-shaped scarf that covered most of their hair, sometimes leaving the forehead, front hairline, ears, and neck uncovered. This style may be (though certainly is not always) confused with a bohemian fashion choice by passersby not in the know, protecting convert women from social stigma, even for those who, unlike the woman quoted earlier, would never dream of removing their headscarves. Much like Homa Hoodfar's famous example in Canada (1997), European Muslim

women find that their headscarves are often read as "fashion" despite being intended as pious dress, while North African migrant women who
cover their hair, even if only as "fashion," are read by the public as wearing
Islamic headscarves. Muslim visibility, then, affects women differently
than men, and migrant women differently than convert women.

Non-Muslim Spaniards increasingly articulate their discomfort with
Muslims' perceived religious, racial, and cultural difference through criticism of Muslims' failure to embody appropriate gender norms. When
secular and Catholic Spaniards express anxiety about Muslims, they frequently presuppose inherent gender inequality as evidence that Muslims'
beliefs, practices, and presence hinder Spain's consolidation as a modern,
progressive nation. These presuppositions translate into practical calam-
ities for Muslims who encounter them. Several weeks after the fight described at the outset of this chapter, Mairame was abruptly let go from
her live-in job caring for an elderly Spanish couple on the city's outskirts.
Mairame found herself out of work and home, a risk facing many migrant
women employed in live-in domestic jobs (Hondagneu-Sotelo 2001; Zontini 2004). Mairame began looking for work in restaurants and hotels.
She was repeatedly told that "it wouldn't be good for business" to have a
Moroccan up front working with customers. Her experiences mirrored
those described to me by many Moroccan women in Granada, and like
other undocumented migrants, Mairame could not report discrimination to authorities for fear of deportation. In these kinds of cases, racial
and gendered anxieties combine with women's structural vulnerability
as undocumented migrants to compound their socioeconomic exclusion
(Raissiguier 2010).

Migrant Muslim men routinely reported feeling criminalized by Andalusians who understood them as *machista* and domineering based on
globally circulating stereotypes of Islam and of Arab men (Ewing 2008;
Inhorn 2012). During the fight in the *Albayzín*, one of the Andalusian
men called the Moroccan waiters involved "*moro*" and "*maricón*" (faggot).
Although *maricón* is a widely used insult in Spain, it is significant that it
was paired here with *moro*, a pejorative that racializes Muslim men in part
by conjuring a particularly hyperaggressive, overly sexual masculinity as
well. In the fight, *moro* marked the Spanish man's Moroccan opponent
as a threatening intruder while *maricón* was simultaneously intended to

emasculate him, with the alliterative quality of the two words reinforcing the weight of the insult. These gendered stereotypes about Islam certainly affected convert Muslims as well. Yet for the reasons discussed earlier, converts were able to sometimes evade such interpellations.

Even the ways the terms *convert* and *migrant* are used in Granada reflect unequal multiculturalism. Converts, migrants, and non-Muslims in Granada use these titles to signify ethnic, racial, national, and class differences more than to refer to divisions between those born into Islam and those who adopt the religion. In Granada, people use *convert* to refer to residents they identify—usually through racialized perceptions of physical appearance rather than place of origin or legal citizenship status—as Spanish and European Muslims, even if those individuals are not converts in the technical sense of the term. For example, children born to convert parents refer to themselves as converts, despite being born into the faith. Similarly, people who otherwise might be considered migrants are termed (and call themselves) converts instead if they are associated with certain ethnic or class status. While many converts in Granada are Andalusian or from northern Spain, others are from elsewhere in Western and northern Europe. But these Europeans, despite having moved across national borders to live in Spain, are never referred to as migrants, a term reserved for foreign-born residents considered nonwhite and from countries deemed politically and economically "below" Spain (cf. Holmes 2013, 187). The terms *convert* and *migrant* have become social categories tied to relations of inequality; they are indexical of institutionalized ethnic, racial, national, gender, and class boundaries among Muslims in Granada that make converts and migrants experience starkly different placement within competing, historically rooted imaginaries of Muslim Spain.

HISTORICAL ANXIETY AND AMBIVALENT INCLUSION

Examining migration and conversion together also facilitates an exploration of Islamophobia, Islamophilia, and the historical roots of their convergence. Granada is home to conspicuous cultivation of the city's Islamic past and sustained efforts to silence Muslim history and limit Muslim presence. Recent anthropological work on Islam includes excellent

histories of the term *Islamophobia,* as well as the concept's political and
analytical benefits and drawbacks (Bunzl 2005). The term's emphasis on
fear may be myopically psychological (Özyürek 2005), and it may "reduce
complex historical patterns to ideologically useful concepts" (Shryock
2010, 2–3). Islamophobia as a universal explanation of European attitudes
toward Muslims risks becoming the next in a long line of diagnoses of
European exclusion. Some of these focus on race, ethnicity, and migratory
or citizenship status (e.g., Balibar 1991; Gilroy 1990; Modood 2005), some
on cultural fundamentalism (e.g., Stolcke 1995), and others emphasize
questions of religion and European secularisms (e.g., Asad 2003; Bowen
2008). As Mayanthi Fernando helpfully points out in a study of Muslim French, these are actually false distinctions, both because "race and
religion have always formed a nexus" (2014, 18) and because complexly
intertwined processes producing the meanings of racial and religious difference in Europe are long-standing, not suddenly new.

My goal in this book is not to identify or diagnose the one real way
in which Muslims are excluded. Instead, I use the term *Islamophobia* on
the one hand to highlight a recent intensification of the focus on Islam
and Muslims in discussions of cultural and racial difference in Europe
(Hirschkind 2011), but on the other hand to demonstrate the specificity and historicity of this process in Granada, where regional history
drives interfaith relations in the present. Further, fear of Islam there
has always been met by, and intertwined with, celebrations of Islam in
ways that are distinct from other European contexts. I use *Islamophilia*
to discuss the way born Muslims, convert Muslims, and non-Muslims
alike extol Islam as a central (and often glorious) aspect of Andalusianness, past and present. Because my interlocutors imagine Islam and
its role in Granada in many ways (as a religion, a historical sensibility, a
multicultural aesthetic, or a regional identity), Islamophilia manifests
variously as conversion to Islam, simple kindnesses toward Muslims, political mobilization for Muslim and migrant rights, or praise for Moorish
architecture. The idea of *Islamophobia* becomes a less rudimentary tool
when paired with *Islamophilia*; in other words, the Spanish context can
help expand the ways we understand Muslim inclusion and exclusion
in Europe. Rather than reifying either phobia or philia as diagnostic,
juxtaposing them actually points to the complex and incomplete nature

of both terms, as phobia and philia work not just in tandem, but as one joint process (cf. Shryock 2010).

Examining Islamophobia and Islamophilia together builds on anthropological research on multiculturalism in Europe and elsewhere that has demonstrated the overlapping technologies of inclusion and exclusion that shape migrants' and minorities' lives (e.g., Carter 1997; Cole 1997; Coutin 2007; Ong 2003; Povinelli 2002; Ticktin 2011). In the growing body of literature on Muslims in Europe, anthropologists have productively demonstrated how limitations intrinsic to various forms of European secularism and liberalism engender different degrees and modes of sociopolitical exclusion for Muslims (Asad 2003; Ewing 2008; Fernando 2014). Recent work also shows that European efforts to include and engage Muslim minorities have often used incorporation as a means of containing perceived Islamic threats by regulating which Muslim organizations and sensibilities thrive in Europe and which do not (Bowen 2008, 2010).

Attending to Islamophobia and Islamophilia in the Andalusian case offers a new vision of Islam in Europe that goes beyond choosing between exclusion and inclusion-as-containment. Muslims in Andalusia and Spain are constructed as a problem for Spanish secularism, modernity, gender equality, and European membership. Yet in southern Spain, the celebration of Muslim identity as a source of local pride (even among non-Muslims) is just as strong as vehemently secular, anti-Muslim sentiment. Calls for Muslim inclusion often go further than common European calls for tolerance, which tend to advocate acceptance of Muslims, primarily conceived of as migrants or children of migrants, on economic grounds (by invoking labor discourse) or on moral grounds (by invoking universal human rights ideals). In other words, economic and human rights logics often engender arguments for Muslims' inclusion in Europe in spite of their perceived religious and cultural difference. In contrast, in Andalusia Islam itself sometimes becomes grounds for Muslims' inclusion because of their Muslim identity and their claims to the region's Muslim past. The existence of an Islamic tourism sector, political overtures toward cross-Mediterranean initiatives with Moroccan cities, and a highly vocal convert community of Spaniards and other Europeans who have chosen Granada as a "natural" site for developing what they call a "European Islam" all help complicate the image common in European political discourse of a secular Europe facing off against an influx of non-European Muslims, an image popularized by Samuel Huntington's 1998 "clash of civilizations" model (Arigita 2009).

At the same time, inclusion of Islam in Granada also entails new, unanticipated forms of Muslim marginalization. Some Spanish converts to Islam adopt Muslim precepts and practices but socially shun Muslim migrants, or are themselves rejected by other Europeans. The local government encourages tourists to consume Moroccan food and Moorish architecture in the Islamic heritage tourism sector, while simultaneously ordering police crackdowns on undocumented Muslim migrants working in the industry. The chapters that follow explore the complicated ways that Islamophobic and Islamophilic discourses bleed into one another in *Granadino* social life.

A Brief History of Phobia and Philia

We might start by asking, from where does this pervasive blend of Islamophobia and Islamophilia arise? In Granada, the pendulum swing between pride in and embarrassment by Moorish history results from the slow accretion of both welcoming and xenophobic impulses toward Muslim minorities over many years. How to grapple with the legacy of Spain's eight-hundred-year Moorish period is one of the oldest questions of Spanish national (and Andalusian regional) historiography and politics (Soifer 2009), particularly for Granada (Calderwood 2014; González Alcantud 2005). As a result, debates about the city's Muslim minority today are refracted through "stubbornly persistent conjurings of the Muslim past in local debates over Granada's civic identity from the seventeenth century to the present" (D. Coleman 2008, 164). While Islamophobia and Islamophilia have shaped views of Islam since at least the inception of the Spanish nation-state (Fuchs 2009), social encounters across terrains of race, religion, and nationality have changed over time, with key historical moments occasionally shifting the characteristics or stakes of debate about Moorishness in Andalusia and Spain. Anxieties about Islam in Spain are not the same today, when European police forces routinely search for Al-Qaeda terror cells in Spain, as they were forty years ago in the twilight of Franco's dictatorship and enforced national Catholicism, or five hundred years ago during the Inquisition.

A century after the anti-Muslim genocide of the Inquisition, early evidence of contemporary forms of phobia and philia comes from the late nineteenth century, when the loss of most of Spain's colonies in the Americas provoked widespread debates about national essence and destiny. In this context, a newly emerging field of historians sought to explain Spain's loss of global standing by searching for the roots of national character in Islamic history. This so-called generation of '98 was followed by romantic poets and travel writers. The American author Washington Irving famously occupied the abandoned Alhambra for a period, and played up the figure of the historic Moor in his exoticized depictions of Spain as non-European (e.g., Irving 2007 [1851]; Tofiño-Quesada 2003). Irving famously wrote:

> I delight in those quaint histories which treat of the times when the Moslems maintained a foothold in the Peninsula. With all their bigotry and occasional intolerance, they are full of noble acts and generous sentiments, and have a high, spicy, oriental flavor, not to be found in other records of the times, which were merely European. In fact, Spain, even at the present day, is a country apart, severed in history, habits, manners, and modes of thinking, from all the rest of Europe. It is a romantic country, but its romance has none of the sentimentality of modern European romance; it is chiefly derived from the brilliant regions of the East, and from the high-minded Saracenic chivalry (Irving 2007 [1851], 351).

Irving's description is more than mere historical anecdote; quotations from his descriptions of the Alhambra are sprinkled throughout the official audio guide provided to tourists visiting the monument today, helping to shape their consumption of Granada's Muslim past.

In the early twentieth century, regional politicians were able to parlay public disapproval of the central government's colonial failures into support for political regionalisms across Spain. The Andalusian public intellectual and regional hero Blas Infante led the first movement of Andalusian regionalism, known as *Andalucismo Histórico*, or Historical Andalusianism, a project built on the idea that Andalusian culture was shaped by the legacy of *al-Andalus*. Infante initiated Moorish-focused cultural institutions, became president of the local government, and penned the first Statute of Andalusian Autonomy. He is now warmly memorialized across the region in history books, statues, and dedicated parks, streets, and buildings. Roughly a century after Irving described Spain as a country apart from Europe, Infante declared of the Andalusian region in particular:

> We cannot, we don't want to be, we will never become Europeans. Externally, in our dress and in certain ecumenical customs imposed with inexorable rigor, we have come to resemble that which our dominators demanded of us. But we have never stopped being what we truly are: that is, *Andalusians*; Euro-Africans, Euro-Orientals, universalist men, harmonious syntheses of men (quoted in Calderwood 2014, 14).

Beloved Andalusian artists of the time, including the composer Manuel de Falla and the poet Federico García Lorca, from Granada, echoed Infante's "*Andalucismo*," composing songs and poems honoring *al-Andalus* and organizing cultural events celebrating Andalusia's Arab, Muslim roots (Shannon 2015).

While the outbreak of the civil war abbreviated Infante's regionalism (both he and Lorca were executed by Franco's nationalists), the war returned images of the historic *moro* to public view in new and contradictory ways. Franco took charge of the Spanish protectorate in Morocco and brought thousands of Moroccan soldiers from the "Army of Africa" to fight under him.[5] Wartime propaganda alternated between images of Moors as Spanish and Moors as eternal outsiders and enemies of Spain. Nationalist representations of Moors and of contemporary Moroccans were aimed at justifying and garnering support for Franco's use of Moroccan troops and his plans to continue the Spanish protectorate in Morocco. While Franco's dictatorship is well known for its enforced Catholicism, his civil war media campaign championed a colonial, paternalist notion of brotherhood with Morocco, based on a shared racial-cultural ancestry between Moroccans and Spaniards since *al-Andalus* (Madariaga 2006). In contrast, Republican media portrayed Moroccan troops as a new wave of Moorish "invasion." Sensationalist news articles warned of Moroccan soldiers committing atrocities against Spaniards, including headhunting and extracting gold teeth from the dead (Goytisolo 1981; Sotomayor Blázquez 2005).

These tropes of Moroccans and Moors in the civil war are especially important because Spaniards today continue to discuss them frequently.

In Andalusia, where civil war casualties were particularly severe, resentment toward Moroccans for their compatriots' participation in the war is still palpable. Andalusians who complained to me about Moroccan immigration in hyperbolic tones often recalled both the "invasion of the Moors" in the medieval period and what some of my interlocutors called the "second invasion" during the civil war (cf. García Sánchez 2014). In this conflation, they cast Moroccans as "eternal invaders" and argued that Moroccan migration today is yet another invasion that must be stopped. Even Andalusians who professed to support immigration and migrant rights in Spain also sometimes excused racism toward Moroccans by explaining that anti-Moroccan sentiment, if unfortunate, was understandable given their role in the civil war. This is a period with remaining emotional significance, particularly for older Andalusians who witnessed the bloodshed firsthand.

Perhaps the most consequential turning point in the modern era was the mid-twentieth-century work of dueling historians. In his seminal 1948 publication, *España en Su Historia: Cristianos, Moros y Judíos*, historian and philologist Américo Castro made famous term *convivencia* (1977 [1948]). Castro meant for *convivencia* to capture what he saw as a unique historical trajectory in Spain, born out of Jews, Muslims, and Christians living together under Islamic rule. Castro believed that the multifaith society had left an indelible mark on Spain. Claudio Sánchez-Albornoz held the opposite view. A staunch defender of the Castilian narrative of Spanish identity and destiny, he argued that all things authentically Spanish and Catholic had their source in Castile, an area "untouched" by Spain's medieval Moorish invaders (Sánchez-Albornoz 1976). Castro's biggest detractor, Sánchez-Albornoz saw the Moorish period as a perfunctory blip in a teleological Spanish national history. Historians since Castro and Sánchez-Albornoz have deconstructed and built on both of their arguments, but nearly all still engage with this debate over the existence of *convivencia*, which has become the central conceptual framing for modern understandings of Spanish history among scholars of diverse persuasions (e.g., Aïdi 2003; Beckwith 2000; Catlos 2002; Doubleday and Coleman 2008; Fletcher 2006; Fuchs 2009; Harvey 2005; Menócal 1987, 2002).

In recent years, this historical debate has been reshaped by the co-emergence of two often-linked phenomena: the global war on terror and a perceived (Muslim) migration crisis in Europe. Spain's participation in U.S.-led military interventions in the Middle East following the attacks of September 11, 2001, are widely considered to have helped motivate the Madrid train bombings of 2004, attributed to Al-Qaeda. As in the United States, European Muslim and Arab minorities in this period became objects of fear; they also became objects of fascination, garnering public interest and political attention, often in the form of governmental efforts to control Muslims and migrants through punitive or inclusive-but-regulatory measures such as mosque oversight (Howell and Shryock 2003). Public opinion in Spain has responded significantly to these events, as well as to terror attacks in Casablanca and elsewhere in North Africa. Following the Madrid bombings, Muslims, especially Moroccans, were routinely ranked lowest in opinion polls tracking attitudes toward minorities in Spain (Zapata-Barrero 2006). As of this writing, the ongoing Syrian refugee crisis has further heightened debates about Islam and migration in Granada and Spain at large. The war on terror and the broad characterization of migration in Europe as a "Muslim" issue make anxiety over Muslim migration and conversion highly public issues in Granada today, bringing out both Islamophilic and Islamophobic voices. This dynamic, then, endures even as it evolves over time. Today, the ambivalence about Islam evinced by *Granadinos* who both laud and lament their city's Muslim history still resembles what Engseng Ho terms the characteristic "cultural schizophrenia" (2006, xxi) of societies with long histories of population mobility and entanglement with outsiders.

THE MARGINS OF EUROPE

Attending to my research participants' ambivalent framing of Granada and Andalusia as a semi-European, semi-Moorish, and ambiguously Mediterranean space helps move this book's analysis beyond (or, more precisely, between) the usual local-global dyad. The phrase *margins of Europe* calls attention to the particularities of Muslim inclusion and exclusion in a doubly marginalized region—Andalusia within Spain, and Spain within Europe. Because of my interlocutors' ambivalence about their belonging in Europe, many orient discussions about Islam and identity toward intensely local scales of belonging focused on the city of Granada or the region of Andalusia or toward the Mediterranean and sometimes an imagined "Muslim world." In both cases, their rhetorics of belonging bypass the Spanish state in favor of subnational and supranational regions as they articulate alternative cultural belongings. Tracing peoples' sense of attachment to the Andalusian region (rather than Spain) and to a broadly conceived Mediterranean configuration (rather than to the scale of global humanity) furthers recent attempts to make sense of ethnographically grounded visions of Mediterranean connections and discourses of Mediterraneanness that interrupt and complicate the local-global or particular-universal schematic common to discussions of diversity and globalization (e.g., Ben-Yehoyada 2014; Candea 2010; Silverstein 2004).[6]

My research participants' Mediterraneanist discourse often involves a strong spatial metaphor of *betweenness* with respect to Europe and North Africa. Yet just as often, people feel constrained by a spatial metaphor of *nestedness* within expanding scales of political belonging, moving outward from Granada to Andalusia to Spain (or bypassing Spain) to the Mediterranean and/or Europe. Like many marginal communities, my interlocutors imagine that outside observers care about and assess their community, with consequences for Andalusian belonging in Europe (Borneman and Fowler 1997). This schematic imbues anxieties about Islam in Granada with the urgency of what Michael Herzfeld calls "cultural intimacy," the idea that stereotypes or signifiers of identity that embarrass a social group in the face of outside observers may also be the factors that most strongly create a sense of community within the group (2005). From the perspective of many *Granadinos*, the experience of being seen as heirs to an Islamic cultural foundation provides a sense of local identity and pride that is hugely important to peoples' sense of self and community, but it has also marginalized Andalusia from Spain and Europe at large. Islamophobia and Islamophilia in Granada thus respond to a broader European "genealogy of desire/disdain" for southern Europe and the Mediterranean (Shannon 2015, 8). My research participants are highly aware of European and North African interests in the multicultural encounters taking place in their city, and debates about Islam in Granada are shaped by ever-anticipated outsider scrutiny.

The play of cultural intimacy across nested scales of belonging thus contributes to the heightened sense of anxiety about Islam in the city, and the ways it becomes central to Granada's self-promotion in the *Albayzín* and to fears of a Muslim reinvasion. Many political-economic and historical factors shape this dynamic of cultural intimacy, but a pervasive desire to demonstrate full membership in the club of Western Europe is critical in fostering the tension between Islamophobia and Islamophilia. Since the transition to democracy, along with other Spaniards, many Andalusians have focused on demonstrating emergence from the isolation of the fascist years, establishing Spain (and here, Andalusia) as fully modern and European (Collier 1997; Dietz 2004; Maddox 2004a). While sometimes a liability, claiming Muslim heritage and including Muslim residents demonstrate both the regional cultural uniqueness and cosmopolitan tolerance that are increasingly part of cultural definitions of what it means to be European (Rogozen-Soltar 2007). In this way, the predicate conditions of European membership create a tightrope for the display of difference. Andalusians ranging from government officials to tourism entrepreneurs to lay citizens must assert productive local heritage but refrain from implying too much dangerous difference.

If claiming Europeanness requires a delicately balanced cultivation and disavowal of religious diversity, this is made all the more complex by the strong Andalusian tradition of proudly refusing European status (or reveling in Europe's refusal to bestow it). This tradition is grounded in characterizations of southern Spain as more connected to North Africa than Europe, first promoted by the likes of Irving and Infante, quoted earlier. More recently, the 1980s transition to democracy encouraged Andalusians to capitalize on their Moorish heritage as a means of promoting Andalusian autonomy. Within Spain's newly federalized state, the degree of political autonomy afforded to each Spanish region was dependent on proof of regional cultural uniqueness, a factor that has played into movements for regional autonomy and cultural recognition in regions across Spain, most famously in Catalonia and the Basque region (Frekko 2009; Urla 2012) Lacking a recognized regional language like Catalán or Euskera, Andalusians called on their historical religious difference to claim regional autonomy (Dietz 2004). Combined with the postdictatorship ambience of experimentation with new lifestyles and cultural openness, these political conditions inspired Andalusian residents and local politicians maneuvering for regional autonomy to revive *al-Andalus* in "branding" democratic Andalusia (e.g., Comaroff and Comaroff 2009) since the late 1970s. Residents interested in Islam formed the *Yama'a Islámica de al-Andalus* (The *al-Andalus* Muslim Community), a cultural group to foment visibility of the region's Moorish legacy, and the affiliated political group *Liberación Andaluza* (Andalusian Liberation) went so far as to call for Andalusian independence from Spain on the basis of the region's Moorish legacy. Even more conservative politicians came on board. According to converts I worked with, in the mid-1980s, it was the mayor of Granada who invited members of the emerging Murabitun convert community, then dispersed across Andalusia, to come settle in the city in the hopes that their presence might help cement Granada as a key political and economic link between Europe and Morocco.

Ambivalence about belonging in Europe thus partially structures Andalusians' ambivalence about the place of Islam in their region, and this in turn shapes their interactions with new Muslim residents. But the city's new Muslims also reshape these interactions by adding their own voices to the fray, rekindling old anxieties about Andalusia's place between Europe and Africa. In the *Albayzín* fight, it was no coincidence that in response to his Spanish opponent's claims that he and his fellow Muslim migrants should leave and go back to their "own country," one of the Moroccans retorted by making fun of the Andalusian man's accent. Andalusian Spanish has a long history of signifying Andalusians' regional alterity within Spain and is often associated with tropes of backwardness that chalk marginality up to southerners' "semi-Arab" character. What better way, then, for a Moroccan-born man to counter a Spaniard's claims that "*moros*" do not belong in Spain than to question the belonging of that "native" Spanish interlocutor instead, calling out the aspect of identity that indexes Andalusians' outsiderness as former Muslims themselves?

FIELDWORK IN A ZONE OF ENCOUNTER

I conducted the research for this book among Muslim migrants, converts, and Catholic and secular Spaniards in a variety of institutional, neighborhood, and social settings between 2001 and 2011, including two consecutive years from 2007 to 2009.[7] Through long-term engagement with Granada and the generosity of ethnographic research participants who became close colleagues and put up with repeat interviews and continued participation in their lives, I was able to access rich ethnographic information even while moving among a variety of field sites within the city. These included a convert-run mosque and Islamic Studies Center, a convert women's association, a Moroccan women's association, shops in the *Albayzín* tourism neighborhood, the streets and cafés of migrant neighborhoods like the Polígono, and two NGOs where I worked as a volunteer. One was a large, Spanish-run migrant social services agency and the other a smaller antiracism association.

It was through these NGOs that I met many of my non-Muslim, Andalusian, and Spanish research participants. These were largely a mix of philanthropic nuns and middle- and working-class, leftist political activists but also included the growing sector of unemployed *Granadino* youth who end up working in social services institutions because they offer low paid or unpaid internships to students and recent university graduates with limited economic opportunities because of the economic crisis.[8] This meant that I had access to the old guard of *Granadino* political activism but was also able to learn about attitudes toward religious and migrant minorities among previously unpoliticized Andalusians experiencing their first concrete engagement with the politics of diversity. In the NGO context I also came into contact with hundreds of non-Muslim migrant clients from across sub-Saharan Africa, Asia, Latin America, and Eastern Europe. This work, along with my apartment's location in a neighborhood with many Andean migrant residents, introduced me to the broader landscape of migration in the city and Muslims' place within it.

I am particularly interested in the way gender politics infuses debates about Islam in Europe. Not wanting to reductively equate the study of gender with "women's experiences," I initially planned to conduct fieldwork with men and women. Yet, following my research participants' understandings of appropriateness, among converts, as a young unmarried woman I was able to work with far more women than men. Among Muslim migrants, I had more male interlocutors, though most were still women and I generally interacted with men and women separately. Among non-Muslims, my research was evenly split among men and women, most of them lifelong *Granadinos* but some from elsewhere in Andalusia or northern Spain.

While this book is about interreligious social encounters among residents of Granada, my interlocutors' encounters with me as a fieldworker also shed light on some of the political and representational anxieties about Islam that shape Muslim lives in Granada. These anxieties were often refracted through people's assessments of who I was or what I might become (was I an innocent young anthropologist, a useful expert, a potential Muslim convert, a CIA agent, or an American critic of Islam?). These appraisals facilitated and delimited the nature of my research access.

Most converts, whom I first met by attending their mosque and public events at their women's association, apprehended me through the lens of "potential convert." I was the age of many of the Spanish and other European women who frequently showed up at the mosque asking questions about Islam, and within months (or sometimes weeks) said the *Shahada* (the profession of Muslim faith) and adopted Islam. Because of this, converts tended to treat me as a new or prospective member of their community, hopeful that bringing me into the fold socially would eventually bring me the religious truth that they desired for me. Our conversations moved between my questions and converts' religious entreaties, inviting me to pray with them, offering me readings about conversion, extolling the Truth of Islam, and even trying to set me up with unmarried men in the community, hoping a marriage might result in my conversion. Most of my Moroccan and other migrant research participants came to know me through my solidarity efforts in a Moroccan women's association where I helped teach introductory Arabic to the toddlers of Moroccan migrant parents and as a volunteer at NGOs where they were participants or clients. They treated me as a political ally and sometimes as a sort of culture broker with assumed knowledge of laws and policies, or a messenger who could share their stories with people in North America.

Despite the overwhelming openness of my research participants and the generosity with which they allowed me into their worlds, the possibility that I might fall into the category of "untrustworthy observer" did surface on a few occasions. Rare moments of suspicion primarily manifested in jokes whose lightheartedness did not disguise the real insecurities behind them. At my first day observing in an antiracism NGO, the head of the organization jokingly asked when I would report back to the CIA. Never having heard the CIA acronym spoken aloud before in Spanish, I frowned in confusion at the word "*la thee-ya*" and only understood the joke when the man said each letter individually and persisted, "You know . . . Osama bin Laden. George Bush. Secret assassinations." At the convert-run Islamic Studies Center one day, a friend jokingly threw an extra scarf she carried in her purse around me saying, "Here, cover your hair. That way you can go unnoticed, just like a spy!" Her comment did double duty, as a reference to the ability of a piece of material to easily change a woman's status and interpellation, while also slyly riffing on the image of American spies infiltrating Muslim spaces abroad. She was joking, but several weeks later she informed me that two older convert women wanted to see my University of Michigan ID, because it had occurred to them that while I said I was from "*Mee-shee-gans*" and "had the face of a sweet innocent," they had no way of knowing for sure. I believe these sudden concerns arose because my research participants had viewed a plethora of news reports around that time about the increased (and sometimes undercover) policing of Islam in Spain, reminding them that they were always suspect in the eyes of outsiders, and that any potential observers must be thoroughly vetted to protect their increasingly vulnerable community. These kinds of interactions happened rarely, but they are useful reminders of the politicized nature of Muslim representation in Granada and in ethnography. My interlocutors' anxieties reveal converts' and migrants' awareness of global attention to Muslims and their concerns about Muslims' international reputation in addition to their local plight in Granada.

Conducting ethnography in a zone of encounter shaped by unequal multiculturalism also presents unique challenges with respect to the ethics of representing inequalities (cf. Arkin 2014). Moving between diverse communities of Muslim migrants, European converts to Islam, and Catholic and secular Spaniards, my research brought me into contact with many different people and allowed me insight into both their social encounters and their mutual avoidances. This work required that I make constant shifts—for example, between field sites at opposite ends of a city, between languages, and between modes of socializing in which alcohol consumption was either taboo or practically required. I also had to cope with some of my interlocutors' reciprocal disdain, which at times made my own actions and associations appear suspect, and I had to find strategies to conduct thorough fieldwork while also convincing people that I was not "taking sides" with those they found abhorrent. This meant frequently navigating conversations in which my research participants talked about one another in ways that exhibited racial, class-based, gendered, and religious prejudice.

Through a focus on unequal multiculturalism, I hope to expose relationships of inequality and injustice, but I aim to do so in a way that does not simply offer up Spaniards, Andalusians, convert Muslims, or anyone else as a spectacle of one-dimensional racism or xenophobia. A reductionist denunciation of Andalusians' discrimination toward Muslims, for instance, would facilitate the kind of easy, self-righteous response that allows authors and readers to replace difficult analysis of the complexities of racially charged social interactions with an uncritical sense of superiority. Oversimplifying racism in southern Spain simply defers the problem of racism and Islamophobia onto the region, absolving the rest of Spain from questions of exclusion, a pattern that besets other marginalized urban spaces in Europe that have become designated as the "racist cities" of their countries, such as Liverpool in Britain (Brown 2005). This approach to Andalusia might also bolster regionalist discourses already in circulation in Spain that position Andalusians as backward or unmodern because of their purported racial or religious intolerance, a trope that ironically often goes hand in hand with racialized depictions of Andalusians themselves as semi-Moorish, non-Europeans and presupposes relative equality in the rest of Spain. Just as those intolerant of Islam leverage Muslims' supposed fundamentalism or intolerance as evidence of their inassimilable nature (Brown 2006), Andalusians' presumed racism sometimes appears as justification for the racialization of Andalusians within Spain. On the other hand, softening accounts of racism because they are perpetrated by groups that are themselves marginalized may be politically tempting but does nothing to foster a sharper analytic or a place for theories of justice in anthropology.

The Andalusian context calls for reconfiguring prevalent scholarly modes of distinguishing between how identity and identification work for people in social mainstreams and at the margins. In Granada, non-Muslim, non-migrant residents experience shifts between majority and minority status, and they articulate identities that are just as fluid and unstable as those of people who have migrated across national, geographic, or religious boundaries. By attending to this, I aim to illustrate the moral complexities of inclusion and exclusion in zones of encounter where victim-perpetrator analyses of social conflict are destabilized as the result of overlapping, nested histories of marginality. Such complexities demand scrutiny, as Andalusia is but one example of an increasingly common scenario in marginal regions of Europe, ranging from Mediterranean to post-Soviet spaces, where people who have historically been positioned outside or on the outskirts of Europe are newly finding themselves as the gatekeepers to migrants and religious minorities (Ben-Yehoyada 2011; Cabot 2013; Candea 2010; Ghodsee 2009).

In what follows, I take up Matei Candea's suggestion that when faced with "zone[s] of "moral discomfort and confusion" (2006, 370), anthropologists avoid adjudication of victimhood and instead treat categories like "victim," "majority," and "minority" as objects of ethnographic inquiry rather than taken for granted analytical categories (371). My own sympathies are often surely visible on the page, as my goal is not to be objective or "sideless," but rather to avoid hasty assignations of blame in favor of explaining inequalities carefully, historically, and with ethnographic detail that captures the complexity of relationships across social difference. Anthropological inquiry partly depends on a willingness not to shy away from "uncomfortable" representations, as "principled tactlessness may be ethically useful, because, in the reactions that it provokes as well as the insights that it generates more directly, it can expose powerful hegemonies" (Herzfeld 2004, 324). This is not a story about victims and perpetrators, or about a conversation in which all participants enjoy equal footing. Instead, I investigate debates about the place of Islam in Andalusia involving multiple voices that sometimes overlap, sometimes disagree, and are always marked by different relationships to power.

OVERVIEW OF CHAPTERS

I begin this ethnography by describing how residents of Granada differently invoke medieval Islamic Spain in competing claims about how to manage multiculturalism and religious pluralism today. In chapter 1, "Historical Anxiety and Everyday Historiography," I argue that ongoing negotiations of Andalusian regional identity are intimately connected to long-standing debates about the place of Islam in the region's past and present. Through ethnography of what I call "everyday historiography," I trace how residents differently remember the long-ago Muslim past, which figures centrally in both analyses of Andalusia's modern marginality and arguments about the place of Islam in the region today. Historical anxiety about Islamic Spain conditions Muslim migrants' and converts' experiences of belonging and difference in Granada, and in chapter 2, "Paradoxes of Muslim Belonging and Difference," I describe their various strategies for carving out space for Islam in the city. Rather than understanding migrants or religious minorities as dislocated, existing "between" cultures, I explore how Granada's Muslims, particularly women, create a sense of "double rootedness" both in the city of Granada and in global communities. The chapter illustrates how converts and migrants differently negotiate claiming rootedness in Granada despite dominant perceptions of Andalusian regional and Spanish national identity that are explicitly linked to Catholicism. While converts achieve a limited but real sense of rootedness and belonging by situating Islamic conversion as inherently Spanish, migrants' claims of belonging are cast as dangerous and unacceptable.

Chapter 3, "Muslim Disneyland and Moroccan Danger Zones: Islam, Race, and Space," explores the complex social hierarchies through which convert and migrant Muslims are incorporated as minority subjects in Granada. In this chapter I take up the spatialization of religious and racial inequalities across two neighborhoods: the touristy *Albayzín*, sometimes called "Little Morocco" or "Muslim Disneyland," and an outlying, postindustrial zone called the Polígono, that houses many Muslim migrants. While on the surface, Islamophilia may seem to map onto the *Albayzín* and Islamophobia onto the Polígono, I argue that exclusion of Muslims occurs within the celebratory context of the *Albayzín* and that Muslim migrants are included as members of the neighborhood in the marginal Polígono. Converts' and migrants' tensions over the racial and gender politics of minority representation and related questions of religious authenticity and authority are the subject of chapter 4, "A Reluctant *Convivencia*: Minority Representation and Unequal Multiculturalism," where I compare converts' and migrants' efforts to represent Islam to wider publics in Granada. For converts, this process centers on a public-oriented mosque and a discourse of "culture-free Islam" that posits European superiority and distances converts from migrants. For migrants, representational work is based on careful performances of acceptability in everyday social encounters and a critique of converts' religious and representational practices. The chapter illustrates how locals' racial and gender anxieties about Islam and persistent outsider scrutiny of Muslims foster tensions within the Muslim community and how the diversity of Islam in Europe shapes struggles for inclusion.

In chapter 5, "Embodied Encounters: Gender, Islam, and Public Space," I explore how unequal multiculturalism shapes and responds to prevalent racial and gendered discourses in emergent Andalusian debates about Islam, the body, and proper public sociality. The chapter discusses headscarf controversies in Andalusia, reframing the now ubiquitous topic by considering it in relation to other bodily practices central to the embodiment of normative sociality in urban Granada, including socializing in public places, consuming pork and wine, and public displays of affection. While headscarves garner most public attention as bodily practices that create "obstacles" to inclusion, Andalusian embodied social norms themselves often create gendered, raced zones of subtle but pernicious social exclusion. The chapter asks how convert and migrant women differently respond to this exclusionary challenge.

Finally, in the conclusion, "Granada Moored and Unmoored," I consider this ethnography's global political relevance. Because of its association with historical imaginaries of the Moors, Granada has been perpetually unmoored from traditional conceptualizations of Europe. I suggest that analyzing Andalusia's enduring, awkward positioning between Europe and North Africa creates space to unpack how people in this European periphery have at times sought to redress the perceived distance between themselves and "real Europeans" and at times to accept, exploit, and celebrate their fringe Mediterranean status. This ambiguity, in turn, has facilitated the uptake of al-Andalus and contemporary Granada as symbols of pluralism, both as idealized examples of successful multiculturalism and as threatening warnings of dangerous civilizational conflicts, in contemporary global conversations about Islam and the West.

NOTES

1. By "Catholic and secular" I mean people who identify as devout Catholics, practicing but secularized Catholics, and non-Catholic secular or nonreligious people.

2. Here, I take my cue from other successful research on historical memory among connected but disparate communities, such as Pamela Ballinger's study of memory and identity across exiled and non-exiled ethnic Italians in Trieste and the Istrian Peninsula (2003).

3. Of course, there are many other religious groups present in Spain, including Protestants, Mormons, Jehovah's Witnesses, Baha'i, and Jews. But the nexus of Islam, Catholicism, and secularism remains most salient in discussions of social difference in Granada.

4. Many anthropologists and historians have studied Muslim mobility, in research on trade and diaspora (Ho 2006; Khater 2001), medical tourism (Inhorn 2011), displacement (Feldman 2008; Peteet 2005), and migration to Western spaces (Bowen 2008, 2010; Ewing 2008; Jamal and Naber 2008; Shryock et al. 2011; Silverstein 2004; Werbner 2002). Other researchers have begun investigating the growing numbers of conversions to Islam across the globe (Özyürek 2009, 2014; van Nieuwkerk 2006), and there is a growing anthropological body of work on religious conversion more broadly, though it primarily focuses on Christianity (Chua 2012; Engelke 2004; Keane 2007; Robbins 2011). In many of these cases, studies of migration take place in contexts where converts are also present, or vice versa. Yet the interactions of converts and migrants are usually mentioned in passing, rather than as a central focus. Exceptions to this pattern are few, though Attiya Ahmad (2010) and Mara Leichtman (2015) both explore conversion and migration together, in Kuwait and Senegal, respectively.

5. The circumstances (particularly whether Moroccans participated as free volunteers versus coerced victims) have been contested, as has the exact number of Moroccans who fought under Franco, probably ranging from 60,000 to 120,000 (Madariaga 2006; Sotomayor Blázquez 2005). As with the numbers of Moroccan migrants in Spain today, the social importance of Moroccan soldiers' presence in the civil war stemmed from their visibility and Spanish perceptions of their role, rather than their actual numbers.

6. Anthropologists have done this variously through attention to cross-Mediterranean, postcolonial legacies between Algeria and France (Silverstein 2004), political metaphors of kinship and "relatedness across difference" among North Africans and Sicilians (Ben-Yehoyada 2011), and historical narratives of entangled Moroccan-Spanish identities (Rogozen-Soltar 2007; 2012b). This growing body of work takes seriously the way North Africans and southern Europeans draw on religious, cultural, and political imaginings of Mediterranean entanglements to navigate contemporary multicultural zones of encounter.

7. Fieldwork included participant observation, media analysis, historical research, and ethnographic interviews. Some of my initial conversations with native Arabic speakers were in Arabic, and interviews occasionally involved Arabic, but most were conducted in Spanish.

8. This growing cadre of unpaid and underpaid volunteer labor results both from youth unemployment and what Andrea Muehlebach has termed a "new voluntary labor regime" in the Italian context, cultivated by neoliberal governance to replace the receding welfare

state (2012, 6). For a detailed panorama of the NGO sector that emerged to address migration in Granada during the transition to democracy, see Gunther Dietz's comprehensive study (2000).

1

❖

HISTORICAL ANXIETY AND
EVERYDAY HISTORIOGRAPHY

INVOKING *AL-ANDALUS*

Much recent scholarship on Islam and migration in Spain takes as its starting point the late 1970s, when Spain became a democracy and transitioned from being a "labor-exporting" country to a "labor-importing" country, with the first migrants to Spain coming mainly from Morocco (Cornelius 2004, 387). Perusing a random stack of books and articles on migration and Islam in Spain, one finds that nearly all begin with a proclamation of this demographic shift. As a result, scholars and politicians alike often consider the Muslim minority in Spain a "new" phenomenon, a fresh challenge of democracy and Europeanization. However, in the course of conducting ethnographic fieldwork, I have been consistently struck by the fact that people in Granada overwhelmingly understand questions of migration and religious pluralism as being shaped by encounters between Spain and Morocco not since the 1970s, but since the 700s. Through *longue-durée* historical narratives that foreground cultural connections and population movements between Spain and Morocco since the eighth century, my research participants conceptualize North Africa and southern Iberia as a semicontiguous space of Mediterranean entanglement. Ideas about local Muslim history are central to understandings of what it means to be *Granadino* and Andalusian today, with high stakes for the politics of multiculturalism.

These stakes are clearly expressed in popular Andalusian music. In October 2009 the beloved Andalusian pop star David Bisbal released the hit song *"Al-Andalus,"* in which he serenades medieval Islamic Spain and contemporary Andalusia, conflating them in an exotic, powerful goddess he calls *al-Andalus*. See the lyrics that follow.

Esta es la historia de una diosa
como nunca hubo ninguna.
Corría el arte en su mirada de color
verde aceituna.
De padre moro y de mujer Cristiana,
con piel de reina y cuerpo de
sultana, movía sus manos como
una gitana, y su embrujo te
robaba el alma.
Dicen que hubo muchos que in-
tentaron conquistarla, y otros
tantos se quedaron hechizados
solo por mirarla.
Aunque hace tiempo nadie ha
vuelto a verla yo sé que ella no
es una leyenda
y sé muy bien donde podré encon-
trarla, a esa que todos llamaban:
Al-Andalus, Al-Andalus.

This is the story of a goddess like
no other.
With artistry running through her
olive green gaze.
From a *"moro"* father and a Christian mother, with the skin of a
queen and the body of a sultan's
wife, she would move her hands
like a Gypsy, and her spell
would steal your soul.
They say there were many who
tried to conquer her, and still
others were bewitched simply
by looking at her.
Although no one has seen her in a
long time, I know that she is not
just a legend. And I know exactly where I can find her,
That woman who everyone used
to call:
Al-Andalus, Al-Andalus.

Bisbal's ode to *al-Andalus* nicely captures the competing historiog-raphies of medieval Islam that pervade social life in Granada. First, his lyrics demonstrate the enduring centrality of Andalusia's Muslim past, transposing historical *al-Andalus* onto the contemporary region. As Bisbal searches for the goddess *al-Andalus*, he casually lists the Moorish mon-uments of each modern Andalusian city in passing. By mentioning that "no one has seen her in a long time," Bisbal acknowledges the official si-lencing of medieval Islam in dominant Castilian history telling. But he intimates the limitations of that silence by insisting that it is nevertheless obvious where he "can find her," since Andalusia is simply a present-day incarnation of *al-Andalus*. Second, the song indexes Andalusians' profound ambivalence about this legacy. The protagonist unequivocally celebrates *al-Andalus* but also makes clear her alterity—referencing her mixed parentage, likening her to "a Gypsy," and personifying her in markedly orientalist and gendered fashion with references to her desirability (later lyrics state outright: "You are desire, *al-Andalus*") and unnatural danger (she bewitches onlookers and robs them of their souls).

In sum, Bisbal's song is both an ode to the marginality of *al-Andalus* and an anthem of southern pride. Bisbal is known for trumpeting his regional pride in other songs about modern Andalusian identity as well. His earlier hits included *"Corazón Latino"* (Latin Heart), a dance number that unabashedly advertises Andalusia as a playground for northern Europeans, inviting them to visit the "nonstop party by the shore" to enjoy "wine," "rum," "hot-bloodedness," and "tanned bodies" (Vale Music 2002). The song *"Al-Andalus"* invokes the imprint of medieval Islam on Andalusia, while *"Corazón Latino"* offers up Andalusia as a place for Europeans to consume southern difference and debauchery.

These two images—of an Andalusia marked by its Islamic past and of the contemporary region's otherness within Spain and Europe—are intimately connected. Together, Bisbal's songs tell a story familiar to many Andalusians, linking marginality today to the region's disproportionately long Muslim period. In this chapter, I pick up this conceptual link, examining both historical memories of *al-Andalus* and historical narratives of more recent Andalusian experiences of poverty, mass emigration, and regional stigma. While these "old" and "new" histories are separated by centuries, I unite them here because, like Bisbal's lyrics, my research participants predominantly understood Andalusia's medieval and modern histories as intertwined, and this "structuring narrative" (e.g., Bourdieu 1977) set the parameters for discussions of Islam in the city.

To explore this discursive linkage, I trace "everyday historiography," that is, the ways in which Granada's nonacademic public engages in the same kinds of fierce debates about the meaning of Spain's Muslim past that have animated the historical scholarship of Spain discussed in the introduction.[1] While their narratives may not be canonized or institutionalized as a part of official history, in the course of everyday social interactions, they commonly drew on the city's Muslim past to make sense of religious pluralism in the present. They did so in ambivalent narratives that involved both historical description and political prescription and expressed both Islamophilic and Islamophobic sensibilities. "Everyday historiography" ultimately refers to the ways people in Granada marshaled history to make moral claims about the meanings of Islam and Andalusianness in the present.

I use ethnography of everyday historiography to illustrate people's often heartfelt sense of political urgency in discussing the contemporary weight of Spain's Muslim past. Other scholars frame the persistence of this past in terms of Freudian and Derridian ghosts and hauntings (e.g., Flesler 2008a, 2008b) or emphasize instrumentalized economic and political uses of the Moorish past (Dietz 2004; Rosón Lorente 2008). I have tried to take my interlocutors' historical claims seriously and to assess them in the present. Their discussions of *al-Andalus* (as idea, identity, memory, or trope) seemed to me to reflect deeply felt beliefs and anxieties about Islam and local identity that inform social life with immediacy and with serious political consequences.

Historical memory always implies a particular—even if unacknowledged—ethics or politics, and often a particular configuration of time and space (Huyssen 2000). In particular, historical memory often becomes an especially politicized component of place-making in cities like Granada, where urban politics are inextricably linked to the production and consumption of local heritage (Herzfeld 2009). In Granada, everyday historiography becomes the cornerstone of what Jonathan Shannon calls "nostalgic dwelling," the "ways of inhabiting and articulating lived experience in places embedded with a heightened awareness of the past" (2015, 8).[2] Everyday historiography, with its shades of Islamophobia and Islamophilia, exudes both anxiety and nostalgia for *al-Andalus*, shaping future-oriented political projects as well as animating relationships to the past (cf. Boym 2001).

While the politics of historical narrative are crucial to local, urban place-making in Granada, my research participants also engage with time and space in broader scope, impacting conversations about Islam and migration in politically significant ways by radically shifting the political frames that are most meaningful, or even possible (cf. Tilly 1994). Their deep historical framing explodes common truisms about border crossing, local belonging, and the dichotomy of place that takes for granted a clear distinction between homelands and hostlands, hosts and guests in the study of mobility. The places that are now Morocco and Spain have been in near-constant historical encounter, with populations moving both north and south, and each alternating between dominant and subordinate colonial positions. Depending on when one begins the story of Spanish-Moroccan entanglement, designations of "homeland" and "host country," "host" and "guest" will change (Nair 2005; cf. Rosello 2001). This is why Moroccans' arrival in Granada may be referred to as a rightful "return" of those wrongfully expelled during the Inquisition in addition to a process of "immigration." Through their actual population mobility and their manner of characterizing it, Granada's residents socially and temporally reconstruct Mediterranean geography (Tsing 2005), often discursively transforming Granada "from a destination to an origin" (Ho 2006, 48). The intersection of these spatial and historical tensions creates palimpsestic and chronotypic (Mandel 2008) relationships between historical and contemporary actors and events, fueling anxiety over religious and cultural difference (Flesler and Melgosa 2003).

The remainder of this chapter is divided into two parts. The first section traces celebratory and anxious narratives that invoke Granada's medieval Muslim past. The second half focuses on narratives about the more recent past, showing how ambivalence about Moorish heritage has been central to the construction of Andalusia as unmodern and stigmatized but also as Europe's greatest hope for multiculturalism.

HISTORICAL ANXIETY IN THE LAST MUSLIM KINGDOM

From the first days of my field research, residents of Granada from all walks of life continually invoked Granada's Moorish period, construing Granada as an indelibly Muslim and Arab space. References to Islam and assertions that Granada was Spain's "most Muslim city" were the single most common topic of first conversations I had with people I met in all kinds of contexts, even those not aware of my research focus. Each person had his or her own understanding of Andalusian history and its contemporary meanings, but running through most of them was a deep ambivalence about *al-Andalus*. Andalusia's supposedly Moorish character was felt as both deeply prideful and painfully embarrassing, and as both an indisputable aspect of Granada's city identity and unresolved, debatable history.

I interviewed Marta, a woman in her twenties born to Spanish convert parents, in a shop where she worked near the Alhambra in the old, Moorish-built quarter. For much of our talk, Marta criticized racism toward Muslims, including toward Muslim migrants. After a sigh and a pregnant pause from recounting incidents of discrimination she had seen or heard of, she said thoughtfully, "The truth is, this city was Muslim for a very, very long time, and that's something that can never be undone . . . . What I mean to say is that, we have this in our blood, I think. I think we have Arabness in our blood." Speaking in ironic tones about Spaniards' rejection of Arab migrants, she mused, "If surely their great-great-great-grandparents had Arab blood, why are they acting this way?" The first part of Marta's commentary tells a clear and conclusive history of Islam in Granada. Extrapolating from the "Arab blood" running through the veins of the population to the level of the city itself, Granada is by nature a Muslim space, and this fact is irreversible and undeniable. Yet Marta's final comments also acknowledge the contingency of history-telling: despite the "fact" of their Arab blood, some of her fellow residents choose not to recognize Granada's Muslim history as a basis for openness toward Muslims today.

The narratives of history and regional identity that I encountered fell roughly into two categories that reflect each of the two sides of Marta's comments. Some narratives interwove discourses about biology, the senses, and inevitability to naturalize present-day *Granadinos'* attitudes (both positive and negative) toward Islam and migration. Others insisted on contingency and responsibility, framing the contemporary importance of *al-Andalus* and *convivencia* in terms of history, politics, and calls for social responsibility in interpreting the past. Though their narratives differently constructed the meaning of medieval Spanish history, people in both cases were navigating contemporary social life in Granada through active cultivation of particular relationships to the past.

"Natural" Histories of al-Andalus

The notion that contemporary Granada's built landscapes, cultural norms, and sensibilities flow inevitably from (and are explained by) the city's

Moorish history appeared in the narratives of both those who lauded and who lamented the city's "Muslimness." Residents' biological commentary sometimes naturalized Granada as open and accepting of Islam, and sometimes explained exclusion. Those who understood contemporary Granada as a "natural" product of the city's Muslim history often used words like *ancestry, nature, biology, blood,* and *genetics* to describe how Arab and Muslim cultural traits had been passed down, working their narratives of Granada's "natural" Muslimness into descriptions of the city and its social issues.

While discussions of blood lines in assessments of ethnic and national heritage are more commonly found in nationalist discourses that emphasize purity or essence, in Granada, invocations of blood were leveraged in multiple ways. Some people discussed blood to emphasize shared descent and relatedness between contemporary Muslims and Christians, denying religious and cultural differences between them by insisting that all current residents share blood lines. Others discussed blood and ancestry in narratives that posited mixing, but among discretely understood populations, imagining Christians, Muslims, and Jews as ancestral communities that mapped onto racial categories of people who shared a city. In this view, Granada was shaped by a history of successful relationships across lines of social-racial-religious difference, rather than a space of sameness. Still others discussed blood as an indication of danger; shared ancestry was something unpleasant to avoid re-creating today.

In addition to emphasizing blood and ancestry, these narratives also illustrate how a sense of natural social relations becomes infused into people's experience of city spaces. Research participants focused on sensory experiences of Granada's material culture, heralding the Moorish aesthetics of the city's built landscape, the *"rasgos"* (phenotypical characteristics) of contemporary *Granadinos,* and what one young woman called the "feeling of being" in Granada, a city she said was made from Moorish scientific, architectural, culinary, and social building blocks. Noelia, a now self-identified "semi-secular" woman who was raised in a Catholic family that "went back generations" in Granada, worked with me at a nonprofit antiracism association. She considered herself an authority on Granada because of her family's longevity in the city and their roots in local political activism. She frequently described Granada as essentially formed by *convivencia.*

One afternoon we were talking about *convivencia* and I asked her how she had come to know this history, whether she had read about it, studied it at school, or encountered it elsewhere. Opening with the authority-claiming statement, "Well, I'm very *Granadina*. I'm as Granada as they come," she answered that knowledge of Granada's Muslim history was much simpler and also more profound than what might be gleaned from textbooks. It came from simply being there, from using one's senses to take in the material remnants of *convivencia*, and from acknowledging one's place in relation to this history. She said,

> It's a natural thing. My family is from the area of Carrera del Darro street. That means we're right in front of the Alhambra, in the *Albayzín*. That whole area has narrow streets and so many names that are Jewish and Arab. It's the Jewish-Arab culture. So, it's normal. It's not something that you study, no. It's that, this is what Granada *is*! From my grandmother's apartment, you have the Alhambra in front, Santa Ana church to the right, and then the Arab baths. So, you know, for me, it's not, "Oooh, the three cultures of Granada!" [in a voice mimicking a sudden, self-aware realization]. I just *know* it. What's more, it's just my culture. All of this is mine, too. Because I'm from Granada.

In Noelia's estimation, experiencing daily life amid the Muslim- and Jewish-built architecture meant that the city's history of religious pluralism became part of *Granadinos*' very constitution—forming their surroundings, feelings, and embodied experiences of city space. To be from Granada was to unconsciously internalize its multicultural nature into an essential selfhood that included tacit knowledge of place, social identity, and lineage, all expressed through sensory appreciation of Moorish architectural remains. Noelia exemplifies the way Granada's urban materiality facilitates its consolidation as a place that makes and is made by historical memory. Her analysis included a kind of double synchronicity—a temporal one between Moorish and contemporary Granada, and a scalar one between her personal, internal sense of self as a *Granadina* and her view of the kinds of social dispositions and relations that should exist in the city.

New Muslim residents often echoed Noelia's emphasis on the built landscape and shared social background of "the three cultures" when they told me why they initially chose to live in Granada. A Moroccan woman who had lived in Madrid before moving to Granada said she had come south to visit friends there but decided to stay "because here it's like my country . . . there are so many Arab things. . . . When I got here and I saw it [the Moorish architecture], and I saw that Arabs and Muslims had been here before, in Andalusia and all, I loved it and I said, 'We are going to live here.'" Another Moroccan woman told me she felt she had a right to live in Granada because "the Andalusians are kind of like my people." Many migrants told me similar stories of choosing Granada. Many Muslims I knew, regardless of later experiences, had an initial sense that the city exuded a Muslim essence that must portend inclusion, and this influenced decisions to move there.

Some residents of Granada, usually non-Muslims, saw historically produced cultural affinities between Muslims and non-Muslims as so all-encompassing that they even precluded discrimination, making Granada a kind of special, tolerant haven of *convivencia* in the present. They positioned themselves as inheriting Granada's Muslim past and therefore being uniquely suited to understanding and promoting tolerance and modern pluralism. Such narratives often took the form of simple assertions that because Andalusia had been Muslim in the past, there was no racism or religious discrimination there today. People with this view did not just ignore race or deny racism; they actively claimed a locally produced antiracism.

When I interviewed Mamen, an Andalusian social worker at a migrant social services NGO where we both worked, she discussed migration policy at length. I concluded our interview by asking if she thought Andalusia's migration policies and practices were different from other parts of Spain. She replied,

> Here in Andalusia, it's a little more—there's been, culturally, historically, more contact between certain cultures like those of the north of Africa, so there's been more ties. . . . Historically, Granada was the last Muslim kingdom, you know? So they were here, established and everything. And a lot of that culture and tradition has been conserved and I think this helps. [long pause] I think Andalusia has to be different from the north because of this, right? Simply because of the culture, history, being right next to the Mediterranean, the passing of civilizations, and cultures. Yes, yes. It's like, because of the proximity, the Moroccans for example; in Andalusia they're much more at ease. I'm telling you, they feel much more comfortable here. And besides, they're closer to their country.

Mamen's comments reflect an assumption about the natural productivity of intercultural contact, common to many forms of liberal multiculturalism, which posit that proximity and contact lead not only to influence or familiarity between social groups, but also to affinity. This liberal vision underlies, for instance, the Spanish government's ongoing efforts to build cultural ties with Morocco under the umbrella program of the Alliance of Civilizations, based on the idea that Spanish-Moroccan ties provide a natural site for common ground between Europe, the Middle East, and North Africa. Mamen was referring here to a kind of historically rooted, intercultural friendship between cultures on northern and southern Mediterranean shores, and at first glance, this seems like a very inclusive gesture.

But this rhetoric of trans-Mediterranean friendship is often limited in effect, even when ambitious in scope. The Alliance of Civilizations Initiative, while predicated on an idea of trans-Mediterranean sameness, is also enacted to counteract feared civilizational conflicts; even the name itself implies a separation between different civilizations in the region. The logic is inherently ambivalent, reflecting the "deeply rooted polarized understanding of Spain, which is defined either as a conflicted border zone that keeps back the Islamic threat from Christendom (or the West), or a fruitful crossroads" (Arigita 2009, 232). Mamen concluded the preceding comment by referencing "their country," placing Andalusian residents of Moroccan origin outside the Spanish national or Andalusian regional space even while professing to include them. While Noelia understood Muslim and Christian residents of Granada as members of one shared trans-Mediterranean civilization, Mamen's Mediterranean vision had room for affinity *between* proximate but distinct religio-cultural entities, illustrating the varying ways people understood relatedness across social difference (cf. Ben-Yehoyada 2014).

Further, Mamen positively invoked Granada's Muslim history as a basis for tolerance today, but this led to her refusal to recognize Granada's very real problem of discrimination toward Muslims and migrants. This kind of discursive denial of racism illustrates how "Islamophilic" historical memory can actually contribute to the further exclusion of Muslims. Part of Mamen's job was to help direct NGO programs for Muslim migrants. This made it especially problematic that her romantic view of Granada's history kept her from acknowledging racism as a problem in the city.[3] Clearly, not only are there both "Islamophobic" and "Islamophilic" narratives, but even inclusive narratives like Mamen's can actually entail exclusionary social effects.

Some Andalusians disputed claims of historically rooted tolerance and instead argued that Granada's Moorish legacy actually naturalized exclusion. Ichazo, Mamen's fellow NGO worker, disagreed heartily with her in an interview, saying,

> Now, as for the theme of "Oh, since we used to be Muslims a long time ago, this makes us less racist," well, I don't believe that for a minute. Not at all! Because it's precisely the Moroccan population here that has the most problems. In all areas: when it comes to finding work; finding someone who will rent them an apartment; for a ton of things.

Others attributed fear of Muslims to an immutable *Granadino* essence, linking individuals' and groups' expressions of anti-Muslim or antimigrant sentiment to an inevitable, citywide, inherited racism, invoking the famed *malafollá* (unwelcoming) character of Granada. A convert woman explaining locals' reactions to the emergence of her community in the 1980s had this view: "When we became Muslim the people of Granada were terrified. I mean they did NOT. LIKE. US. And they thought, I think, that we were going to take over or something. I think [it's] somewhere in their genetic memory, the thing with the Muslims being here in the past." Many non-Muslims seconded this perspective, telling me that anti-Muslim sentiment was inevitable, because the medieval Muslim invasion was "in the memory" of Granada.

This tactic of naturalizing antipathy toward Muslims sometimes moved from explanation to excuse, leading some *Granadinos* to deny the importance of Islamophobia. In some cases, downplaying Muslim exclusion rested on rhetorical minimization of not only *al-Andalus* but also historical acts of religious exclusion. Older *Granadinos* surprised me periodically by referring to the events of the fifteenth and sixteenth centuries in depoliticizing language, referring to when the Muslims and Jews "left" Spain or to periods when they "weren't in Spain anymore," as though religious diversity had evaporated with the weather instead of the Inquisition. Such rhetoric also reflects official, institutionalized ways of remembering the violent past in neutralizing tones. On the outskirts of downtown Granada, the Museum of Andalusian Memory houses a four-room, horizontal wall panel of text and images depicting regional history in Spanish and English. Each panel lists a year or set of years, along with a headline and a short paragraph describing historical events for the designated period. Every so often, a year or range of years is bolded, indicating its significance, but most of the text is identical across all the panels, giving observers a sense of smooth, linear progression through time, with all periods and events being equally impactful. Three side-by-side panels are titled "1487: The Spanish Inquisition is created"; "1502: The Mudéjars must convert to Christianity or be expelled"; and "1550: There's nothing like a good rice pudding."[4] The former two panels depict the horrific events of the Inquisition, while the third panel lauds the development of regionally particular cuisine during the sixteenth century, a time when the Muslims of Andalusia were still being persecuted. The side-by-side placement of one of the most famous genocidal episodes in global history and the popularization of a beloved local dessert recipe presents the political as neutral, slotting the Inquisition in alongside accounts of happy region-making events and processes like the creation of Andalusian cuisine. Spatially, this implies that expulsion (and later execution) of Muslims and Jews is just one more element of local folklore and casts all these events as equally consequential parts of an inevitable flow of linear time. This exhibit illustrates how memory and amnesia work in tandem in public representations of the past, especially in palimpsestic urban spaces like Granada (Huyssen 2003).

Political Histories of al-Andalus

Some of my research participants were acutely aware of the way everyday historiography can reveal underlying political stances. They worked to capitalize on the politicization of historical memory in an effort to refashion themselves as modern, democratic Andalusians. Their historical narratives, particularly among critics of religious intolerance, often emphasized historical contingency, social responsibility, and political decision making over naturalizing rhetorics of genetics, essence, or inevitability. They cast remembrance itself as a locus of political possibility, arguing that people today have a moral and political choice about how to remember (or not) the city's Muslim heritage. Because much of Spanish official history has silenced or minimized the presence of Islam, residents of Granada who embraced this history felt that they were enacting a politically revolutionary counternarrative.

For some Andalusians, reframing history to call for the inclusion of Muslims was a way of fully leaving behind the recent past of Franco's dictatorship, enforced Catholicism, and strict Castilian narratives of a homogeneous Spain. It is true that across Europe, broad conceptual linkages between tolerance, modernity, and Europeanness often produce an exclusionary discourse in which Muslims become the limit of secular European tolerance (Asad 2003; Brown 2006). However, within the context of a broader Spanish embrace of tolerance as modern and democratic, Andalusians often used historically based reasoning to make strong calls for Muslim inclusion—or calls to recognize Muslims as *already* included in Andalusia, as its founders. They tied celebration of *al-Andalus* and acts of solidarity with Muslims to becoming responsible, moral, democratic citizens through a reworking of local history (Rogozen-Soltar 2007, 2012a).

When these self-fashioned modern Andalusians spoke about the past, they tethered their narratives to claims about responsible history telling. As María, a Catholic, lifelong *Granadina* put it,

> Granada has been *al-Andalus*. By *al-Andalus*, I mean to say that it's Muslim land. So, there shouldn't be racism here. It's not that it doesn't happen, just that it shouldn't. Because really this land was the land of the three cultures, where the Arabs, Jews, and Christians coexisted. And they never killed each other. Well, until they did because they wanted the land, I guess. But today, who can say that I'm not Muslim, that I'm not Jewish? Because I could have been. Or I could be. You never know.

María's historical reasoning entailed two related reasons for respecting Muslims in Granada today. First, she positioned interfaith tolerance as a social legacy of the region, insisting that historical "coexistence" should guide interaction among plurireligious residents. Second, she invoked the potential for all non-Muslim *Granadinos* to be descendants of former Muslims. Although she herself was not Muslim, she (and many other Andalusians) did not see Muslim religious affiliation as a necessary condition for recognizing their region's Islamic legacy or promoting tolerance of Muslims. It sufficed that her ancestors *could have been* Muslim or Jewish, and that had history unfolded differently, her present-day family could be either.

This reasoning highlights the weight many of my interlocutors placed on local history, above other possible resources for parsing multiculturalism, such as contemporary religious affiliation, nationality, or cultural background. Andalusia's particular history became the basis of an argument for respectful treatment of religious minorities that transcended other frameworks for understanding difference. María's argument was based on both belief in a local, successful pluralism and a constant reminder that the true condition of cultural or religious "Other" was suspect given the highly possible Muslim or Jewish ancestry of all city residents. In other words, recognizing Granada's interfaith history meant erasing or at least blurring lines of modern social categories that mark mainstream from minority groups, acknowledging constant slippage between them.

Despite recognizing that her idealized *al-Andalus* also experienced violence, María chose to emphasize a notion of harmonious history and warned that refusal to recognize this legacy of tolerance and enact compassion toward Muslims was precisely what had historically made Andalusia "backwards." She and other Andalusians countered their fellow citizens' fears that a Muslim and migrant presence would jeopardize Spain's membership in modern, secular Europe by insisting that it is instead the open-minded tolerance of Muslim difference that will solidify Andalusia's European status.

For Muslims themselves, historically based assertions of Muslim belonging in Granada often contained a pointed, political critique of Andalusian racism. Muslims criticized other Andalusians for harboring immoral prejudice toward Islam, and for misunderstanding or failing to appreciate their own national and regional histories. These critiques ranged from disappointed accusations of Andalusians' willful ignorance of the past, as in the often-repeated phrase "*No quieren saber*" (They don't want to know), to sharper condemnations of the cynicism and hypocrisy of official histories that exclude Islam. As one Moroccan woman put it, "Despite the history of *al-Andalus*, the people here are racist and they don't accept Islam."

Muslims offered a range of explanations for what they saw as Andalusians' historically incongruous insistence on rejecting Islam. A twenty-two-year-old Senegalese Muslim student who had lived in both France and Britain before coming to Spain told me she was dismayed that Granada was "so racist despite *al-Andalus*," as she had looked forward to precisely the opposite, having chosen to study in Granada because she expected to find tolerance of Muslims there. She thought perhaps racism prevailed because today's Muslim population was relatively new and had not had time to educate the local population, which had been misled by "racist history books." Belén Martínez, a convert Muslim, echoed her in a separate interview, arguing that *Granadinos* were racist because of "the Inquisition. And years and years of, like, a marketing job, to erase eight hundred years of Muslims that founded and shaped Granada." She continued,

> It's very strange because, you realize, they were here for eight hundred years. *EIGHT HUNDRED YEARS, living here, Muslims!* We're not talking about eighty years or five years. No. Eight hundred. It's incredible how a country can turn around and renounce its past, its origins. When the Catholic Kings finally captured Granada, they started this promotional campaign to replace Islam with Christianity. So that people would forget Islam. It's like they said to themselves, "We're going to have to work hard so the people forget their roots." And this is at a time when Muslims had brought science, math, thousands of things to Spain and they destroyed it all. It was like the Catholic Kings reprogrammed the people. And now it's stuck there in people's heads. So now we have a huge job.

Belén's use of marketing and promotional language here highlights the strong representational dimension of everyday historiography, explored at length in chapter 4. Historical narratives are not just about describing interreligious sociality. For many people, these deliberations are also about efforts to reshape public discourse, and marginalized Muslims experience these efforts as high-stakes attempts at inclusion.

Muslim migrants and converts frequently emphasized the cruel irony of persistent racism toward Muslims in the former *al-Andalus.* They juxtaposed what they saw as the purposeful erasure of Muslims' historical contributions with the cultural insensitivity of those historical remembrances in which Andalusians did participate, especially festivals that commemorated the Catholic "reconquest" of Granada. *La Toma de Granada* (The Taking), which celebrates the Catholic Kings' 1492 capture of the city with costumed battle reenactments and street processions, is held every January 2, despite protests (García Castaño 2000). The public

processions and other festivities of *Semana Santa* (Easter week) also produced frustration among Muslims, who frequently pointed out that in
Easter week's heavily touristed processions, participants actually wear
ceremonial costumes derived from the robes of the Inquisition.[5] Criticizing Granada's government for supporting the January 2 and Easter
Week festivities, a Muslim woman named Sana echoed my Arabic teacher
from the introduction, saying, "These things are all part of the Inquisition!" She charged, "They should know about it. Because the Muslims of
al-Andalus were tolerant of all groups, while the Spaniards were over in
the Americas just killing off all the people!" Claiming tolerance for Islam
rather than Catholic Spain, Sana turned European critiques of Islamic
fundamentalism—which often reject Islam on the grounds of its supposed intolerance—on their head. She also invoked not only the racial
and religious violence of the Inquisition, but also the Black Legend, a
tradition of anti-Spanish propaganda from Spain's colonial rivals that
vilified Spanish colonial practices as more cruel, barbaric, and excessive
than those of neighboring European empires like Britain or France. The
Black Legend's image of a barbaric Spanish sensibility has historically
been central to Euro-American depictions of Spain's "off-whiteness," its
exotic ties to the Muslim world, and its cultural difference from European
"civilization" (DeGuzmán 2005; Fuchs 2009).

When Muslims glossed contemporary Andalusians' anti-Muslim attitudes as extensions of the racist violence of Spanish colonialism and
the Inquisition, they collapsed past and present and critiqued modern
Andalusians' civic failures through invocations of the specter of Andalusian backwardness. These critiques cast intolerant Andalusians as non-
normative Europeans, but not by contrasting them to contemporary
pan-European ideals of universal human rights or normative tolerance.
Rather, in calling up old histories of violent religious and cultural encounters such as Spanish colonialism and the Inquisition, they drew on
historically rooted tropes of backwardness that cast Spain as Europe's
internal racial other. The second half of this chapter demonstrates that
widely circulating tropes of Andalusian backwardness stem from historical memories of Muslim Spain, and influence multiculturalism today, as
diverse residents of Granada leverage invocations and denials of Andalusian backwardness in arguments about contemporary pluralism.

ANDALUSIAN *"RETRASO"* (BACKWARDNESS)

My interlocutors often drew on understandings of the region's recent history of marginality, which they linked to older Muslim history, to define contemporary Andalusian and *Granadino* character and to assess questions of Muslim inclusion and exclusion. Stigmatizing narratives of *retraso* (slowness, behindness, or backwardness) often blame Andalusia's Muslim ancestry for its modern socioeconomic woes, or use an idiom of Muslimness to index Andalusia's marginality. Since the advent of democracy and economic growth in the 1980s, many of the socioeconomic indicators originally tied to narratives of Andalusia's backwardness (such as income, education levels, and prevalence of labor emigration) have vastly improved. Yet stereotypes about Andalusia remain salient in Spain and elsewhere, and Andalusians are keenly aware of this persistence, particularly as the ongoing economic crisis re-creates conditions reminiscent of prior decades, with new waves of Andalusian emigration and plummeting employment levels. Notions of Andalusia as a semi-Moorish, marginal region circulate among northern Spanish transplants, lifelong Catholic and secular Andalusians, and Muslim residents of Granada, all of whom differently rework tropes about the region's retraso.

Almost without fail, when Andalusians, other Spaniards, and migrants described Granada and *Granadinos*, they would mention Andalusia's medieval Muslim history. Often, they would link this with the more recent history of poverty, emigration, and marginalization within the nation-state, emphasizing disenfranchisement and stigma as historically powerful signifiers of Andalusia. The most common maxims about Andalusians were that they were rural, lazy, unmodern and traditional, unsophisticated, uneducated or uncultured, speakers of incorrect Spanish, sexist, brutal to animals (as in bullfighting), fanatical Catholics prone to excessively graphic or fervent expressions of religiosity, overindulgent in alcohol and parties, and racially suspect. In expressing this last trope, speakers often melded several of the others, asserting that Andalusians were racially contaminated by historical Moors and/or "Gypsies," and that the proof of this was in their unsophisticated love of bullfighting, flamenco music, and parties.

Along with these negative qualities, Andalusians were also described— and described themselves (as in the music of David Bisbal)—through positive but no less essentialist claims that they are good at throwing parties and artistically gifted practitioners of flamenco. Indeed, while Andalusia has been marginalized in Spain, many of the tropes that circulate as cornerstones of Spain's identity in global contexts, epitomized in tourism promotional campaigns, are actually artistic genres and practices that within Spain are most closely associated with Andalusia (Dietz 2004). In this way, widely recognized symbols of Andalusianness recall other contexts in which cultural and artistic forms associated with marginal groups are appropriated as national symbols for global consumption while their practitioners are stigmatized, as is the case for belly dancing in Turkey (Potuoğlu-Cook 2006), Roma performance in Russia (Lemon 2000), or Tamil popular theater in India (Seizer 2005).

The idea that an Andalusian character marked by *al-Andalus* influences current and recent regional events has been codified and politicized by official historical and political narratives, including those of early anthropologists in the region. Early structural-functionalist and psychosocial research from proponents of the idea of a Mediterranean honor-shame complex, for instance, contributed to circulating notions of Andalusians' traditional, rural, religiously fervent, and *"machista"* character (Mozo González and Tena Díaz 2003). In my research, whether speakers presented these signifiers as fair or inaccurate varied. Sometimes research participants (often northern Spaniards and migrants) invoked these traits uncritically, to describe what Andalusians were like. Others (often Andalusians) included them in metadiscursive descriptions of how they believed others saw them. But Andalusians also accepted some of these maxims as true, while non-Andalusians occasionally questioned them as potential *"tópicos"* (stereotypes) irrelevant to actual Andalusian life. Here, I trace tropes of Andalusianness through their replications among northern Spaniards, non-Muslim Andalusians, and new Muslim residents of Granada, exploring their linkages to ideas of Andalusian Moorishness.

"Northern" Imaginaries of Andalusia

In Granada I interviewed and conducted participant observation with many Spaniards from central and northern Spain who invoked the stereotypes of Andalusia, in both serious and joking, endearing and insulting ways. It is important to caution here that, like Andalusians, northern

Spaniards are not homogeneous, including in their views of southerners. However, most were aware of nationally circulating narratives of Andalusia's uniqueness and many took them up as ways of commenting on regional difference. Here I offer a few short but illustrative examples of common tropes.

The first trope, that of Andalusia as an exotic, tourist playground for northerners was clear in the way several of my acquaintances from northern regions of Spain approached Andalusian regional festivals. One woman reveled in purchasing and donning flamenco dresses around the time of local festivities. She would wear the dresses over her regular clothes and romp around her apartment, giggling at their ruffled absurdity, affecting an exaggerated, faux Andalusian accent, and dancing made-up flamenco-like choreography to the delight of her friends. Her impersonations reflected Andalusia's reputation for flamenco, bull-fighting, and *fiesta*. Conchi, a Madrid-born business owner, espoused the second common trope I encountered, that of Andalusia as Spain's unmodern past. Conchi would frequently engage in denials of Andalusians' coevalness, cautioning me that Andalusia still had the problems that most of Spain had left behind, such as poverty, the need to emigrate, political corruption, and most of all, problems with *"machismo"* (sexism) and overpopulation.

Finally, the image of Andalusia as a gendered, racialized internal other akin to the orientalized goddess in Bisbal's song *Al-Andalus* was a third major trope. A humorous but unsettling encounter early in my fieldwork during a weekend trip to Madrid to visit friends illustrates the circulation of ideas about Andalusia as Spain's exotic frontier. At a bar where I waited while a friend was in the restroom, an elderly, intoxicated man began to clumsily and crudely speak to me in a style associated with what Spaniards call *"viejos verdes"* (dirty old men). Mistaking me for an Andalusian woman upon hearing my accent, he responded to my polite disinterest by snarling with what appeared to be real anger, "All you Andalusian women are the same, temptresses put on earth to make men suffer." Melding gendered discourse reminiscent of orientalist fantasies of Muslim women with tropes of Andalusians' artistic and fiery natures, he went on about the suffering inflicted by Andalusian women on non-Andalusian men until thankfully my friend returned from the restroom. These are just a few ways that tropes of Andalusianness circulate among Spaniards not from the region.

In Granada, one woman stood out for the persistence with which she offered commentary about Andalusians' essential character and its implications for Muslims in the city. An elderly nun from northern Spain who had lived for many years in Granada working with migrant populations and other "marginal groups," as she put it, Claudia saw her role at the migrant social services NGO where we worked together as one of civic duty and spiritually informed pastoral care. She worked endless hours as a volunteer, freely handing out advice and judgment to migrants and coworkers with a boldness that others sometimes chalked up to tactlessness, but she to righteousness and wisdom. Claudia considered herself my educator about all things Spanish. We often jointly staffed the front desk at the NGO, and when we were not busy attending to clients, Claudia would talk with me at length about her views of Andalusian history, immigration policy, religion, and whatever else she deemed important for my research.

One day, Claudia sent a client to visit another office located in the Polígono, a neighborhood known for housing working-class Andalusian Roma and, increasingly, Moroccans. Incidentally, Claudia also lived in this part of town with a group of fellow nuns whose order worked on social projects in the area. I asked for her thoughts on the neighborhood and she said it was an area "in decline," a "typical, poor, difficult Andalusian *barrio*."[6] Claudia attributed the area's downward class mobility to *Granadinos'* lack of work ethic or civic-mindedness, saying, "The society here is very much about 'Gimme, gimme, gimme,' and there's very little conversation about people's obligations. Just the right to "Receive, receive, receive,' but it's lacking in responsibility." Claudia said she sometimes even worried that the Andalusians in Granada's poorer neighborhoods would "contaminate" migrants with the desire to live off unemployment benefits rather than finding work. She was concerned that despite being officially part of Spain's new democracy, Andalusians were not properly embodying the role of rights-having individuals in a modern welfare state. She went on to say that she advocated "abandoning" all government subsidies and welfare programs in Andalusia. This remark surprised me, considering the time and effort Claudia devoted to this social services organization, which she knew was funded through state-subsidized grants. But Claudia's concern about Andalusians' perceived failure to rise to the occasion of democratic citizenship reflects ongoing national and regional dilemmas in Spain concerning what it means to become European and democratic, and whether Andalusia has really done so.

Later that day, Claudia explicitly linked this narrative of modern Andalusian civic failure to the history of Islam in the region. She asserted that Granada's Moorish-influenced difference within Spain actually made it an ideal place for new Muslim migrants' well-being. As we sat at the front desk chatting, she confided in me her concern for a Moroccan migrant woman who that morning had announced her plan to move to Bilbao, an industrial city in Spain's Basque region. Relaying the woman's decision to head north, Claudia shook her head, theatrically pretended to pull her hair out, and groaned loudly, "Bilbao, uuuggghhh." When I asked why she thought Bilbao was a bad destination for this Moroccan woman, Claudia raised her eyebrows and peered at me as though the answer was obvious. "The thing is, you have no idea, the north—it's just that here, they tend to see the Moroccans as a little more similar to themselves," she said, chuckling. "It's just that, goodness, here, the people are practically suited to [having Muslim migrants], the Arabs were here for such a long time, you can see it in the . . ." gesturing to our surroundings with one arm and trailing off as if to indicate "in everything," Claudia elbowed me in the ribs with her other arm and chuckled heartily.

To convey that Andalusians were "suited" to living with Muslim migrants, Claudia had said, "they're, you know, *medio apañaaaooo,*" in a mock Andalusian pronunciation of *"medio apañado,"* a polyvalent phrase that translates roughly as being able to perform, suited to, or prepared for a task, in this case that of receiving and living with Muslims. But Claudia made her point as much in linguistic form as in lexicon. She eliminated the final *d* from the word and stretched her vowels out while smirking and rolling her eyes, in a clear imitation of Andalusians' accents. On the one hand, Claudia was saying that despite their "lazy" influence, she felt Andalusia offered Muslim migrants a better quality of life, something that mattered deeply to her. On the other hand, she also tied Andalusians' supposedly favorable treatment of migrants to an essentialized, stigmatized regional character, one she attributed to the lasting stamp of Moorish rule and indexed through a mocking use of Andalusian speech.

Claudia's use of this mock Andalusian to deride the region was perhaps unsurprising given the pervasiveness of Andalusian accents as signifiers of regional stigma. This is just one way that circulating discourses of Moorish-inflected retraso figured into my research participants' negotiations of identity, status, and belonging in the context of a growing Muslim minority. As the following sections demonstrate, these forms of discourse circulation moved along many vectors, in many directions. Here, Claudia revoiced the speech of a group she wished to deride, if gently. But Andalusians, including Muslims, also replicated (and rejected) stigmatizing discourse about themselves.

Proud Andalusian "Half-Moors"

Northerners' views of Andalusia of course varied dramatically. Yet most Andalusians I worked with, while proud of Andalusia's desirability to northern tourists, strongly believed that northerners also harbored a sense of superiority over and disdain for their home region. This is often the case with "cultural intimacy," that is, "the recognition of those aspects of cultural identity that are considered a source of external embarrassment but which nevertheless provide insiders with their assurance of common sociality" (Herzfeld 2005, 3). Andalusians' belief in "northerners" as a collective "external observer whose opinion is imagined *and imagined to matter*" (Shryock 2004b, 11) was far more important for their experience of what it meant to be Andalusian, and for the stakes of Andalusia's connections to Islam, than any actually documented northern attitudes. In Granada, anxieties about regional reputation helped shape anxieties about Muslim presence, past and present.

Far from a consistent strategy of denying Andalusian backwardness or embracing it via strategic essentialism, Catholic-secular Andalusians' and Muslims' revoicings of the retraso (backwardness) trope varied widely but always reflected deep-seated ambivalence. Some Andalusians responded to notions of regional backwardness by directly rejecting them; some by embracing them as positive, in both calculated and heartfelt self-reifying turns; and some by regretfully admitting stigmatizing stereotypes as their unfortunate lot in life. The most common Andalusian response to discourses of regional backwardness (always presumed by *Granadinos* to have originated in the north) was to recirculate the tropes in a prideful manner, while excising any racial undertones that pejoratively implied Andalusians' Muslim or Arab character. Andalusians' response to a highly publicized northern criticism of their dialect provides a useful example. In October 2009, the same month that David Bisbal released his hit song lauding Andalusia's Moorish heritage, Montserrat Nebrera, a Catalán conservative politician, resigned from her post in the Spanish parliament. Nebrera had been heavily criticized since the preceding January, when she denounced the Andalusian-born socialist politician Magdalena Álvarez's handling of a crisis at Madrid's airport by saying on national radio that Álvarez had "an accent that sounds like a joke." Nebrera had gone on to insist that talking (and she implied, working) with Andalusians in general was impossible due to their "low class, choking, bewildered" manner of communicating (20 Minutos 2009).

News of Nebrera's slight to Andalusians spread like wildfire and moved many *Granadinos* I knew to vehemently denounce "those northerners" for perpetually trying to humiliate and shame Andalusians by talking about their poverty, accents, and supposed lack of organizational skills. Andalusian politicians encouraged Nebrera's superiors to fire her, homemade videos defending Andalusian speech and criticizing Nebrera sprang up on YouTube, and Nebrera's sin against Andalusians was recounted later in media discussions of the Andalusian government's 2009 launching of *Plan Andalucía 10*, a government initiative meant to dispel negative stereotypes about the region (Ramos 2010). José Antonio Griñán, then president of the Andalusian regional government, hoped the plan would "debunk the stereotype of 'Andalusia: the subsidized region'" by dispelling myths of economic dependence and underdevelopment. According to media reports, the plan aimed to showcase regional "advances and modernization in areas of new knowledge, research, sustainability, and equality" (Rivera 2009).

Noelia, the woman quoted earlier who felt that the legacy of *al-Andalus* in Granada was "a natural thing," told me about Nebrera's comments and in the process, lost her temper. Like many other recent college graduates in their midtwenties, Noelia was underemployed. She had recently told me that a major difference between Andalusia's past and present was that her grandparents' and parents' generations had to emigrate for work and she did not. But on this day Noelia had given up on that narrative of progress. She had spent the morning perusing job openings in Catalonia and was dismayed to find that most advertised positions required applicants to speak Catalán. She exclaimed,

> Who do they think they are? They think they're better than the rest of Spain! They say Andalusia is in Morocco, that once you get past a certain point southern Spain is Morocco, and that offends me. Why do they have to say that? And why should I have to learn Catalán if I want to apply for a job in Catalonia?

Noelia's outrage reflects the relational nature of regional identity claims in Spain. Many Andalusians resent the fact that while Catalonia enjoys relative independence and, in their opinion, flaunts its regional language, their own region is stigmatized in comparison and their accent mocked.

Noelia frequently brought up such regional comparisons. She countered stereotypical critiques of Andalusia with prideful assertions of Andalusian cultural superiority. In particular, she felt that people from Madrid and farther north were "cold" and "rude." After weekends in Madrid visiting friends, she would complain that in Madrid, one witnesses "terrible things that would never happen in Granada," such as people refusing to give strangers directions, or young people declining to cede public transportation seats to pregnant or elderly riders. Such practices of course occur in Granada as well, but Noelia's comparisons reveal the deep importance that regional representation holds for people's notions of self, community, and morality. Noelia's response to stigmatizing discourse about Andalusia was thus to deny vigorously the racial aspect of that stigma by scoffing at the notion that Andalusians could be Arabs. She also asserted an Andalusian moral superiority rooted in correct interpersonal behavior, that compensates for relative poverty and lower status compared with other regions. She constructed Andalusia as a moral community where care for humanity was not dimmed by the greed and individualism she imagined in the north.

However, when discussing Andalusian identity in other contexts, without an immediate example (like Nebrera's) of northern discourse as a referent, Noelia was one of the Andalusians I knew who most frequently asserted the importance of Moorish heritage and the need for solidarity with Moroccans, to whom she felt *Granadinos* were historically related. The discrepancy between that position and her rejection of a northerner's assertion of Andalusian Arabness in the Nebrera case signals the extent to which *Granadinos'* discourse about whether they have (or should admit) a Muslim character is inextricable from their frustration over asymmetrical relationships among Spain's regions.

Many Andalusians echoed Noelia's strategy of melding prideful reification of certain tropes of regional identity with rejection of others in their engagements with stereotypical discourse about the region. A middle-aged, male *Granadino* taxi driver, for instance, did so in a monologue that stretched the length of our twenty-minute drive through the city. On a rare snowy day, recovering from the flu, I hailed a cab to ride what was usually my forty-minute walk from the home of a convert research participant in the uppermost hills of the Moorish-built *Albayzín* to the working-class and migrant neighborhood where I lived, near the city center. The driver commented that no one was out in the street, and I suggested that perhaps it was the unusual winter weather (it almost never snows in Granada and is front-page news when it does) or the economic crisis (which had just recently begun to make headlines at that time) that were keeping people at home. He shook his head vigorously and retorted that nothing keeps Andalusians at home. He had been out the previous Sunday with his family, he said, and the city was so crowded they had to search for a restaurant with a free table. He explained,

> "From Madrid on down, we're like that. It's our philosophy. We don't have much money but we like to spend it. To enjoy life." I might have less land and less power than someone else who hoards his money, but what do I care about land and power? I have fun and enjoy life with the people I love. The other day when I went out to that restaurant, we spent ninety euros. I had a good cut of meat, and my wife had a nice big plate of food and we had a great time, enjoying ourselves together. It's important. What is life without being able to do this, to spend money on your family, on a good, quality glass of wine? In other parts of Spain they care more about saving money and earning lots of money and things. "They say we don't work, that we're lazy, that we only like to party and have fun, that we're lazy. But it's not true. In Andalusia we work more than in any other part of Spain, it's just that we get paid less." We work more, and get paid less! And we spend all our money.[7]

My taxi driver clearly incorporated some of the tropes usually glossed as negative in narratives of Andalusianness, asserting them as the foundations of a morally superior Andalusian philosophy of the good life, based on family, humility, and an almost romantic view of the landless, Andalusian working class. Like Noelia, he buffeted back critiques of Andalusian backwardness with an insistence on the morality of the region.

Yet he also politicized Andalusians' working-class image, for even as he inverted the stereotype of Andalusians' frivolity by recasting it as familial love and contrasting it to a conjured northern acquisitiveness, he was careful to explicitly correct the elements of the discourse that offended him, insisting that Andalusians in fact worked hard but were poorer because they were unfairly paid. In doing so he casually invoked Andalusia's particular political-economic history. Prior to the emergence of today's tourism-oriented service industry and the arrival of a migrant workforce in agriculture, the Andalusian majority worked as wage laborers on large landowners' properties. In contrast, northern Spain has a stronger tradition of small-plot land ownership supporting family farms, as well as more and better-remunerated jobs in the industrial sector, which was and is limited in Andalusia. Note that in direct contrast to Noelia, who decried northerners for believing the old, derisive adage that below a certain point, Spain becomes Morocco, the taxi driver took up this geographic axiom, proudly claiming that the family-oriented, antimaterialistic moral philosophy of Andalusians reigns "from Madrid on down." While he did not draw an overt link to Moorish heritage as the cause of Andalusian particularities, he celebrated the very qualities of Andalusianness often associated with being "*medio moro*" (half-Moors) in more derogatory narratives. My taxi driver's commentary illustrates how multifaceted self-reifying discourse can be—he incorporated essentializing tropes of Andalusianness as part of a meaningful way of understanding and valuing his regional norms of sociability, while also carefully parsing out those aspects with which he disagreed. In other words, he did not have to choose between a full rejection of stereotypes and a romantic but self-defeating rehearsal of demeaning tropes.

Still other Andalusians accepted the notion that they, as a region, have been marked by the lasting influence of their Moorish heritage in pained admissions of ineptitude chalked up to backwardness. In his research in the Andalusian capital city of Seville, Richard Maddox perfectly captures this sentiment in what he terms a research participant's "rueful confession of an open secret," as in "'Yes, it has taken thirty years to fix the highway;

well, we are *medio moro*'" (2004b, 131). Andalusians in Granada also occasionally sided with the narrative that despite recent economic growth and development, they remain *medio moro* and outside the bounds of Europe.

Migrant Critiques: Andalusians as "Practically African"

This uncertainty over Andalusia's Europeanness provided an opening for Muslims to join in the circulation of discourses of Andalusian retraso. Granada's new Muslim residents, especially Moroccan migrants, invoked the specter of Andalusian retraso as a way of criticizing Andalusians and deflecting Andalusian antimigrant or anti-Muslim discrimination. Their comments recall other European regions that have served as exotic, internal others, such as in Corsica, where mainland French employ accusations of Corsican racism toward Maghrebi migrants to reinforce claims of Corsican alterity and to delegitimize Corsican complaints about regional marginalization within France (Candea 2006). The Andalusian context is strikingly similar, though here it is Moroccans and other migrants who are picking up on broader Spanish critiques of Andalusia in their own defense. Often fully aware that Andalusia's historical outsiderness has stemmed from the region's associations with Islam and North Africa, Moroccan migrants' invocations of Andalusians' non-Europeanness are at once novel political inversions and reifications of Islam's and North Africans' inferiority and otherness with respect to secular-Christian Europe.

In an interview, a Moroccan cook who had lived in Granada for nearly twenty years when we met complained about Andalusians' discrimination toward Muslim migrants. When I asked her opinion about the causes of this discrimination, she expressed her belief that Andalusians act out of a defensive obsession with their new status and a desire to escape their recent history of marginalization and stigma:

> The thing is that here, before, they had very little, *very little*, you understand? They were poor, and now that they have more, they're worried that we're coming here to take it away from them. There are good and bad people from Morocco, and good and bad people everywhere, but they want to see it as though they're all good, and all of us are bad. The majority of them think this way.

For this Moroccan, invoking the narrative of Andalusia's recent history of stigma and poverty served as a powerful counternarrative to Andalusians' claims of racial or cultural superiority, pathologizing them as sufferers of a kind of historically produced inferiority complex.

Moroccans often critiqued Andalusians as non-Europeans when re-counting stories of their day-to-day experiences of discrimination. This was common among the participants at *Asociación Najma* (the Najma Association, hereafter Najma), a Moroccan women's association. One day, several new Moroccan members were in attendance, and the group of newly acquainted women immediately began to complain about not being able to find jobs, claiming Andalusians stigmatized them because of their religion and migratory status. Several of these women had lived in central and northern Spain before moving to Granada, and they launched into a series of regional comparisons that reveal Moroccans' common disappointment in Granada's failure to live up to their expectations of the "Muslim city." Safa, a particularly outspoken and jocular young mother of two toddlers, reminisced about life in northern Spain:

> The people there are much more cultured; they respect you. There, you're in Europe. It's just that, there, maybe there are also racist people, who don't like Muslims, but they don't say anything to you, they don't express it. But here, they air it out. They look at you strangely on the bus and they say things to you. Here in Granada, they say Morocco is the Third World, but here, supposedly we're in Europe. But if this is Europe, why are the people so unrefined and why is the city covered in dog shit?

Here, Safa invokes an image of Andalusians who lack the social sophistica-tion and refined comportment of northerners: they make awkward public comments; they cannot keep their city streets clean; and they are racist. Because the crux of Andalusian regional stigma hinges on the idea that Andalusians are less modern, cosmopolitan, and worldly than northern-ers, accusations of Andalusian racism are often folded into commentaries that cast aspersion on the region's "character." After a lengthy critique of Andalusians' vocal, public racism, Safa added, "The farther north in Eu-rope you go, the more cultured the people are, and the farther south you go, the less cultured people are—here, they're practically Africans!" She said this last part while grinning mischievously, perhaps demonstrating her reflexivity about the self-reifying racial implications of using "African" as an insult among an audience of North Africans. The rest of the women giggled.

Many Moroccans are actually quite ambivalent about identifying as African, and a racial discourse separating Moroccans from "black Africans" is long-standing and widespread in Morocco (El Hamel 2013). Yet Moroccans in Spain are highly aware that Spaniards see them as African and as racially distinct from Europeans. By calling Andalusians "practically Africans," Safa implicitly invoked locals' disparaging attitudes toward her own provenance and her national community. This self-reification is perhaps not as surprising or contradictory as it might seem. Safa's critique is not meant only to insult Andalusians but also to delegitimize their attempts to distance themselves from African migrants, calling into question the boundaries between them. Safa seemed to be impugning Andalusians' intolerance of Muslim and African migrants not by implying that racism per se was morally wrong, but rather that Andalusians had mistaken their own position in a racial hierarchy in which they really were aligned more with Africans than Europeans. As a political counternarrative, Safa's use of the discourse of Andalusian backwardness calls for Andalusians to improve their treatment toward Muslims, not by dismantling that hierarchy itself through appeals to racial equality or universal human rights, but rather by recognizing their shared heritage of racialized exclusion from Europe and low status in a global racial hierarchy.

This does not mean Safa believes this racial hierarchy to be good or just. Safa and other Moroccans may draw on this discourse of Andalusians' otherness as a means of advocating for their own equality in Andalusia because it circulates freely in Spain and is readily available to them, and effective in ways that other means of political redress and antiracist, paradigm-changing discourses are not. Her usage points both to the political centrality of locally focused historical discourse in Granada and to the instability of reifying labels for marginalized groups. They fail to map cleanly onto discrete, fully formed, unchanging groups of people in the world, despite their near-universal recognition and continual circulation. In Granada, the multiple and context-dependent uses of the identity labels *Andalusian, backward,* and *African* became linguistic shifters; they "pointed to *relations* among 'us' and 'them' more than [they] referenced a

stable group" (Lemon 2000, 78). This relational nature of boundary drawing and (self)-stereotypy in Granada is unique in its orientation toward
a Moorish-Andalusian and Mediterranean center, rather than Europe or
a global scale of value. It underlays all of the engagements with notions
of regional retraso explored here: those of non-Andalusian Spaniards,
Andalusian-born residents, and migrants.

Cultural Intimacy at a "European Celebration"

This chapter opened with singer David Bisbal, who achieved fame during
his participation in the 2002 season of *Operación Triunfo* (Operation Triumph), a televised singing competition whose winner represents Spain
in the annual European-wide competition Eurovision. The Eurovision
contest has become a forum where political, economic, and cultural questions about the nature of Europe and Europeans literally take center stage
(Baker 2008; S. Coleman 2008). This performance arena is particularly
fraught for historically peripheral countries, which struggle to display
cosmopolitanism and cultural heritage while avoiding displays of difference that reinforce their marginality to Europe (Sieg 2010). Bisbal was
one of several Andalusians to succeed on the show in 2002. Rosa López,
a young woman from a rural town in the province of Granada, eventually
won the *Triunfo* contest. During the weeks leading up to Rosa's victory, her
presence on the show inspired intense local pride. Her photos were posted
in public spaces, street parties celebrated her, and the city was abuzz with
discussions of her success, which felt to many like an Andalusian coup of
sorts. However, *Granadinos'* pride in Rosa's talent was accompanied by
embarrassment over how she represented Granada.

   At the time, I lived in the home of a *Granadino* family that included two
sisters in their early twenties. The night Rosa was announced as winner of
Operación Triunfo, the sisters were two bundles of nerves as they sat on the
couch holding hands in anticipation, waiting for a woman from Granada
province to win a nationally televised competition. When she won, we
heard cheers erupt throughout the apartment building, its interior patio,
and out in the street of the family's lower-middle-class neighborhood.
Yet once the initial joy wore off, the sisters became nervous about Rosa's
upcoming Eurovision performance for a European, even global audience.
They were amazed by Rosa's powerful singing voice. But they were also

apprehensive that it sounded "too black" and "too *moro*." Moreover, Rosa wore "ugly clothes," was overweight, had snaggled front teeth, and stammered shyly in a pronounced rural Andalusian accent when she spoke. Months later, when Rosa represented Spain at the Eurovision competition, they were relieved to see that she had lost weight, she was outfitted *"muy de moda"* (very stylishly), and she had traded in her penchant for Andalusian *copla* folk songs for an English-Spanish number with a Europe-oriented, English title, "Europe Is Living a Celebration."

Bisbal and Rosa are both beloved in Andalusia. But while Bisbal's hit song *"Al-Andalus"* foregrounds Moorish history as a foundational and positive (if romanticized and exoticized) legacy for Andalusia today, Rosa's success among the *Granadinos* I knew partially hinged on ridding herself of the *"moro"* trappings they felt initially marked her as a rural *Granadina*. Their anxieties about Rosa's representation of Granada did not stem from any documented critiques of Rosa, Andalusia, or Granada on the part of Spaniards from elsewhere, who seemed to embrace Rosa as well. Yet the *Granadinos* I knew, while proud that a "local girl" had made it big, saw in the "local" aspects of Rosa a risky representation of Andalusia. In this way, my Spanish friends' and neighbors' reactions to Rosa and their appreciation of Bisbal reflect the same fundamental ambivalence exhibited by their everyday historical narratives of their region's long-ago and more recent pasts.

CONCLUSION

Andalusian residents' everyday historiography of both the region's medieval Muslim past and its more recent political-economic and social marginalization within Spain and Europe reveal a deeply embedded ambivalence about Islam. This ambivalence points to the limitations of common models used to explain multicultural societies. Western social science has long drawn on two contrasting stories about how pluralism generally works. One is the liberal narrative that contact and familiarity between social groups eventually begets understanding, appreciation, and tolerance, illustrated in the Alliance of Civilizations Initiative and some *Granadinos'* confidence that their city is fundamentally nonracist because of its long intercultural history. This story also undergirds contemporary political discourse in Europe that calls for unity in diversity, the now common idea that a productive, sanitized harnessing of "local culture" creates economic prosperity, civilized tolerance, and peace (Herzfeld 2004, 2009; Maddox 2004a; McDonald 1996; Shore 2000). An alternate model predicts the opposite. Some see a "threshold of tolerance," the idea that after reaching a certain percentage of the overall population, minority presence will provoke the natural ire of any mainstream society. This idea is similar to the theories of popular political pundits who envision strife among communities that are not carefully maintained as homogeneous (e.g., Huntington 1996). In Europe, this perspective engenders a vision of Europe-as-fortress that has taken hold among some of the political far right (Candea 2006; Partridge 2012).

The ethnographic material in this chapter indicates that both of these models fall short of capturing the complexities of multicultural encounters. Everyday historiography does not fit squarely into hopeful liberal narratives of tolerance or dire predictions of strife. Instead, Granada's residents' experiences of belonging to social mainstreams and minorities, or to both, are fundamentally relational, shifting, and overlapping. Conceptual links between Islam's place in Andalusia, and Andalusia's place in Spain and Europe, shape Spanish commentary on Andalusianness, *Granadinos'* own self-stereotypy, and Muslims' revoicings of tropes of Andalusian retraso that themselves are rooted in depictions of Andalusia as racially marked by its Muslim associations.

While representational anxieties may be interconnected at different scales, Andalusia's seemingly recursive debates about belonging do not unfold in a predictable, concentric manner. Recall Noelia, the woman who in one interview told me that embracing Islam and the legacy of *convivencia* was "a natural thing" that belonged to all *Granadinos*, but who in the face of perceived northern disparagement of Andalusia fiercely denied any natural linkages between Andalusia and Morocco or Islam. Others shared this duality—in contexts shaped by questions about Andalusia's place in Europe, they defensively downplayed Arab and Muslim influence, while in conversations focused on Muslims in Andalusia without reference to Europe, they celebrated the Moorish legacy in Granada. But some people consistently touted Muslim heritage in all contexts, or persistently denied it. Andalusians' concerns about the place of Muslims in the region are linked to questions about Andalusia's place in Spain, and in turn, Spain's role in Europe, but these concerns are not a straightforward nesting of Russian dolls; anxieties about Islam in Andalusia reflect broader Spanish and European scales but, like most politics, take on their own particular valences according to scale and context (Silverstein 2011, 2013).

The everyday historiography described in this chapter has complex political ramifications for the inclusion and exclusion of Muslims. My research participants' layered uses and complex circulations of historical narratives and discourses of Andalusian history and identity reflect how Andalusians' sense of stigma clearly structures their attitudes and actions toward Muslims, with whom they sometimes align themselves, and from whom they sometimes intently create distance. Michael Herzfeld writes that for some marginalized social groups, "embarrassment can become the ironic basis of intimacy and affection, a fellowship of the flawed" (2005, 29). This certainly seems to be the case for Andalusians who ruefully accept the notion of their region's stigma, bonding over the idea of their "*moro*" ancestry, a sense of real regional suffering and marginalization, and resentment toward perceived disrespect from "northerners." Further, who exactly belongs to this Mediterranean "fellowship of the flawed" is in flux. Through the repeated but variable historical narratives that circulate in Granada, residents of the city assert, analyze, and reformulate the social groups to which they see themselves and others belonging, and their relationships to one another. Andalusians sometimes invoke historical narratives that lead them to invite Muslim converts and migrants to join the Andalusian "fellowship," while Muslims themselves sometimes attempt to join it (or join northerners in critiquing it), whether invited or not.

Finally, everyday historiography also shows how anxieties about Islam in the region are both reflective of and divergent from broader conversations about Islam in Europe. My interlocutors are approaching questions of migration and religious pluralism not primarily through commonly studied European discourses about Islam and secularism, liberal multiculturalism, or citizenship and universal human rights. Rather, they use a framework based on Andalusia's regionally particular relationship to North Africa, and to an imagined Mediterranean, Muslim past. Perhaps ironically, in their historical narratives Andalusians seem at once to refuse European-led terms for understanding social difference, instead emphasizing the regional historical uniqueness of *al-Andalus* and trans-Mediterranean sociality (cf. Ben-Yehoyada 2011), and at the same time, in their trumpeting of *convivencia*, to claim ownership over the "best" model of precisely the values and social arrangements that many Western European nations seek—those of multicultural harmony, peace, tolerance, and successful pluralism.

NOTES

1. My historical approach in this book builds on a tradition of ethnographies of historical memory and history in Spain (Behar 1991; Roseman 1996); recent work incorporating more historicized perspectives in the study of diaspora and mobility to and from Spain (Berg 2011); and an outpouring of work on the politics and laws of historical memory surrounding the civil war and the Franco regime (Ferrándiz 2008; Labanyi 2007). Most of this work, however, begins with the nineteenth century or the civil war and postwar period. Here, I am interested in a more regionally specific and *longue durée* variation of historical memory.

2. In an expansive, comparative study of musical remembrance and performance of *al-Andalus* across the Mediterranean, Jonathan Shannon links Spanish political and musical nostalgia for the Moorish period to parallel discourses in Syria and Morocco (2015).

3. Similar moves occur on a broader political scale. The Alliance of Civilizations and other government attempts to officialize *convivencia* are largely seen as a joke by my research participants in Andalusia, a governmental folly that provides no actual cultural bridges across the Mediterranean. Aomar Boum (2012) finds similar sentiments in Morocco.

4. Mudéjar refers to Muslims who remained in Iberia after the defeat of Granada and the Catholic unification of the country.

5. The costumes consist of robes and pointed hats that are similar in appearance to traditional Ku Klux Klan costumes in the United States, also thought to be derived from Inquisitorial wear.

6. The word *barrio* here is not a neutral word for "neighborhood." In Granada, "neighborhoods" are *zonas* (zones), and *barrio* denotes areas understood as lower class and marginalized.

7. This conversation was not digitally recorded and is reconstructed as accurately as possible from field notes. Quotation marks indicate the portions of text I am certain are word-for-word quotations.

2

❁

PARADOXES OF MUSLIM
BELONGING AND DIFFERENCE

"People at the restaurant are always asking me where I'm from, what's my background and honestly, sometimes I just give up and tell them I'm Brazilian![1] I mean, sometimes I'm in a hurry." Yassmin, normally quiet and not particularly emotive, cracked a rare, wry grin as she recalled pulling one over on diners at the touristy restaurant in the *Albayzín* where she waitressed. Somehow "Brazilian" appeased questioners, placing Yassmin's light brown skin and ever so slightly accented Spanish in an identity box that seemed to fit, perhaps because of Brazil's global reputation as an interracial society par excellence. Yassmin, twenty-two when I met her in 2007, could not explain her background in a hurry because, as she put it, "it's complicated." Yassmin was born in Germany and raised primarily in Spain by her mother, a German convert to Islam who settled in Andalusia after divorcing Yassmin's father, who returned to his native Senegal. Yassmin spent a few years as a child in Germany and visits her Senegalese family periodically but cannot communicate well with them because she does not speak Wolof. She brought up this intersection of nationalities during a long conversation on a winter afternoon, offering me the extended answer she lacked the time or patience to give inquisitive restaurant diners. She said slowly, ruminating,

> German traditions—I don't have any of that. And I don't consider myself
> Senegalese. Spanish, yes, a little bit yes. Since I've been living here for
> so long, my way of being, of thinking seems a lot like the Spaniards. But
> then sometimes I ask myself, "Am I really Spanish?" And, no. No, I'm not

Spanish either. So truthfully, I identify as Muslim, and that's it. Because it's the only thing I know I am for sure.

Claiming to be Brazilian is Yassmin's humorous way of skirting the difficulties of explaining her German-Senegalese-Spanish (and Muslim) upbringing to strangers. The answer resolves diners' discomfort with her apparently ambiguous race and nationality. While "Brazilian" satisfies others' desire to know and place her, "Muslim" resolves similar issues for Yassmin herself. Both answers reveal the underlying difficulty Muslims face in Granada, where historical anxiety about the relationship between national and religious identities structures Muslim inclusion and exclusion. Despite public attention to the city's Moorish legacy, Granada still forms part of a nation-state where normative understandings of national identity are strongly linked to Catholicism (and now increasingly to secularism as well), with Andalusia often cast as the most fervently Catholic region. While Catholic and secular Andalusians may ruminate at length on their own Muslim roots and are sometimes scapegoated as "half-Moors," it is far more difficult for Muslims to identify as Muslims and also successfully claim belonging in Spain. Many of my Muslim research participants had similar trouble answering the question Yassmin asked herself: "Am I really Spanish?" The last chapter demonstrated that Andalusia may be one of the few places in Western Europe where there is a real, palpable recognition of Islam as something indigenous and local. Yet Andalusian social life is also marked by expectations of Catholic and secular identification that make Spanish or Andalusian Islam unthinkable for many.

This is the fundamental paradox of Muslim belonging and difference in Granada. This chapter explores how Granada's new Muslim residents work to carve out space for Muslim belonging in a city where public expectations of a linkage between religious, regional, and national identifications shape the question "Am I really Spanish?" and its possible answers. The normative link between Andalusianness and Catholicism pervades Andalusian social imaginaries, such that Spanish converts to Islam are easily recognized as Spanish but find it difficult to be taken seriously or accepted as Muslim by other Spaniards and other Muslims.

Muslim migrants and their Spanish-born children, in turn, are presumed to be Muslim but are rarely seen as Andalusian or Spanish, regardless of their citizenship status.

Still, Muslim belonging and exclusion in Granada are far more complex than a simple story in which European converts get to be European but not fully Muslim, with migrants easily claiming belonging in the Muslim religion but excluded from Spain. For both converts and migrants, failure to fit easily into the locally normative Catholic-Andalusian-Spanish identity nexus creates problems of belonging that affect their experiences of attachment to and dislocation from both Spain and other, far-flung communities such as the Moroccan nation-state or the *ummah* (the global Muslim community). Andrew Shryock, based on work with Arab-Americans, suggests that Arabs in the United States experience a "double remoteness" with respect to both their origins and destinations, because while not fully emplaced in the mainstream U.S. host society, they are nevertheless also distanced from places of birth or ancestral origin (2004b, 291). This is also true in Granada, where Muslims feel marginalized from Andalusian social life and insufficiently connected to other places and communities, especially North Africa (for migrants) and the ummah (for converts).

Despite such dislocations, my goal in this chapter is to emphasize rootedness and belonging as equally important. In other words, I ask how converts and migrants claim rootedness in Granada and how they struggle to maintain and create connections to dispersed communities (the global ummah, Morocco, and the Moroccan diaspora). I focus on the specific ways Muslims claim, strive for, and experience rootedness in the city of Granada in particular, but I suggest that more emphasis on the rootedness of mobile and marginalized people (sometimes in multiple places at once) can correct overemphasis on remoteness, exclusion, and betweenness in scholarship of mobility more broadly. Unlike the common metaphor of betweenness, which relegates migrants and minorities to a kind of unnaturally permanent liminality, thinking about the simultaneity and intersections of rootedness and remoteness fosters attention to the important insight that minorities can live not "*between* 'two worlds' but *in* one world of many overlapping spaces" (Lemon 2000, 11).

Further, I am interested in how these dual dynamics of belonging and nonbelonging shape life *in* Granada, even when the relevant attachments in question are to other places. Muslims' rootedness in Granada works at different levels and in various degrees. Sometimes Muslims deeply feel a sense of belonging and rootedness; sometimes they feel remote from *Granadino* social life, from North Africa, or from the global Muslim world, intently working toward a sense of rootedness that remains incomplete; and sometimes rootedness appears in brief glimpses, as a momentary, personal sense of being in place that is nevertheless unrecognized by wider publics. For example, this is the case for Muslim migrants who breathe with ease amid Granada's Moorish architecture, feeling ownership over the city in one moment, only to be mistreated in a government office or harassed by police fifteen minutes later. By focusing on how the intersections between Muslims' rootedness in and remoteness from multiple places and communities all play out through lives lived *in* Granada, I seek to complicate both flat descriptions of Islamophobic exclusion and linear models of "integration" that ignore the hiccups, paradoxes, and partial exclusions inherent to processes of inclusion.

As I trace how converts and migrants strive for rootedness and manage remoteness, I pay special attention to how assumptions of Andalusian Catholicism engender and reverberate against the different ways converts and migrants claim belonging. Converts primarily tapped into nostalgic ideals of medieval Islam and *convivencia* to envision conversion as the revival of a glorious, past version of Spanishness. They emphasized social values, sensibilities, and styles of urban living that appealed to and resonated with broader social and political efforts to refashion Andalusian and Spanish global brands of cosmopolitan, sophisticated, intercultural harmony. In contrast, migrant Muslims, especially Moroccans, tended to claim belonging in terms of ownership over territory, contributions to the city's built landscape, and ancestry, emphasizing their forebears' presence in the city. Unfortunately for migrants, these rationales, intended to buttress claims of migrant inclusion, found easy uptake among less celebratory, more Islamophobic currents in the city. After introducing how remoteness and rootedness are built into Spanish governance of Muslims and migrants, I delve into the ethnography of these processes, first exploring the experiences of converts and then migrants.

ARRAIGO: SPANISH POLITICS OF EXCLUSIONARY INCLUSION

Even the specifically Andalusian debates about Muslims' regional belonging explored in this book draw some of their symbolic weight from Spanish national political frameworks for incorporating minorities—especially migrants and Muslims. The ideas of rootedness and remoteness have been central to the Spanish approach to Islam and migration and are formally expressed in the historical, social, and juridical concept of *arraigo* (rootedness) and its complements: *arraigo social* (social rootedness) and *notorio arraigo* (official or historical rootedness). This concept governs decisions about inclusion, which often turn on the degree to which Islam is interpreted as having deep historical roots in Spain.

Arraigo has dual implications for sociality and politics. The reflexive verb *arraigarse* can mean to create strong roots or to firmly embed or establish oneself; in social contexts, *arraigo* and its derivative forms can positively convey deeply felt social norms or refer to pillars of the community. However, *arraigo* can also refer to something undesirable that is stuck, dangerously affixed, or difficult to be rid of, like a tenacious weed. In other words, the Spanish concept of arraigo has a built-in allowance for overlap between rootedness as a social good and rootedness as a dangerous presence, the kind that must be eradicated at all costs. Unsurprisingly, then, in policies directed at both migrants and religious minorities, arraigo is an organizing principle that fosters both inclusive and exclusionary politics. Measuring minorities' arraigo emerged as a basis for policy decisions in the years following the Spanish transition to democracy, when the end of fascism heralded new challenges for a government that rapidly had to come up with governing strategies for its growing minority populations.

The tensions inherent in the arraigo concept are on display in Spanish governance of religious minorities. The 1978 constitution broke the official ties between the state and the Catholic Church that had characterized the Franco years, yet also reflected the ongoing importance of Catholicism. The constitution officially called for separation of church and state, but it also explicitly named the Catholic Church as an example of a religious organization with which the state would cooperate. This produced a kind of institutionalized ambivalence about the relationship between the state, nationality, and religion. Over the next decade, state officials met periodically with representatives of Spain's minority religions. In 1989, Islam was officially granted recognition as a religion of Spain, and in 1992 the government formalized the Agreement of Cooperation with the Islamic Commission of Spain. Recognition was made on the grounds of Islam's notorio arraigo, or deep historical (and official) rootedness in Spain. Normally, the status of notorio arraigo is awarded to religions with strong institutionalization and scope, usually measured in numbers of adherents and organizations. An exception was made for Islam. Despite the incipient nature of the religion's membership and institutions in the late 1980s and early 1990s, the government included Spain's Islamic history in its determination of Islam's scope, invoking the historical dimension of arraigo. Elena Arigita (2009) suggests that the state's legal recognition of Islam's arraigo must be understood within the politicized, commemorative mode of the years leading up to 1992, when Spain hosted the Olympics and celebrated the quincentenary of the 1492 "discovery" of the New World. Hoping to nudge public discussion away from memories of fifteenth-century colonial violence abroad and the Inquisition at home, recognizing Islam's notorio arraigo seemed a useful antidote.

Despite what may well have been good-faith efforts to recognize and integrate Islam, the Catholic Church remains the government's model for state-religion interaction. This means that successive Spanish administrations (and Andalusian policy makers) have complained about the inability to find a singular Muslim representative body resembling the Church and have blamed Muslims themselves for lack of communication, explaining away failure to deliver on commitments made to Muslim communities. In conversations during fieldwork, imams and Muslim association leaders frequently mentioned promised but unrealized accommodations for Muslims. These ranged from provisions for imams in prisons to Qur'anic classes for schoolchildren as alternatives to Catholicism classes, halal food options in schools, Muslim cemetery space, and permits to construct mosques, which are often stymied when regional and city governments cave to public opposition (Astor 2012).

The concept of arraigo, with its inherent logic of "exclusionary incorporation" (Partridge 2012, 21), has been equally foundational to democratic Spain's governance of migration. In 1985, a year before joining the

European Economic Community (EEC, the precursor to the European Union [EU]), Spain passed the first Foreigners Law to begin monitoring and controlling migration and has enacted two large-scale amnesties since then (Calavita 2005; Suárez-Navaz 2004). Spain provides a path to legal residence for undocumented migrants through a program called Arraigo Social (social rootedness, as assessed by lawyers and social workers). Undocumented migrants who can document three continuous years of residence in Spain, have registered with local municipal government offices, and are determined by officials to have put down social roots may apply for legal residence status. Until recently, undocumented migrants were also eligible for programs offering them access to public education and public health care. Some observers see in this a benevolent "Iberian model" in which Spain and Portugal are supposedly more tolerant of outsiders than other European nation-states because of their own histories of mass emigration and religious difference from Protestant Europe (Howe 2012).

However, despite some apparent leniency, Spanish political economy has depended on including migrants as labor, population, and social security buffers, not as full citizens (Calavita 2005). Even the most inclusive programs aimed at extending public services to migrants are enforced unevenly, often along racial, gendered, and religious lines (Rogozen-Soltar 2012a). Today, amid severe economic crisis, as the welfare state recedes in successive waves of privatization, migrants—especially the undocumented—are the first to be left unemployed and to be cut from services like health care (Colectivo IOÉ 2012). In this economically difficult context, even arraigo social as a route to legal residence has been drastically curtailed.[2] This exclusionary impulse reshaping treatment of migrants within Spain extends to its borders as well. Policing has become increasingly militarized, technologically complex, and geographically expansive, as Spanish border patrol is at once aided by EU-wide technology and surveillance initiatives and outsourced to North and sub-Saharan African forces (Andersson 2014). In coordination with its EU partners, the Spanish government periodically alters migration law and comprehensive programs for migrant integration, but the tendency has been toward more contradictory and restrictive laws aimed at curtailing migration, under both conservative and socialist governments (Calavita 2005; Suárez-Navaz 2004).[3] Restrictive policies and expanded border policing have not been successful. They have simply driven migrants to travel more dangerous routes to Spain, or to Italy, Greece, or Eastern Europe, and to live more in the political and social margins upon arrival (Cabot 2014; Lucht 2012). The so-called "Iberian model" of inclusion does not seem to deliver on its promises.

Arraigo, then, expresses Spanish and Andalusian historically rooted ambivalence about Islam and migration. In Granada, arraigo echoes both the promise of *convivencia* achieved through recognition and inclusion and the specter of *malafollá* in the form of persistent exclusions. While the logic of arraigo is often discussed in relation to policy, the same contradiction between the promise of real social belonging and its impossibility shapes how my research participants responded to that ever-present question Yassmin posed: "Am I really Spanish?" This question always figures as a dual provocation—at once referring to Muslims' senses of self and to others' perceptions and (mis)recognitions of them. The question implicitly also asks, "Am I really *accepted as* Spanish?" I turn now to ethnographic discussion of how Muslims variously manage this anxiety about belonging in Granada.

CONVERSION AND COSMOPOLITAN ROOTEDNESS

Converts' experiences are structured by the fact that they adopt Islam, a stigmatized minority religion, in a context in which regional, national, and religious identities are overwhelmingly conflated in public discourse. This means that many converts struggle to convince themselves and their families and friends that they are *still* Spanish (or European, if not born in Spain) despite converting. This is more straightforwardly the case for converts who see Islam as compatible with Spanish life, but even those converts who see conversion as a purposeful departure from normative Spanishness or Europeanness, described shortly, ultimately draw on and are constrained by prevailing tendencies to think about religion in terms of nationality. Converts negotiate this tension on a slippery terrain that moves between questions about the essence of individuals and groups of people (are *converts* still Spanish?) and the region of Andalusia itself (is *southern Spain* still Catholic? Or still becoming sufficiently secular?).

These anxieties around conversion in Granada recall other contexts in which conversion causes what Esra Özyürek calls a particular kind of public "alert" by virtue of uncoupling national and religious identities in uncomfortable ways. This anxiety is often related to the power of conversion to reveal the unsutured nature of national histories, particularly when converts become awkward "reminders of multifaith pasts" (Özyürek 2009, 95). In Germany, for example, conversion to Islam reminds Germans of the unfinished nature of post–Cold War projects to create cultural homogeneity and successfully put to rest racial, ethnic, and religious divides (Özyürek 2014).

In Granada, conversion provokes especially sharp historical fears by re-invoking the religious conflicts that shook Andalusia and Spain in the medieval period. Here, both the act of conversion in general and the adoption of Islam in particular foster anxiety. Historically, for the Catholic Kings who "reconquered" Muslim Spain, conversion was central to the project of creating a Catholic Spanish nation-state in which religious and national identities uniformly matched (Nirenberg 2004). Forced conversions of Jews and Muslims to Catholicism were meant to solve the problem of mismatched national and religious affiliations. Yet new converts in medieval Spain were constantly suspect and scrutinized (Woolard 2013), so much so that insecurities about their sincerity ultimately propelled the Inquisition toward its now-infamous racial logic of blood purity—eventually seen as a more rigorous way of evaluating eligibility for national belonging (Fuchs 2002; Lea 1988; Root 1988). Thus, while conversion was a key government strategy for disciplining the population, religious converts were also understood as a dangerous, somewhat inscrutable category.

Today, converts to Islam are suspect for being out of place in a Catholic-turned-secular state, but are also threatening because of the possibility that they may in fact be perfectly in place. In this sense, conversion represents an age-old threat to a homogeneity that was never established. Because many Spanish converts overtly claim to *return* to their Andalusian Muslim roots, the implication is one of reversing the effects of earlier centuries' forced conversions to Catholicism, which were foundational to the creation of the Spanish state. Conversion to Islam today thus literally threatens to undo the nation. Converts doubly evoke anxiety by reintroducing Islam and by adopting a historically suspect subject position of *convert* that produces suspicion and unwelcome reminders of violent religious and racial conflict.

Belén: Convert Continuity and Belonging

When I first met Belén Martínez, the woman from chapter 1 who referred to Catholic historiography as a "marketing job" meant to erase eight hundred years of Spanish Islam, she was a Catholic who could not imagine becoming Muslim. It was the summer of 2006, and we were both leaving a convert-built mosque high in the hills of the *Albayzín*. Introducing herself, she explained that her husband was inside praying, but she was heading home. He was a Muslim from the Middle East, but she was Catholic, "like all Spaniards," she said. A small, vivacious woman dressed in a trendy pink and purple pantsuit with black spike heels, Belén enthusiastically insisted we walk back toward downtown together. The sun was setting behind the Alhambra, splendidly visible across a shallow valley from the mosque, and the path through the narrow, winding, cobblestone streets of the medieval, Moorish quarter was long and best traversed with company.

As we left, we ran into one of the leaders of the mosque and his wife, both Spanish converts to Islam. Knowing that Belén was married to a man inside praying, they asked if she was thinking of converting to Islam. "No!" Belén replied emphatically. She smiled and said Islam was great, but that she was "just too typically Spanish" to consider becoming Muslim. Despite their protestations that they had managed to convert, Belén was steadfast. Matter-of-factly, she reasoned aloud that she couldn't possibly give up the Spanish traditions of consuming pork, wine, and beer, all beloved in Granada but prohibited in Islam. "Impossible. I can't even think about it," she concluded. And with that, we headed toward downtown.

Fast-forward two years. In 2008, newly back in Granada, I knocked on the door of an antiracism NGO where I had arranged to conduct research, and to my surprise, Belén opened it. We had not kept in touch, but I recognized her immediately and we became fast friends as I worked with her at the NGO where she served as a volunteer lawyer, helping with cases involving Muslims and migrants who had suffered racial and religious discrimination. My first day there, Belén confided that despite her earlier certainty that as a Spanish woman, she could never convert to Islam, she had in fact become Muslim. After much reading, thinking, and discussing with her husband, she had surprised him by converting at their Islamic wedding ceremony, held at a local mosque, three years after their initial marriage in a civil ceremony. She now attended a mosque on a semiweekly basis, she was studying Arabic to read the Qur'an "properly," and she was an avid advocate for Islam in Granada, taking every opportunity to explain and defend Islam to her fellow Spaniards, insisting on Islam's normalcy and compatibility with Andalusian life.

How, one might ask, did Belén change her mind? The story of Belén's romance with a Muslim man, her initial belief that being Spanish and converting to Islam were incompatible, and her gradual adoption of the religion exemplify the social processes that structure converts' desire for rootedness in Granada. Converts must overcome a prevalent understanding of national and religious identities as fundamentally linked, and this shapes their possibilities and limitations for claiming belonging as Spanish and European Muslims.

Belén's account of her own initial doubts about conversion and her eventual change of heart illustrate in particular how race, class, and gender ideologies create assumptions about the incompatibility of Islam and Andalusianness or Spanishness. Belén recalled that she initially had no idea that Spanish Muslims existed, and everything she knew about Islam had to do with images of "*machismo.*" One of her favorite topics to discuss with me was her initial rejection of Ahmet, her husband. "The first thing I said to my husband when we met was, 'So, you're Arab? Well, they say you Arabs are terrible, you know!' And he said, 'Oh really?' And I said, 'Yes, they say you treat your women very badly!'" This began an antagonism that would morph into flirtation and ultimately love and marriage. Belén would often repeat this exchange and then laugh; she found her prior naïveté hilarious. But she also brought it up in more serious tones as a cautionary tale about Spaniards' pervasive ignorance about the Muslim world. She would scold herself for having conflated Arabs with Muslims, and for holding such strong "*tópicos*" (stereotypes) about Muslim gender inequality. Belén now spoke frequently about her husband's kindness, patience, and support of her career because she wanted me and everyone else around to know that their marriage was characterized by gender equality and that he had not forced her to convert.

In describing her conversion process to me, Belén emphasized two major turning points that cemented the idea of conversion for her after the first eye-opening realization that her husband was Muslim, Arab, and yet in her words, "not *machista*." The first was her growing sense that, despite initial apparent differences, Islam and Catholicism had some theological and practical continuities. While Ahmet did not pressure her to convert, it was through him—initially watching and observing his practice, and eventually talking to him at length about Islam—that Belén decided to become Muslim. At the beginning of their time together, Belén was surprised by her husband's pious practices, and above all, his routine commitment to religiosity, which she saw as a marked improvement over most Spaniards' "Sunday Catholicism."

> Living your life with a Muslim is really different than if you marry an atheist, or an Italian. The hours of the day are organized by prayer. I remember that early on we would go out with my husband, and say we'd leave around seven p.m. and I'd think that we'd be out until eleven at night, and when eight o'clock came around, he'd say, "Sweetie, can we go home? I have to pray." Your life is marked out by the five daily prayers. And that's what I liked most, was seeing his daily relationship with God, it's like a permanent dialogue . . . and I had a certain envy of this.

This admiration led Belén to ask questions about Islam, and a few initial questions eventually became regular evening discussions about theology in which she would quiz her husband about Muslim beliefs and practices, ruminating at length on their potential implications for Spanish life.

After many discussions with her husband and other local Muslims, Belén felt convinced of Islam's compatibility with Spanish lifestyles. In making this point, she emphasized that Islam can be adopted gradually, working new practices into one's life according to the common Spanish phrase *poco a poco* (little by little) without pressure to be perfect or to immediately wear a headscarf (hijab) or do all the daily prayers. Equally important was her sense that Islam "doesn't prevent women from anything," including having careers, in her case from being a lawyer. Most of all, both religions profess belief in one God. She summed this up by saying she had realized that Islam "just wasn't that weird (*raro*) after all." Finally, Belén even found similarities between what were in her estimation the less appealing aspects of both Muslim and Spanish Catholic life. When I asked her how she resolved some of her doubts about gender and Islam, she brought up her initial worry that Islam might involve polygyny. But, she said, polygyny was rare, and after all, not very different in her mind from the common practice in twentieth-century Spain of "men having two women, the wife, and the mistress!"

The second pivotal moment for Belén was her discovery of Spanish converts, and importantly, female Spanish converts who were well-to-do and had successful careers.

One of the first times this happened was when she attended a mosque with her husband and visited the women's section. "I asked the women if I could look around, and I asked one fair-skinned woman where she was from. She said, 'I'm Irish!' and I said, 'And you're a *Muslim*?!?' And she goes, 'Yeah, and this woman over here is Spanish, and this one, too.' And I was shocked, obviously. I was like, 'There are Muslims that aren't Arab?' It was the first time I realized that." Belén's and other women's anxieties about Islam's foreignness reflected a powerful interlocking of ideas about gender, race, and class that shaped their understandings of national identity and belonging. Belén said that discovering Spanish Muslim women was hugely important, but even more so was meeting educated, high-achieving career women. A friend of hers concurred in an interview, saying she only felt comfortable converting once she met "professional" Muslim women at the local university:

> Of course at the beginning I had a lot of doubts about Islam. But the Muslim women I met were so highly educated and had fellowships and impressive CVs and spoke French and Spanish. I liked what they said about Islam. I saw that Islam wasn't so strange [*extraño*] after all; that the women didn't have to be locked up, they could work and be active, not passive at all, but active women.

This woman's observation that she was swayed by seeing that Islam "wasn't so strange after all," is strikingly similar to Belén's realization that Islam "just wasn't that weird after all." Belén's and her friend's gradual opening to the idea of Islam reflects local investment in the alignment between nationality and religion, and the ways it is shaded by racial and gendered beliefs about Islam as a foreign religion characterized above all by gender inequality and migrant socioeconomic marginality. For these women, at least initially, becoming Muslim was doable because it did not seem to entail radical changes to their gendered and class-specific senses of self.

Today, Belén is on a mission to convince others that Islam fits with Catholic (and secular) *Granadino* social norms. Her approach illustrates one way converts try to claim rootedness for Islam in Andalusia—by accommodating local understandings of regional identity. When talking about Islamic practices, she almost always describes them using carefully chosen phrases that normalize Islam as part of Andalusian life. She describes how Islamic prayer fits into "*la vida quotidiana*" (everyday life), and how Muslim Spanish girls are "*chicas muy normales y corrientes*" (very normal and ordinary girls) who attend Spanish schools, speak Spanish, and have non-Muslim Spanish friends, a far cry from the popular image among some Spaniards of Muslim women and girls closed off from society, secluded at home. When asked by coworkers about the hijab (which she does not wear except when praying at a mosque), she compares it to scarves worn by pious Catholic women in Spain, who—like some Muslim women—covered their heads out of modesty. When Muslims use the Arabic phrase insha'Allah (God willing) in reference to something they hope for, Belén turns to any non-Muslims present to point out that this is just like Catholics' penchant for adding "*si Dios lo quiere*" (God willing) to the end of hypothetical statements, such as "My favorite soccer team will win tonight, God willing!" In this way, Belén tries to demystify Islam and defuse fears of its foreignness by pointing out that Catholic and Muslim Spaniards actually engage in many similar practices on a daily basis, such as ways of talking and covering for modesty. She talks about these issues with me and with anyone else in earshot, and uploads videos of herself commenting on these and other topics to YouTube. Belén believes strongly in Islam's compatibility with Spanishness, and she sees her activities as necessary to counter Catholic historiography's "marketing job."

Indeed, her efforts are clearly shaped by her knowledge of Andalusians' frequent inability to recognize the existence of Andalusian or Spanish Muslims. Underlying Belén's insistence on Islam's normalcy is the idea that Islam is something dangerously abnormal. Consider the way Belén described to me how some of her Catholic friends came to accept her conversion. Musing over some of her friends' nonchalance about her conversion, she said, "I think it's because I really represent for them the idea that—I'm a perfect example of someone who even though I converted, no one has locked me up in my house, I don't *have* to veil, and they can see that I continue to be a normal person. They can say, 'We have a friend who converted and she's the same as always, the same life, just now in an Islamic family, where they celebrate the Muslim holidays, but she continues working, studying.'" Belén even told me that some of her friends chalked her lack of change up to secularity, mentioning to her that they figured she and her husband must be fairly nonpracticing Muslims. Belén took care to let them know that the opposite was true, that he was deeply pious and meticulously practicing, and that she was on her way to adopting more pious practices herself.

While Belén was happy that her friends were unperturbed by her conversion, the implication was also that publicly visible Muslim piety *is* in fact disruptive and unwelcome. Her friends were accepting, she surmised, because they assumed that her Muslim family was a secular one. Her conversion was tolerable because it was largely invisible. Belén seemed ambivalent about this. On the one hand, she celebrated her continued acceptance by these friends and felt like a great ambassador for Islam. After all, she herself had highly valued her ability to remain the same in many ways after converting. On the other hand, she scratched her head at their assumption that, in the absence of a headscarf or total seclusion at home—stereotypical signs of Islamic religiosity within Spanish imaginaries—she was presumed not to care about piety. Belén felt that Islamic values had begun to shape her life at all times, helping to guide her interactions with others and her decisions about home and work life. Her friends' acceptance, then, seemed to endorse her conversion for not standing out, and thus to accept Belén's continued friendship, but not her newfound piety.

Murabitun Converts: Rupture and Rootedness

Other converts, particularly those who identified explicitly as members of the Sufi Murabitun, also claimed rootedness for Islam in Granada, though they diverged significantly from Belén's understandings of conversion, piety, and Spanishness. Like Belén, they saw the relationship between their new religiosity and their sense of national and regional identities as a key question posed by conversion, but they answered it differently. Belén reconciled her newfound Muslim religion with her desire to remain Spanish by insisting on the compatibility of Islam and Spanishness. In contrast, Murabitun converts considered adopting Islam to be a purposeful departure from mainstream Spanish life, a kind of radical rupture with modern Spanish values. However, despite this stance, they also emphasized Islam's resonance with an imagined formerly glorious Islamic Spain shaped by cosmopolitanism and social sophistication. Ultimately, this pulled their narratives back to an underlying insistence on Spain's innate Muslimness and convert Muslims' belonging in Spain. In other words, their claims of purposeful uprooting became—sometimes unwittingly—also claims of cosmopolitan rootedness in Spain, unexpectedly echoing Belén's position. While these converts differed from Belén in many ways, examining how the local imperative for convergence in religious-national-regional identities shapes the identity discourse of converts who are otherwise very diverse reveals its enduring and widespread social power.

Converts who participated in the local group of Sufi Murabitun sometimes considered conversion to Islam to be a theological rejection of the trappings and values of a wide spectrum of modern Spanish life. Some felt that true Islamic piety required a departure from the global capitalist economy, sent their children to unauthorized Muslim schools, embarked on or considered polygynous marriages, and worked to establish new gendered divisions of labor at home and in public, replacing normative Spanish emphasis on the Western conceptions of gender equality that Belén revered with what they saw as Islamic norms of gendered piety. In interviews and casual conversations, their comments often moved back and forth between discussions of Muslim belief and pious practice, and vociferous critiques of Spanish and Andalusian politics, economics, and social norms.

But these converts often circled back to Andalusian and Spanish history when they told me their stories of coming to Islam. One woman, Sylvia, converted to Islam shortly after moving to Granada from central Spain. When I asked her about the process, she explained that living in Granada, with its Moorish ambience "all around you," had produced her conversion. "There's a magic here in Granada for me. I love the history. I feel like I'm returning back to my roots!" Her comments put a regional twist on the spiritual discourse of "return," common among Muslims around the world who see adoption of Islam not as a conversion to a "new" religion but rather as the return to a natural, inherent state of piety accessible to all (Ahmad 2010; Van Nieuwkerk 2006). For Sylvia, conversion to Islam was a return to her religious roots, but that return was induced by a prior recognition of the Muslim roots of Andalusia, whose Moorish-infused ambience inspired Sylvia's spiritual journey. The regional-national here was critical to making sense of the spiritual. In research on conversion to Islam in Germany, Esra Özyürek finds that most of her European interlocutors converted to Islam following a "meaningful relationship" with a Muslim-born migrant (2014, 22). In Granada, conversions were more likely to follow a "meaningful relationship" between converts, the city of Granada, and its imagined history.[4]

This tendency to understand conversion to Islam as a critique of Spanishness, while also situating conversion *as* Spanish or Andalusian and as intrinsically related to Granada as a *place*, began with the "original" converts—men and women now in their fifties, sixties, and seventies who converted during the 1980s, in the midst of Spain's transition to democracy. I interviewed and spent time with many women of this generation, who saw their religious transition as a kind of revolutionary religious homecoming. Lubab, a middle-aged woman born and raised in Granada, explained her 1980s conversion as a natural part of being young during Spain's democratic transition: "We were young, and besides we were coming right out of the dictatorship, and there was this kind of searching going on. We wanted to encounter new things . . . and really what happened was more like a social movement."

Her friend Nahlah, originally from Switzerland, similarly explained her decision to embrace Islam in terms of the political context and social milieu of the democratic transition, saying, "I mean in those days, Franco had just died and it was like [here she made a sound mimicking an explosion and threw her arms in the air]. I mean people were becoming Muslim by the day." I asked Nahlah what prompted so many conversions, and she replied:

> It had a lot to do with freedom. Freedom . . . because Franco had just died. And people were, you know, when they were in the university there was no freedom . . . and this was a Catholic country, with a dictator, with no choice. And Islam was forbidden. And so here we were, this group of

people, and when I arrived in Spain Franco had just died, and Spain was
amazing. I mean it was effervescent! Especially the younger generation . . .
suddenly he died and the whole thing changed, and there was democracy,
so people were trying everything. Right? And the whole Sufism bit was
quite extraordinary. I mean we used to go down to Plaza Bib-Rambla and
do these huge *hadras*.[5] I mean we used to be *outrageous*!

Nahlah thus cast conversion as a radical rupture from the Francoist version of Catholic Spanishness, but included the conversion movement
within a broader swath of bohemian, alternative social experiments in
Granada that accompanied democracy's arrival. Generally, Nahlah ab-
horred what she and others called the Spanish "obsession" with freedom;
like many Muslims involved in various Islamic revival movements around
the world, she felt that upholding a secular ideal of freedom as an ultimate
value prevented people from realizing the benefits of religious practices
that require submission and duty to God (Deeb 2006; Fernando 2014;
Ghodsee 2009; Mahmood 2005). Yet here, she enthusiastically situated
adopting Islam within a special moment of religious and political freedom
in Spain. Her reminiscence casts public Sufi ritual as a provocation that rejected traditional Spanish religious and cultural sensibilities, but also as an
act fitting within the democratic transition's upheaval, figuring conversion
as part of Granada's particular bohemian, alternative, cosmopolitan milieu. Freedom figures here not as the modern, capitalist freedom Nahlah
often criticized but as a religious openness and tolerance reminiscent of
al-Andalus. Conducting mass Sufi rituals in the plaza she mentioned—one
with an Arabic-derived name and a significant role in Granada's Muslim
history—was especially meaningful to her as a way of celebrating this
newfound freedom to embrace Islam and express non-Catholic piety in
public, rerooting Islam in Granada's urban space.[6]

Clearly, Murabitun rejections of Spanishness belied an underlying reconciliation between Islam and Spain. In rejecting modern Spanishness,
they embraced an imagined cosmopolitan Muslim history of *al-Andalus*,
and enshrined themselves and their practice of Islam within it. Many
of my interlocutors accomplished this through a kind of double discursive move. First, they made claims about Islam's rootedness in Spanish and Andalusian history, always in ways that underscored Muslims'

contribution to a long-lost Spanish cosmopolitanism. Then they linked the ideals of this lost past to the convert Muslim community in the present, contrasting their own religious and cultural sensibilities to those of non-Muslim Spaniards. The structure of these comments facilitated a disavowal of modern Spain while also claiming regional rootedness through an embrace of *al-Andalus*.

Amal, the thirty-five-year-old daughter of two northern European parents who had moved to Granada to join Sufi converts there in the 1970s, tethered present-day converts to an imagined cosmopolitanism of *al-Andalus* by emphasizing economic practices. Though born into a Muslim family, she considered herself part of the convert community, a *"converso."* On a spring day, I interviewed Amal over lunch at the convert mosque's adjacent Islamic Studies Center. As with many of my convert research participants, Amal eventually swung our wide-ranging conversation around to the history of Islam in Spain, rebutting official Spanish historiography:

> The official Spanish version is: "The Arabs came, they conquered, and then they were thrown out, okay, by the Catholic Kings." But the true version is that, through trade, and just proximity, and affinity . . . Christians found it easy to accept Islam, because it's part of the same tradition. *Al-Andalus* was then you know, *from here*, and now there are people in North Africa who can trace their ancestors back to Spain. So it's not that the Arabs came here, and then were kicked out. No, it was *Spanish* Muslims who were kicked out.

It was important to Amal that I see Muslims expelled by the Inquisition as real, indigenous Spaniards who were Muslim, not just "invading Arabs." Further, for Amal, trade had been a central feature facilitating and constituting Islam's rootedness in medieval Andalusia. Through economic ties, communities on both sides of the Mediterranean engaged one other, and, she said, they found religious affinities in the process. Since "all of the prophets come from the same God," she said, it was relatively easy to embrace one another's religious beliefs, leading to a kind of cosmopolitan mixing that was ended only by the Inquisition.

Several minutes later, Amal firmly placed her own present-day convert community within the legacy of this cosmopolitan *al-Andalus* when I asked where she lived. Like many converts, Amal lived on the outskirts of the *Albayzín*, in a neighborhood she characterized as cosmopolitan.

Oh, I like the *Albayzín*. Definitely. You know, historically, that's the
Muslim part of the city. I'm pretty cosmopolitan, and I like neighborhoods
where you see a lot, where not everybody looks the same, you know.
I mean it's actually quite multicultural where I live. I have the Moroccan
shop in front, the Chinese supermarket next door, so yeah, that's my favorite sort of area is the historical center.

Amal went on to laud her own and other converts' cosmopolitan outlook
in contrast to what she presented as the provincial closed-mindedness
of Catholic *Granadinos*. Earlier in our conversation she had faulted the
Inquisition for putting a sad end to the cosmopolitanism of *al-Andalus*.
Now, she complained about other neighborhoods in Granada that were
gearing up for *Semana Santa* (Holy Week and Easter), scoffing at the local
street processions' use of costumes derived from inquisitorial clothing.
For Amal, living in the *Albayzín* and appreciating its ethnic businesses
became a way of situating her current Muslim life in the city within the
imagined—and lauded—cosmopolitan ethos of medieval *convivencia*. Just
as Spaniards in Amal's historical narrative became cosmopolitan through
cross-Mediterranean trade that led to religious pluralism, so today, many
converts consciously chose to live in the historic city center, where engagement with internationalism in the guise of ethnic businesses figured
prominently in their sense of themselves as a cosmopolitan community
that rejected the stale remnants of Franco's Catholic public sociality. Amal
seemed to reject modern Spanish Catholicism by embracing an interna-
tionalist, cosmopolitan ethos—but in doing so, she actually insisted on its
very Spanishness. Rather than really turning away from identification as
Spanish, her critique of Spanishness was more an insistence on cosmopolitan Muslim sensibilities as the revival of a long-lost, better Spanishness,
one that honors the Spanish Muslims who were expelled so long ago.

While Amal claimed cosmopolitan rootedness for Islam in Spain by
emphasizing links between past and present trans-Mediterranean economic trade and religious pluralism, Maha, another young convert, articulated similar claims of Islam's Spanishness through a discussion of
morality and aesthetics. She saw a historical Islamic essence in flamenco
music and dance, aesthetic practices that are widely seen as archetypically
Andalusian. Born in Granada to parents who converted when she was
very young, Maha had moved with her extended family to Mexico as a

young woman to help spread Islam there as a part of a Murabitun *dawa* movement, and she returned to Granada around the same time I moved there. We had many conversations about the joys and difficulties of moving (back) to Granada. Maha was having a hard time socially. She often strongly critiqued "mainstream modern Spanish life," complaining that she could not identify with "Andalusian women of today," and felt lonely and isolated from her young adult peers since returning. She felt that her Andalusian peers were *vacío* (empty) and obsessed with personal freedom to the detriment of family values. She worried about drug use, homosexuality, premarital sex, violence in schools, disrespect for the elderly, and materialism, which she felt European political and economic systems perpetuated. Maha hoped that turning away from modern moral poverty and "filling" herself with "the light of Allah" would insulate her and her future children from Spanish "*cultura*" (culture).

One day, as she complained about Andalusian youth, Maha said that unlike "modern Andalusian women," she identified much more with the long-lost "*mujer Andaluza antigua*" (the ancient Andalusian woman). I asked her who that woman was, and she described the ancient Andalusian woman nostalgically as a "real" Andalusian, a practitioner of the musical genre flamenco, which she went on to characterize as both deeply shaped by Islamic and Arab influence and foundational to the authentic essence of medieval Andalusians.

> Well, I don't know, I've always really liked flamenco music, since I was little, and I think [the ancient Andalusian woman] is that—I mean flamenco varies a lot nowadays, but it's that pure flamenco, that just comes out of your soul, I think that's really beautiful and very connected to spirituality, you know? It forms a real part of the peoples from here, from Granada and Andalusia. The song, the dance, all of it, I think that a *large* part of it is related to the Arabs, too. The way [flamenco artists] sing is just like the way the Qur'an is recited. So I think the ancient flamenco singers, they listened and they tried to imitate [Muslims]. It isn't empty [*vacío*], it's full of an essence. And even still today flamenco retains that state of *fitra. Fitra* is the relationship you have with your closest life, with your real self or nature. All of this is being lost now and exploited for tourism too.

Many scholars have noted a tendency to associate Andalusian music with the mythical resonances of a medieval "golden era and lost paradise"

(Paetzold 2009, 208; Shannon 2015). In Granada and throughout Spain, flamenco performance, often associated with Roma communities, has long been discursively linked with the essence of *al-Andalus*. Debates among scholars, musicians, and Andalusians about the possible Arab or Islamic roots of flamenco are intense and serve as a kind of musical metonym for debates about the Moorishness of Granada, a key city in the flamenco world (Chuse 2003; Cruces-Roldán 2003; Labajo 2003; Washabaugh 2012). Indeed, the early-twentieth-century Andalusian regionalists described in the introduction—the poet Federico García Lorca, the politician Blas Infante, and the composer Manuel de Falla—all championed flamenco music as an excellent way of linking the Roma traditions of Granada and Andalusia to older forms of Moorish and Islamic artistic expression. Flamenco was central to these early, Islamophilic regionalist projects (Shannon 2015).

Maha likely drew on this broader discourse that positions contemporary flamenco as flowing from Moorish performance genres. From her position as a pious convert, she emphasized the spirituality within these musical genres across time. She located the Islamic concept of fitra, which usually means a kind of natural disposition or constitution, within (and as accessible through) flamenco performance. Because flamenco has been, in the eyes of many, diluted by the demands of the tourism economy, flamenco artists considered "pure" and unadulterated by touristy pop or world music trends have come to stand for a rarefied, authentic Andalusianness for many people.[7] By associating fitra with this vision of a pure flamenco that expresses Andalusianness, Maha wove Islam into the very fabric of authentic Andalusian identity and belonging. In the image of fitra-infused flamenco, she saw glimmering flickers of a long-lost medieval Islam.

Maha also saw in the aesthetic practices of flamenco artists the last remnant of real (Islamic) Andalusianness with which to identify as a young convert today. Her logic parallels the way Amal enshrined converts today within the cosmopolitan glory of *al-Andalus* by citing the relationship between trans-Mediterranean spirituality and economic practices to characterize Muslims in both periods. Attending flamenco performances and working on her own flamenco craft became, for Maha, a way of connecting with the "ancient Andalusian woman" that she admired, as well as a way of developing her faith. Like Amal, for Maha, critiques of Spanish life in the end became articulations of her own authentic Andalusianness, of conversion as a revival of, or protection of, the last traces of older, truer, Islamic practices and values in the face of contemporary Catholic and secular women's commodification-driven lives. Further, aligning Islam with flamenco situated converts' religiosity within a well-received, respected local discourse of Andalusian identity and history, given the immense regional popularity of flamenco and pride in local flamenco expertise. Rejecting mainstream Andalusianness and embracing *al-Andalus* was at once a way of conceptualizing conversion and Islamic practice as a departure from Spain and asserting it as the cornerstone of regional authenticity.

The tendency to situate convert religiosity within local nostalgia for a lauded, cosmopolitan *al-Andalus* means that converts' presence in the city sometimes resonated with popular, institutionalized ways of remembering *al-Andalus* that were comfortable and pleasing to the general public. Converts' self-understanding in terms of cosmopolitan rootedness plays into the discourse and aesthetics of successful local programs—cultural organizations, government initiatives, and economic sectors that champion the legacy of medieval Islam—bringing it safely and acceptably into public life in the present. These programs tend to present Granada as a cross-Mediterranean space of cultural and economic productivity. The prominent cultural organization *El Legado Andalusí Fundación* (the Andalusi Legacy Foundation), for instance, is a hybrid public and non-profit entity with established tourist routes through the Moorish monuments of Andalusia and a museum exhibit in Granada on *al-Andalus* that foregrounds cultural activities, scientific and political achievements, art, architecture, and food. The foundation funds local research about *al-Andalus* as well as workshops for schoolchildren in cooking and art, among other topics.

The recent *Milenio* celebration, promoted by the government in collaboration with the Andalusi Legacy Foundation and similar organizations, involved a full year of programming in 2013 to commemorate a millennium since Granada's 1013 founding. The celebration exemplified the political and economic marshaling of *al-Andalus* in efforts to make Granada the centerpiece of a cross-Mediterranean cultural and geopolitical configuration. The Milenio's most celebrated events were music and dance performances, art exhibits, sporting competitions, business show-case events, and trans-Mediterranean economic ventures. In honor of the Milenio, the Andalusi Legacy Foundation's museum gift shop featured a small book display with tomes reminiscent of Discovery Channel edu-cational programming, some including photographic scenes reenacting *al-Andalus*. In one large coffee-table book, actors had posed in scenes of medieval everyday life in the now-museumified spaces of the Alhambra, bringing them to life with images of how rooms and gardens might have been lived in and used under Moorish rule. Flipping through the pages, I could not help but notice most of the actors were white, and they wore clothing and headscarves identical to the style worn by my European con-vert Muslim interlocutors. I do not suggest a direct or intentional relation-ship between the ways of remembering *al-Andalus* in these local programs and among converts. I do want to suggest that this dominant mode of presenting the Moorish legacy for public consumption—in ways oriented toward the branding of local heritage for tourist consumption and the ap-preciation of art, aesthetics, and scientific achievement, but rarely if ever in terms of religiosity or actual ancestral inheritance—creates the context in which my convert research participants claim belonging as Muslim Spaniards. By insisting on Islam's compatibility with modern Spanish life or by casting Islam as a conduit for recovering an authentic, older Spanish, or particularly Andalusian ethos already widely celebrated by *Granadino* publics, converts' positioning of their presence as Muslims fits nicely into existing, acceptable social and political frames.

"You Lose Your Life!": The Limits of Convert Belonging

There are, however, sometimes profound limits to converts' belonging in Granada. Some who identify as Murabitun socialize mostly with one another, and while Murabitun sometimes expressed sadness over rejec-tion from family or Catholic friends upon conversion, many saw their isolation from non-Muslim Spaniards as inevitable or even necessary, and oriented their new familial and social lives toward relationships with other converts. But for new Muslims intent on maintaining social and family networks from before conversion, or who had to interact daily with Catholic and secular coworkers and neighbors, the limits of convert be-longing, which resulted from normative conceptions of Spanishness and

Andalusianness as definitionally Catholic-secular, were more obvious and painful.

Belén is a prime example of the remoteness into which converts find themselves pushed. Given Belén's optimistic attitude about the compatibility of Spanish and Muslim life, I was surprised when she revealed that she had never told her family about her conversion to Islam. When I arrived at the NGO office one day, Belén's usual, incessantly cheerful disposition was gone, and she seemed rather sad. She explained that she had been looking at pictures of her sister, which always brought her down a bit. I asked why, and Belén told me the story of her family's reaction when she married Ahmet. Belén was from a prominent Catholic family in southwestern Spain with strong ties to local business and to one of the Catholic brotherhoods that works year-round to prepare for annual processions during Holy Week and Easter. When Belén broke the news that she was dating a Muslim Arab, her family was dismayed; they were concerned about their reputation and Belén's safety. Neighborhood gossips clucked their tongues and when they ran into Belén at the butcher shop and fish market, they implored her, "¡¿Pero Belén, con lo que tú vales?!" (literally, "But Belén, with what you're worth?!" That is, "You're above this" or "You can do better") and "Es que él querrá papeles" (Surely he just wants papers). Belén's mother developed heart trouble around this time, and her siblings blamed their mother's ailment on stress over Belén's relationship. Unable to overcome the constant pushback she received from her family, Belén ultimately decided to forgo the huge wedding she had always imagined, and she and Ahmet married in secret at the local courthouse.

When told of the marriage, her siblings were enraged. Her mother wept profusely and nearly fainted, but she slowly came around to a kind of resigned acceptance of her daughter's choice. Belén thought maybe things would improve over time, but the first summer after her marriage, Belén's brother-in-law Juan, whom she described as "the most racist, racist ever," called to say that he wanted to be sure Ahmet did not plan on coming to the family's annual get-together at their summer house in the countryside. Belén insisted that he should be invited, and Juan retorted that there was no way a *moro* was going to be allowed in the pool, to swim in the same water as his vulnerable two-year old son. Several days later, Belén's siblings stopped by her apartment. Juan yelled from outside, "Get out here, Belén!

And you, *moro de mierda* (shit Moor), get out of Spain! You deserve to die!" Ahmet and Juan got in a screaming match and eventually a physical fight in the street, in full view of the local neighbors on their nightly *paseo* (Andalusians' frequent evening strolls). After this fight, Belén felt humiliated and terrified. She was worried about future violence between Ahmet and her family.

Because of this family history, Belén had never told them about her conversion, and since they no longer lived in the same city, they were blissfully unaware. Disallowed from seeing her nephew, she felt that she was already on the verge of losing her relationship with her siblings, and she feared that revealing her new faith would be the last straw. Finally, she was concerned about pushing her mother's heart over the edge and she did not want to "kill my own mother." Throughout the telling of this story, Belén kept repeating at intervals that her family was "very Catholic, after all" and very Andalusian. The family's sense of Andalusian pride seemed to her to explain their agony over having a Muslim, migrant relative.

In the weeks following Juan's and Ahmet's fight, Belén and Ahmet decided to move to Granada, where Ahmet had heard from migrant friends that there were many Muslims. Belén saw the move as an obvious choice. She had never been to Granada, but the city, with its famous Moorish heritage, loomed in her imagination as a self-evident panacea to their problems. Early one morning, she and Ahmet caught an intercity bus to Granada. They arrived at dawn and before even going to a hotel, they caught the number seven bus directly up to the famous *San Nicolás* lookout square in the *Albayzín* to gaze across the valley, watching the sun rise over the Alhambra, suitcases in tow. Now, years later, she looked back at that moment of innocent arrival with a knowing smile. She knew now that being Spanish and Muslim in Granada was no easy task. Belén's decision to move to Granada and her new perspective on life there together indicate the limits of Muslim belonging in the city, but they nevertheless gesture to how Granada stubbornly figures as a beacon of hope for Muslim Spaniards.

Another convert woman, Clara, was also outspoken about the social and emotional consequences of conversion to Islam. Her story highlights the double remoteness converts contend with as they lose a sense of belonging in Spain (when people begin to recognize them as Muslims) but do not feel it immediately replaced by membership in an imagined Muslim world. Clara explained, "Spaniards, in general, don't realize Islam is a religion. Here, being Muslim means being Arab. They ask you, 'Are you Muslim?' and I say, 'Yes.' And they say, 'Oh, well then you're not Spanish.' And it's the same with Arabs.[8] They see this [pointing to her headscarf] and they say, 'Oh, you're an Arab.'" Clara told me many stories of misrecognition, disapproval, and distancing on the part of fellow Spaniards. Shortly before our first interview, she had gone to the post office. A public employee there was rude to her, she told me, and had yelled at her about correct postage. A second employee came to Clara's rescue, but to her dismay, said to the first employee, "Hey, you can't yell at her just because she's a foreigner!" To Clara, this misrecognition from a well-intentioned employee trying to defend her was actually worse than the initial yelling, as it cemented her sense that as a Muslim woman with a headscarf, she was forever to be presumed foreign by the general public.

Clara was most frustrated by the way reactions to her adoption of Islam changed precisely these kinds of day-to-day, small interactions, like conversations in the course of running errands, that had previously helped make up her sense of self and critically, her sense of belonging in the city. While she had faced steep opposition to her conversion from family and friends, one of the stories Clara became most emotional telling me was about how her interactions with the man who ran her local neighborhood grocery store changed after conversion. Grocery stores are an important place for social life in Andalusian cities, which are organized primarily as mixed-use zones, rather than into separate shopping districts and residential areas. While more cities now have large supermarkets, most neighborhoods still have several small grocery stores. Grocers know neighborhood shoppers by face, often by name, and these stores are key threads for the fabric of city sociality. Clara and her grocer had always shared a friendly, witty banter, but the first day she walked in with a headscarf he stared at her, eyes wide, mouth agape. "He was speechless, it was a shock that he just couldn't hide. And the worst part of all was that he spoke to me as *usted* for the first time. He had never called me *usted* before. It was his way of putting distance between us. It was a really tough encounter." *Usted* (you) is used to address someone in the formal register in Spain (in contrast to the familiar *tú*), and is far less common there than in Spanish-speaking

Latin America. People only employ it in news reporting or when speaking to the very elderly or those in high positions of power. Using *usted* with a friend, unless joking, indicates anger and negates intimacy. For Clara, the accumulation of new distancing gestures on the part of friends, family, and other city acquaintances was taxing. After telling me the story of her grocer friend, she paused and then said angrily, summing up, "It sounds like an exaggeration to say it, but what really happens is, you lose your life!" Clara's conundrum was that people either mistook her for a migrant, revealing the unthinkability of a Spanish Muslim, or they realized she was both Spanish and Muslim and responded with anger rather than acceptance over her choice to break from Catholic and secular identification. If Muslim migrants are seen by unwelcoming sectors as invaders, converts are traitors. Clara's assertion that she had lost her life indicates the personal and social upheaval that results from negative responses to conversion.

Despite such difficulties, converts actively and adamantly claimed rootedness and belonging in Granada. Converts like Belén who saw adopting Islam as compatible with Spanishness and those like Amal or Maha who framed conversion as a rupture with normative Spanish cultural practices and politics might seem to hold opposing positions, but they all actually furthered an underlying assumption linking religion and nationality. Even those casting Islam as a departure from Spanishness or Europeanness did so in ways that inscribed conversion, and sometimes Islam, into Spanish politics and history.

Ultimately, converts' efforts to secure Muslim belonging may unintentionally shut the door on a politics of belonging that would also include Muslim migrants. This is because converts' basis for inclusion, however difficult and tenuous, always comes down to a defense of their Spanishness—either in the guise of claims that converts themselves are "still Spanish" or that Spain itself is rightly a Muslim space and that conversion simply reconstitutes it as such by reviving *al-Andalus*. Both moves, while accepting of Islam, still emphasize belonging based on Spanishness or Andalusianness, foregrounding the importance of having national or regional provenance. Despite Belén's heartbreaking experience of familial disapproval and Clara's exclusion from social networks, both were able to hold on to a sense of Spanish belonging and recognition as Andalusians in some contexts, even if it came with sacrifices. In other words, despite some Murabitun critiques of Spanish and European political economy, converts largely acquiesced to (and could manage to sometimes fit themselves within) a discursive landscape that privileges Andalusian and Spanish (and sometimes broader European) origins. This is a litmus test that Muslim migrants are rarely able to pass.

MIGRATION AND TERRITORIAL, ANCESTRAL ROOTEDNESS

Like converts, migrant Muslims' sense of rootedness in Granada is also shaped by the underlying public expectation of linked national and religious identification. While converts sometimes raised ire for breaking this linkage, migrants faced obstacles to inclusion in Granada for seeming to uphold it. Non-Muslim *Granadinos* largely saw Muslim migrants as unproblematically linking religion and nationality. Migrant Muslims' nationality was not in jeopardy for the larger public in the same way as converts', because migrants were considered always already *not Spanish* and *not Andalusian*, regardless of their citizenship status or, in the case of migrants' children, place of birth. For migrants themselves, questions of national belonging produced anxiety because most desired belonging and inclusion in both Spain and Morocco or other countries of origin and they felt disconnected from both places, exemplifying Shryock's "double remoteness." While European publics often uncritically assume migrants' "real" or "ultimate" allegiance to be to "home countries" or to Islam, most migrants I knew actually struggled to retain ties to a Morocco that felt increasingly distant, a common experience in the North African diaspora in Europe (Salih 2003). Migrants faced these tensions by actively working to create belonging in Spain and countries of origin, striving for a kind of double rootedness. Unlike converts, who did so by drawing on discourses of Islam's Spanish compatibility or of cosmopolitan cultural sensibilities, my migrant interlocutors were more likely to emphasize their Moorish ancestry, attachment to territory, and their ancestors' role in creating Granada's built landscape—tropes that resulted in a very different uptake in the wider public imagination.

Jihan: Double Remoteness and Rootedness

The daily life struggles and anxieties of Jihan, a Moroccan migrant, illuminate how migrant Muslims wished and strove for rootedness in Spain and Morocco at once, all the while feeling remote from both places. I met Jihan because we both volunteered at Najma, the Moroccan women's association. Jihan and her husband were from Tetuan, a city in northern Morocco. They had a toddler and a baby and lived just outside downtown Granada, where they moved after a short stint in northern Spain. Jihan's husband had previously lived in Spain for seven years before returning to Morocco to marry Jihan, a distant cousin. Immediately after the wedding, she accompanied him to Spain, a fairly common practice in which marriage facilitates legal migration through "family reunification" policies (Bledsoe and Sow 2011; Pham 2014). After a few weeks of eyeing me quietly, Jihan decided we should be friends and began to ask me questions about my research and my life in America at every opportunity. One day, she invited me to her apartment to interview her for my project. When I arrived, she proudly led me to the sitting room, set up like a Moroccan receiving room with three long, low futon-style cushions piled high with pillows next to elaborate woven rugs, and Moroccan-style mosaic tile art on the walls, all in white and blue. I complimented Jihan on the beauty of the room, and she said, "Oh yes, well, that's how rooms were in the old days in Morocco." She then led me to a Spanish-style living room with couch, TV, and table where we talked over couscous prepared with sugar and cinnamon and homemade cookies.

As she told me about their apartment, Jihan was reminded of a story. Interrupting herself, she said, "Listen to this—it has to do with your stuff, you know, immigration, Muslims." A week or so after moving to Granada, Jihan was getting the apartment in order while her husband was at work in a bookstore. Her daughter was coloring at the dining room table and her son slept in his crib. Jihan's last task before she could finally sit back and relax was to shake out a small throw rug, so she stepped onto the balcony and absentmindedly shut the sliding glass door behind her, not realizing it would automatically lock. She then found herself locked out, stuck on the balcony with her two small children inside. Panicking, she looked out to the street below for help. A man she presumed was Andalusian saw her, made eye contact, and shook his head. She yelled to a woman on the sidewalk, who yelled back, "Give me your husband's phone number and I'll call him so he can come let you in." Jihan, embarrassed, could not remember her husband's phone number without her cell phone. She asked the woman if she could call her mother in Morocco instead. She had her mother's number memorized, and was sure she would know what to do. But the woman refused, saying she didn't want to place an international call to Morocco. Jihan started sizing up other passersby and immediately felt homesick. In Tetuan, she knew everyone and felt safe with strangers, but here, she did not know whom to ask for help. "I kept looking at all of them thinking, 'Oh, maybe that one! No, he has a racist-looking face. Oh, maybe her! No, she looks drunk, or mean,' and I kept thinking that in my country, this would never be happening to me; I would just have yelled at any person on the street to help me and I would already be back in my house!"

Eventually, after a storekeeper across the street threatened to call the police because her children were locked inside, a young woman stepped onto the balcony of a building directly across the street from Jihan's and yelled in Moroccan Arabic, "Hey, what are you doing?" Jihan immediately recognized the woman as a fellow Tetuan native because of her accent. This neighbor called Jihan's mother in Tetuan, who gave her Jihan's husband's phone number. The neighbor called him, and he came home and rescued Jihan. Later, Jihan brought home-baked treats to the woman across the street to thank her. When the woman's housemate opened the door, she turned out to be an old family acquaintance of Jihan's who exclaimed, "Hey, I know you!" Jihan laughed at how this stressful situation had led to her making Moroccan friends in her new Spanish neighborhood. Telling this story made Jihan think of Morocco, and she pivoted toward the TV, saying excitedly that she wanted to show me her home videos. She popped in a VHS cassette of her wedding ceremony and reception. As we watched, she carefully explained to me every detail, who was who, where they were, all the gossip, and the backstory on choosing wedding outfits. Jihan had a gleam in her eye during the whole video, clearly enthralled. She offered me her running commentary without turning her face away from the TV, until we arrived at a later scene in which she and her husband were filmed getting into a car to leave for Spain. Now Jihan abruptly turned off the

TV, eyes lowered, saying that part of the video was too sad. "I don't want to watch that part."

Jihan's recounting of her balcony episode and her wedding video reveals how Moroccan migrant women in Granada lament a kind of double remoteness and strive for double rootedness in the course of mundane daily tasks like chores. She felt disconnected from Morocco, sensing that if only she had been at home in Tetuan, she would not be stuck on a balcony. At the same time, she felt removed from *Granadino* social life, unable to trust her neighbors and secure their help. In the end, the resolution to her balcony entrapment came about by dually forging connections in Tetuan and Granada at once. She connected to Tetuan via her neighbor's phone call to her mother, bringing her mother in Tetuan into the run of her daily chores in Granada. She also ended up feeling more comfortable in her Spanish neighborhood by making Moroccan friends there. Similarly, watching videos of Morocco in an apartment made to look like Morocco helped ease Jihan's homesickness by bringing Tetuan into the space of her Spanish home, but it also made her homesick by visually reminding her that she was far from home, fostering a simultaneous sense of rootedness in and remoteness from Morocco. At the same time, rooting her family's life in the city of Granada was as much about Tetuan as Granada. One day, Jihan let loose, venting about all the things she found difficult about living in Granada. After listening to her, I asked why she and her husband had chosen to live there. She said, "Well, it's so close to Tetuan. I'm almost in my city." Choosing Granada, then, was a way of maintaining ties to northern Morocco. The very city that represented for Jihan all of her feelings of loneliness, homesickness, and frustration was also the best place for her family to live in Spain because of the access it provided to Tetuan.

For Jihan, and for many of my migrant interlocutors, life as a migrant and religious minority in Granada was acutely defined by the intersection of connections to and disconnections from multiple places at once. In many global contexts, migrants' attachments to one place are often oriented equally toward another. For instance, Salvadorans in the United States sometimes celebrate U.S. citizenship, but this is largely for the ease it provides in traveling to and from El Salvador and participating in Salvadoran economic and political life via remittances and pressure on U.S. foreign policy (Coutin 2003). Jihan's ordeal, with its phone call resolution, also recalls Jennifer Cole's finding that in France, through telecommunications, female Malagasy marriage migrants navigate relationships with kin in Madagascar and with fellow migrants in France within one joint process (2014). In Granada, Jihan did not experience her life as one of "betweenness," moving back and forth between connections or allegiances to Moroccan or Spanish cultural identifications or places. Instead, she managed rootedness and remoteness in both at once, always located in Granada, in relation to her immediate life in the city.

Territorial Belonging and Social Difference

Given Jihan's and other Muslim migrants' frustrated efforts to imbue their lives in Granada with a sense of belonging to and rootedness in both Spain and Morocco, it is helpful to contrast their articulations of belonging to those of converts. As described earlier, many converts claimed belonging for Islam in Spain through an emphasis on cosmopolitan cultural sensibilities and lifestyles, invoking international economics, cross-Mediterranean religious influences, flamenco performance, and conversion as a renewal of medieval religious freedom. Early in my fieldwork, I mistakenly assumed that migrant Muslims might create a sense of belonging in Granada in similar ways. In fact, they usually did not. Migrants are largely excluded from this strategy because the sensibilities converts lauded have been recuperated as *Spanish* and *Granadino* through government initiatives like the Milenio, cultural institutions like the Andalusi Legacy Foundation, and the Moorish-themed tourism industry. As people considered categorically *not Spanish*, Muslim migrants have less access to this celebratory romance with *al-Andalus* and its legacy.

I discovered this through pointed responses to my own blunder during a Ramadan *iftar* (fast-breaking meal). On a hot and dry September night near the start of my research, I sat on a low wooden stool with four new Moroccan friends huddled around a small table outside a Moroccan souvenir shop in the *Albayzín*. Lined up and down the cobblestone, pedestrian street, built as a staircase laid into a hillside, were other small groups also breaking the day's Ramadan fast. As we munched on dates, soup, and milk, the desert breeze started to cool the city, bringing one of Granada's signature day-to-night temperature drops, heralding a comfortable evening. I had spent that morning with convert Muslims, learning about their views of Granada's history and their fond imaginings of *al-Andalus*. From where I sat now with my Moroccan companions, we could see tips of the Alhambra's towers peeking through rooftops and trees in the hills above us. Filled with warm soup and warm fuzzy feelings, I remarked on how beautiful it was, and Peque, nicknamed from *pequeño* (small) because of his short stature, replied, "Yeah, well, Granada is the capital of the world. The Alhambra is beautiful—the pinnacle of civilization." This comment sounded to me very similar to the celebrations of *al-Andalus* I had heard in convert quarters, so I excitedly asked Peque and his friends if they felt connections to this so-called civilization of medieval Spain, and what they thought that concept meant for the present.

Immediately, I got four frowns and four shaking heads. "No, no, today is nothing like the past. We have nothing to do with that," Peque insisted, and the others agreed. Today had nothing to do with the civilizational glories of *al-Andalus*. I asked why, and the four of them offered explanations about the differences between medieval Islamic culture in Granada and the present. Peque said, "For example, we don't really have the same ideal Muslim piety, [the] dedicated practice that people had back then, so the religion and values are not the same." Mehdi, a souvenir shop worker and student of Arabic linguistics at the University of Granada, added that with the global war on terror, there was nothing "successful" about Muslim civilization in Spain anymore; everyone was scared and suspect, and Muslims were no longer leaders in society. Ziko, an undocumented shop worker from central Morocco whose family had fled poverty to disperse through Spain and France, said the question itself did not really matter. Regardless of whether there were actually any similarities between Muslims' lives in Granada today and in the past, no one among the general public believed those similarities for migrants, only for converts. Manal, a young Moroccan woman, finished out the resounding disagreement with romantic views of Andalusi (e.g., from *al-Andalus*) values in the present. She said, "Yeah, I guess [the Alhambra is beautiful]. But the thing is, when people here talk about the Alhambra and all the beauty, they say that the Spanish Muslims made it, that Spanish Muslims did all these amazing things, and when they talk about bad stuff like terrorism, then it's 'those Arab Muslims.'" It is helpful to juxtapose Manal's comments here with those of Amal, the convert woman who insisted on the indigenous

Spanishness of Islam. It becomes clear that making a case for Muslim rootedness in Spain on the basis of Andalusi values does little to include migrant Muslims if Spanishness or Andalusianness (often coded racially as whiteness) are the primary criteria for belonging. My migrant research participants recognized and enjoyed the beauty of monuments like the Alhambra and celebrated *al-Andalus* as an idealized place, time, or memory, but even those who occasionally expressed pride in the city's Muslim heritage did not primarily claim local rootedness by enshrining themselves in the cosmopolitan sensibility or cultural values associated with the medieval past.

Instead, migrants tended to articulate belonging through discourses of territory, ancestry, and urban materiality, asserting a rightful presence in Granada through claims of prior Arab or Muslim presence and by invoking the labor of their ancestors in physically building the city. One man told me of the *Albayzín*, "My great-great-great- [etc.] grandparents built this," and another said "This looks just like Morocco because we were here before." These utterances are typical; many migrant Muslims made similar comments that used the linguistic shifter *we* to invoke a legacy of North Africans' legitimate and productive presence in southern Spain. Sometimes this kind of commentary came up when migrant Muslims were rebutting Spanish discrimination toward Muslims, or trying to correct public perceptions that specifically "Spanish" Muslims had built the Alhambra. But just as often, assertions of rightful presence were oriented inward, statements migrants made to themselves and each other that were as much about creating a sense of comfort and a feeling of belonging and being at home as they were about political claims. Many migrants spent hours taking me on tours of their favorite parts of the Moorish-built city or listing off streets with Arabic-derived names. I was often told that people liked Granada because as one woman put it, the Moorish architecture "feels like a Moroccan city," and another said, "It's like I'm still in Morocco." A Moroccan woman I met with periodically for Arabic-Spanish language exchange liked to say, "Here, you can pretend you're in Morocco." Like Jihan, these migrants drew on ideals of ancestry, territory, and urban landscape to create a sense of rootedness in Morocco *in* Spain. This ability to feel connected to Morocco through sensory appreciation of Granada's built landscape was important for migrants setting up lives in a new city.

These comments are not unlike those of Noelia, the Catholic woman in chapter 1 who invoked the architecture of Granada to explain her experience of inheriting and inhabiting *al-Andalus* in the present. This drawing of lines from past to present is also what underlies the sense of authenticity that lends itself so well to the Moorish-themed tourism of the city—a sense of Muslim presence as historically rooted and of Muslims as "in place" in Granada. Yet the limits of migrants' claims of belonging are stark. This is perhaps clearest when the same discursive strategies that make Moroccans feel at home in Granada are recast as dangerous rhetoric in encounters with non-Muslims.

An encounter between Spaniards and Moroccans in a teahouse, recounted to me after the fact, exemplifies this. One day I commented to Olivia, a middle-aged, longtime Granada resident originally from Madrid, that I had spent the morning walking around the *Albayzín* and had been to both the large, beautiful convert community mosque in the upper *Albayzín* and a smaller, less extravagant mosque frequented by Moroccans lower down the hill. She responded with surprise that I had wandered into these out-of-the-way spots, assuring me that the farthest she'd ever been into the *Albayzín* was to a teahouse near the edge of the neighborhood. She said this in an emphatic tone and continued on to explain why she had never returned. When Olivia and her friends went to this teahouse, they had an unexpected altercation with the waiter. Apparently, when he came to take their order, one of her friends ordered "*té Moro*" (*Moro* tea). At this, the Moroccan waiter and his coworkers became irate, telling Olivia and her friends, "That is very rude and inappropriate, you can't say that, it's called 'Moroccan tea'" (as mint tea is called on most menus in the area). According to Olivia, the waiters then

> started going on and on about how Andalusia is really Muslim, really Moroccan territory, that the Moors are the original and authentic inhabitants, that Andalusia isn't really Spain, it's really Africa because it used to be Muslim. They were saying such crazy things, such stupid, ridiculous things. They're from another world, telling us that this is their territory, that we're the ones who aren't in our own territory, when in reality they are the ones in a foreign country!

In her recollection of this encounter, Olivia did not acknowledge the Moroccan waiters' anger over her companion's careless use of a racist insult. She simply expressed her outrage over their claims of authenticity and rootedness in Andalusia, which they had articulated in terms of territory and ancestry. I cannot know how accurately Olivia described the "ridiculous things" these waiters said to her group. But what is certainly clear from her reaction is that even though the Moroccan waiters articulated their claims of belonging and ownership over Andalusia in terms of the very same historical tropes and referents that underlie the tourist industry in the *Albayzín*, they were deemed outlandish. Catholic and secular Andalusians may wax poetical about *al-Andalus*, convert Muslims may invoke nostalgia for the period in their claims of rootedness as Spanish Muslims, and migrant Muslims may create a sense of belonging and recreation of home through experiencing physical similarities between Granada and Morocco and by remembering their ancestors' role in the city's past. But in encounters between these groups of people, the meanings and stakes of such claims shift, and often ultimately result in failures of communication that reflect racialized tensions.

Non-Muslims' tendency to balk at migrants' claims of belonging, centered on references to built landscape or ancestry, reflect ongoing, historically based, racialized anxieties about nationality and the integrity of territory. In the summer of 2011, national and Andalusian regional newspapers found it necessary to declare that a political rumor circulating across the region was false (e.g. ABC [Sevilla] 2011; Calvo and Gómez 2011; Libertad Digital 2011; Vallejo 2011). The rumor was that Morocco's minister of culture had declared Morocco entitled to half of all annual profits from the Alhambra, no small sum, as the Moorish-built palace sustains Granada's tourism industry. As the story went, the minister asserted Moroccan ownership over the profits on the basis that its builders were from what is now Morocco, and that the Alhambra and other Moorish architecture is just as much Morocco's heritage as it is Spain's. The swiftness and ease with which this bit of political gossip spread may simply demonstrate the power of the Internet and twenty-four-hour, sensationalist news cycles. But the seriousness with which Spanish newspapers went about investigating the matter highlights the level of anxiety in Spain about Andalusia's geographic, historical, and cultural proximity to Muslim North Africa and fears that there is real potential for Moroccans to make material claims on Andalusian soil.

CONCLUSION

In chapter 1, residents of Granada used historical narratives to negotiate their ambivalence about the contemporary meanings of Moorish heritage, expressing widespread anxiety about the relevance of medieval Islam for Granada's belonging in Spain and Europe. As those sometimes considered "half-Moors," Catholic and secular non-migrants, the so-called mainstream public, experience their own kind of remoteness despite being "at home" in Granada and Spain. This chapter has continued to probe uneasy questions about Islam, belonging, and exclusion, this time primarily from the perspective of Granada's Muslim minority. In the context of Andalusian ambivalence about Islam, all Muslim residents face obstacles to claiming rootedness in the city, and converts and migrants have different possibilities and strategies for doing so, with diverse outcomes. Given normative emphasis on Catholic and/or secular identity for Andalusians (and Spaniards at large), recognition as Muslims sometimes comes at the expense of recognition and belonging as Spaniards or Andalusians. Other European nations of course also boast long traditions of including minorities on the condition of downplaying their social—especially religious—difference (Arendt 1991 [1951]; Hunt 1996).

What seems unique to Andalusia is the way that Islam both grounds and disqualifies claims of Andalusian or Spanish belonging, reflecting the ambivalence of the arraigo concept. The possibilities for and closures of Muslim claims of belonging highlight the complex paradoxes of belonging and difference in a city where Islam is celebrated and censored, and where city identity is intimately connected to Moorishness, yet insistently imagined as fundamentally Catholic and secular at the same time. And while both converts and migrants undermine notions of minority betweenness by pledging, seeking, and insisting on belonging in Granada, their claims also reflect unequal multiculturalism. Converts are sometimes able to achieve recognition as Andalusians, Spaniards, or Europeans by articulating values and aesthetic styles that coincide with positive popular images of al-Andalus. Many migrants, almost always racialized beyond recognition as Andalusian or Spanish, are more likely to articulate local belonging in terms of themes like ancestry and prior presence on Spanish territory, which are in turn received as threatening by Islamophobic sectors. These predicaments of rootedness and remoteness highlight the diversity of Muslim experiences in Granada.

Just as convert and migrant Muslims differently manage the resulting remoteness and rootedness of minority Muslim life in the city, the social processes of including and excluding Muslims also play out differently across city spaces. In this chapter's discussion of how Muslims claim belonging and rootedness in Granada, I have included more stories about converts than migrants. In the next chapter, which takes up the intersections of race, religion, and urban space, exploring the spatialization of Muslims' racialization in the city, migrants figure far more prominently than converts. This lopsided coverage is not accidental; it is precisely this kind of imbalance that defines the unequal multiculturalism of Andalusian encounters. All Muslims face challenges to their belonging in Granada, but Spanish and European Muslims have more opportunities to claim belonging and discussed the topic with me far more often. Migrant Muslims are the primary face of racialization and the most marked faces of Granada's emerging, marginalized neighborhoods on the city's outskirts. I turn now to the spatial dynamics of race, Islamophobia, and Islamophilia in the city.

NOTES

1. Parts of this chapter appeared in Rogozen-Soltar 2016., "Chapter 21: Becoming Muslim in Europe," in *Conformity and Conflict: Readings in Cultural Anthropology, 15th edition,* ed. David W. McCurdy, Dianna Shandy, and James Spradley (Boston: Pearson, 2016).

2. While the program is still technically running, the state effectively bars otherwise eligible undocumented migrants from applying; many of these migrants are now housed indefinitely in the Spanish CETIs (Temporary Immigrant Residential Centers) of Spain's North African enclaves Ceuta and Melilla. While there, they are prohibited from signing up with the local municipal register (Andersson 2014), a crucial first step in proving the three years of continuous residence required for securing legal residence papers.

3. Kitty Calavita's close analysis of Spanish and EU immigration law has demonstrated that despite frequent small changes instituted by new laws and amendments, a series of inconsistencies persists. The laws treat migrants primarily as an "emergency labor supply" and therefore involve sparse policy provisions for their permanent residence. Even during mass legalization programs, those who obtain legal residence are given temporary permissions that later expire, requiring migrants to "navigate a maze of government bureaucracies to renew their permits" (2005, 5). In my experience, this maze involves such a

complexity of shifting laws that migrants rarely succeed in obtaining long-term legal residence. In the course of many mornings spent in line with migrants at the local *Granadino* police station's office hours for foreigners, the classic case that I saw many times was that of migrants confounded by the law that requires a yearlong work contract in applications for residence permits, and the fact that a yearlong work contract is unattainable for those without residence permits in the first place.

4. This discursive relationship with the city actually parallels a long-standing tradition in Muslim and Arab regions of anthropomorphizing cities—especially those of *al-Andalus*—in Arabic and Andalusi-inspired literature. Elegiac poems dedicated to the lost cities of *al-Andalus* comprise a large genre within classical Arabic poetry (Elinson 2009; Shannon 2015).

5. *Hadra* usually refers to collectively practiced Sufi ritual. For the Murabitun in Granada, an important practice is *Dhikr*, or collective, rhythmic recitations of Qur'anic passages, prayers, and songs.

6. Most of my Arabic-speaking interlocutors in Granada loved to comment on the Plaza Bib-Rambla's Arabic-derived name. Today, the square is a center of tourism to the Catholic part of the city, for its views of the enormous, adjacent cathedral. Local lay historians believe the square was a key site for the burning of Arabic texts during the Inquisition.

7. Flamenco also indexes Andalusian southernness (and otherness) within Spain and has come to stand for an authentically Spanish artistry that figures centrally in national pride even as its practitioners are socially stigmatized as belonging to the marginalized Andalusian region or for being Roma. Lila Ellen Gray has described parallel processes for fado music in Lisbon, Portugal, where music is also connected to ambivalent ideas about Portugal's global connections and southernness within Europe (2013).

8. Of course, even as she criticizes "Spanish" and "Arab" failures to de-essentialize the social category *Muslim*, Clara makes her own elision here, by using "Arab" to refer to all Muslim migrants from North Africa and the Middle East, despite large Amazigh populations well-represented in Spain.

3

◈

MUSLIM DISNEYLAND AND MOROCCAN DANGER ZONES

Islam, Race, and Space

This chapter is about the spatial politics and racialized hierarchies through which Muslims, especially migrants, are categorized in Granada, and their experiences of inhabiting the city as minority subjects. Different places within the city have historically accrued social identities that are more or less associated with the Moorish past and that differently become racialized zones of encounter in the present, engendering diverse intersections of inclusion and exclusion for Muslims. Because it is the historic, Moorish-built quarter and center of the Moorish-themed tourism industry, the *Albayzín* neighborhood is the area of Granada most associated in the public imaginary with Islam and the city's supposedly exemplar Islamophilia. But as Granada's Muslim population grows, with many Muslim migrants residing in the city's outskirts in a geographically, politically, and economically marginalized area called the Polígono, that neighborhood is increasingly seen as the city's "real" Muslim space, in a strikingly different way than the *Albayzín*. The Polígono is a relatively newly constructed area and is not part of the city's medieval history or tourism economy. Instead, the Polígono is fast becoming associated with Islamophobic exclusion and the ghettoization of Muslim residents, as has happened with suburban areas in France (Ossman and Terrio 2006).

To address these contrasts, the chapter unpacks the spatialized social practices and discursive moves that differentially place Islam across the city, tracing the ways racial, migratory, and religious difference are enshrined in the urban landscape. Following Setha Low, I understand *spatialize* to mean "to locate—physically, historically, and conceptually— social relations and social practice in space" (2000, 127). Low considers spatialization a contested process that creates links between urban spaces and social configurations, including the production of social difference. In this chapter, I draw on the idea of spatialization to examine the city as a processual space of political possibility and limitation (e.g., Newman 2015; Selby 2012). Through attention to spatialization across neighborhoods, I explore how the production of social difference in urban Granada is both solidified and challenged.

Moving between the *Albayzín* and the Polígono, I explore how Muslim migrants in particular confront their relationship to various city spaces. While at first glance, the *Albayzín* seems to embody Granada's Islamo- philia and the Polígono Islamophobia, in fact, inclusion and exclusion do not map neatly onto separate neighborhoods; each neighborhood includes and excludes Muslims in spatially inflected ways. The chapter demonstrates the need to ethnographically uncover exclusions inherent in apparent spaces of inclusion, and to ask what happens when spaces of urban social exclusion become the main places where Muslims and migrants are included. As in other contexts, in Granada these spatializ- ing processes are articulated both through spatialized historical memory that shapes religious and ethnic identity in relation to place (e.g., Sawalha 2010; Slyomovics 1998) and through the spatialized dimensions of migrant racialization across borders of both nation-states and neighborhoods (e.g., Chavez 2008; De Genova 2002, 2005; Rome 2008; Sundberg 2008).[1]

I begin the chapter by further discussing the particulars of the racial- ization of Islam in Granada discussed in the introductory chapter. Pan- European anxieties about Islam, secularism, and security combine with local, historically based frameworks for thinking about racial and religious difference to create a nexus of multiple modes of exclusion (along racial, class, gender, ethnic, and migratory dimensions) that I refer to jointly as *casual racism*. I use this term both because my research participants glossed these various forms of "othering" as "*racismo*" (racism) and be- cause of the way discrimination toward Muslims, especially migrants, pervades public space in general, shaping casual interfaith encounters on a daily basis. After tracing the contours of this casual racism, I move to a

comparison of the *Albayzín* and Polígono to examine casual racism's spatial variations, showing how the differentiation of city space is becoming
a key node in the dynamic of Islamophobia and Islamophilia in Granada.

THE RACIALIZATION OF ISLAM IN GRANADA

In this chapter, I follow Alaina Lemon's suggestion that anthropologists "treat race as a discursive practice" (2002, 54). In doing so, I emphasize processes of social interaction and migrants' own experiences and
understanding of their racialized inclusion and exclusion over diagnoses
of kinds or modes of discrimination (cf. McIntosh 2015). My research
participants enact and experience prejudice in terms of racial, cultural,
religious, class, and migratory difference, and they combine and divide
these diacritics contextually, in both tacit and self-conscious ways. I ask
how Muslim migrants describe their experiences of prejudice as they re-
late to urban life and the creation of distinct Muslim spaces in the city.
To start, I situate the way marginalization of Muslims in Granada departs
from other European contexts before elaborating on casual racism.

On the one hand, scholarship of Spain routinely casts the country
as politically inclusive of Islam and Muslims because it lacks the organized anti-Muslim politics of other European countries. Political
scientists point out that Spain has not produced the kind (or scope) of anti-
immigrant, anti-Muslim political movements seen in France, in Germany,
and elsewhere in Western Europe. There have been no successful national
legislative bans of headscarves. Mosques and minarets are not prohibited
by law, and Islam is an officially recognized religion. Scholars of Spanish
politics usually attribute the relative failure of Spain's political far right to
drum up support for overtly racialized anti-Muslim action to the politics
of "reconciliation" that shaped the 1980s transition from dictatorship to
democracy. Embraced by leaders across the spectrum of Spain's deeply
divided political factions, an emphasis on consensus was seen as necessary
to safely usher in a new, fragile democracy without slipping into the divisions that had produced the bloody civil war (Aguilar 2002; Carr and Fusi
1981; Edles 1998; Ellwood 1995). The legacy of this approach, combined
with near-universal disdain for the violence of separatist organizations

like the Basque group ETA, has engendered a political culture that many feel "shuns political extremism" (Encarnación 2004, 178). Indeed, among *Granadinos*, so-called extremist political stances are often subject to scrutiny and social monitoring; one simply needs to refer to an interlocutor as a "*facha*" (fascist), tacitly accusing those with far right or far left views of reviving the Franco years, to effectively shut down certain lines of discussion. In addition to this safeguarding against extremism, Spanish nationalist discourse is not a viable political option for anti-Muslim sectors because it echoes Franco's brutal enforcement of national "*hispanidad*." This is an identity discourse rooted in older Spanish hispanism, "an ideology that posits an essence uniting all current and former Spanish subjects via the Castilian language, the Catholic religion, and above all a talent for the sublation of difference" (Tucker 2014, 910–911). Raw memories of Franco's suppression of autonomous regional cultures within Spain has thus prevented anti-immigrant or anti-Muslim campaigns presented in Spanish nationalist terms from resonating with large publics.

On the other hand, the racialization of Islam and discrimination toward Muslims in Spain and Andalusia is nevertheless widespread (García Sánchez 2014; Serra i Salame 2004). The absence of a strong, nationalist response to migrants and Muslims has not meant that Muslims are uniformly welcome in Spain. Instead, it has meant that in Granada antipathy toward Muslims generally oscillates between two overlapping but distinct perspectives. The first is a Europe-centered discourse of civilizational difference between mutually exclusive categories of Europeans and Muslims, and the second is a highly localized, historically rooted discourse that regards Muslims (understood as a religious, migratory, and ethnoracial category) as eternal Moorish invaders and religious foes bent on reclaiming the region of Andalusia. The civilizational discourse positions Andalusians as members of a generally secular, tolerant, progressive European civilization at odds with a monolithic Islam naturalized as intolerant, fanatical, and violent (Brown 2006; Puar 2007). The more local discourse situates *Granadinos* as tacitly Catholic inheritors of a vanquished *al-Andalus*, struggling against a reincarnation of the city's historic Moors.

Much Spanish commentary about Muslims in Granada reflects a combination of both of these discourses. Aurelia was one of the nuns who volunteered with me at a migrant social services organization, along with

Claudia, the woman who mocked Andalusian accents. One day Aurelia finished attending to a Moroccan client and then turned to me, shaking her head and clucking her tongue. She said, "Here we see so many of them, that I think, 'Wow, they've taken over Granada.' They say there was a reconquest and they left and all, but there are so many of them, if they wanted to retake Granada, like some people say they do, it wouldn't even be that difficult!" Taken aback by her assertion that Moroccans, through large-scale migration, were undoing the Catholic "reconquest" and the Inquisition (whose expulsions she had glossed as "they left"), I asked if she really meant this seriously. She replied slowly, thinking through her words:

> Well, I guess not. But look, right now there are two blocks, the West and the Muslims or the Arabs, or well, I don't know exactly what to call this second block, but there are two distinct blocks facing off and one of these groups has tons of people infiltrated into the world of the other block. [Here she knowingly raised her eyebrows.] We're separated by language, country, culture, but most of all, at the core, by religion. And it's a problem because one of the blocks is very, very, very religious. I mean these Moroccan women are very deeply religious. And that can be one of the easiest ways to manipulate people. And when you have so many of them infiltrated here—I mean I don't like that word, it sounds too sinister— although, actually, some of them really are infiltrated, you know, but I don't just mean those ones.

Here, she trailed off, shaking her head again. Still somewhat confused, I asked Aurelia if she herself was not also very religious. She was, after all, a nun who constantly advocated for a place for religion in the public sphere. She nodded and matter-of-factly explained that of course she was very religious, but in a different way. Andalusian Catholics were "open" and "tolerant" and respected other people and their differences. Then she abruptly changed the subject.

Aurelia's comments reveal the complex mixing of local-historical and European-civilizational discourses about Muslims and migrants in Granada. Her words reflect traces of increasingly common anxieties among secular Europeans about the specificity of Muslim difference— the idea that Muslims are somehow special in their religiosity, intolerance, and fundamentalism, and thus a threat to democracy, stability, and security, in addition to European cultural norms. She refers directly to the facing off of "Muslim" and "Western" civilizational "blocks." But at the same time, she also expresses regionally specific concerns about a Muslim or Moorish "retaking" of Andalusia, in which she situates herself as part of a Catholic region, rather than secular Europe. Her comments are a helpful reminder that in southern Spain, even as pan-European discourses about Islam become more common, secularism is often not the prevailing, or only framework in which Islam becomes unacceptable. In some ways, Aurelia posits a secularized Catholic majority against a non-secular Islam, but she also fears that Islam will disrupt the emphatically Catholic public character of Andalusia, noting that for her, religion is the core opposition between the two "blocks." While Aurelia is a nun, speaking from a distinctly Catholic perspective, her opinion is by no means peculiar to devout Catholics. Many nonreligious and even stridently atheist research participants made comments about Muslim migrants in which they framed the problem of Muslim presence in terms of undoing the Catholic "reconquest" of Andalusia. Finally, Aurelia's remarks show how the production of Muslims' social difference in Granada exceeds scholarly frames focusing primarily on religion and secularism, or on race, ethnicity, and migration. Even as Aurelia emphasizes Islam by identifying an essentialized Muslim religious difference from Christianity as a new, unique delineator between "blocks," her anxiety about Muslim migrants incorporates multiple markers of social difference—language, nationality, race, migratory status, and more.

Casual Racism

Without government policies such as the headscarf bans that have shaken France (Bowen 2008; Scott 2007), mandatory courses in national culture established in Germany (Ewing 2008), or widespread, extreme anti-Muslim violence, my Muslim interlocutors in Spain more often discussed how anti-Muslim attitudes affected them in institutionalized housing and employment discrimination, and in daily interactions in public spaces in the city through casual racism.[2] This phrase unites several related phrases common among my research participants, including *"racismo"* (racism), *"racismo diario"* (daily or everyday racism), and *"racismo de la calle"* (racism of the street). Because the phrase *"en la calle"* generally means "out and about," this last phrase really connotes a racism characterized by its location in public space. Muslims, especially migrants, often used these terms with me when commenting on the way racism toward Muslims pervades everyday social life to a degree that surprised them and felt different than other European places some had previously lived. I use the term *racism* to respect and emphasize my research participants' own analytical framing of their experiences of discrimination as Muslims and migrants, but casual racism is also deeply shaped by ideologies about class, which my research participants sometimes acknowledged in the term *"racismo de dinero"* (money racism), as well as migration, gender, and other dimensions of social difference. *Casual* here denotes not a lesser degree of discrimination than other forms, but rather the ways prejudice manifests in casual, daily encounters, and the nonchalance with which non-Muslims espouse racialized views of Muslims.

The latter aspect of casual racism reflects a particular style of public interaction in Granada that many migrant Muslims saw as unique to *Granadino* and Andalusian urban space. Andalusians are not known for self-conscious political correctness, and bluntness is often seen as a virtue, including in discussions of social difference. In Granada, people are socialized to make conversation with strangers in the course of public, urban life—at bus stops, in store lines, and in cafés. Talkative, outgoing people are appreciatively called *"abierto"* (open), while less loquacious individuals are often seen as *"cerrado"* (closed off) or unforgivably antisocial. In many ways, it is better to be open though blunt or rude, in fitting with the famed *malafollá*, than to be quietly polite. Given this general sensibility about conversations in public space, it is common to overhear, or be abruptly brought into, conversations about all kinds of topics with strangers, including issues people see as current and pressing, like religious diversity or migration.

To illustrate casual racism, consider three instances that I observed in the course of two days. One morning, at my neighborhood produce stand, an elderly non-Muslim woman complained to everyone in line about the Senegalese Muslims who had recently moved into her building. "I tell you, those blacks, well, there's a problem! There's just no living with them. A group of them live upstairs from me now, and if there isn't water leaking through our ceiling, they're holding up the elevator. It's just impossible to live with them!" Her phrasing in Spanish invoked "living together," subtly playing on *convivencia,* which in the context of city politics can refer as much to civic coexistence as to *al-Andalus.* This woman's comments accused the migrants of ruining good neighborly *convivencia* in her building, even as her casual racism belied the limits of *convivencia*-as-multiculturalism. That afternoon my landlord, a generally gentle, kind man who dubbed himself the "Spanish grandfather" for my housemates and me and invited us to dinner at his house on holidays, stopped by to fix an electrical socket in the living room. Struggling to maneuver wires while perched on a ladder, he dropped something and exclaimed in anger, "I shit on the Moors!" (a phrase used similarly to "Shoot!" or "Darn!" in English).

The next day, answering phones in the migrant social services office where I worked as volunteer secretary, I received a call from an olive farm owner in rural Granada who requested referrals for agricultural workers as part of a program we had matching employers with migrant employees. When I mistakenly thought he was asking to be put in touch with workers who "speak Spanish," and told him most of our clients spoke conversational Spanish, he yelled, "No, no, no! I'm not asking that they *speak* Spanish, but that they were *born into* the Spanish language. You know, *bien de color* [of good color]. They can be Bolivian or whatever, but you know, no Moroccans, okay?" Over the two years I spent working with this NGO, many employers called with requests for Latin American migrant workers, believing their language, religion, and temperaments were more suited to working with Spaniards. In this way, the implications of casual racism may be far from casual. Here, it resulted in systemic job discrimination, despite the NGO's best efforts. Many Muslims—both converts and migrants— routinely pointed out to me the shock and insult they felt when hearing other Andalusians say things like "I shit on the Moors" when they missed the bus or stubbed their toes.

The point of sharing these stories is not to imply that all non-Muslim, non-migrant *Granadinos* are constantly spewing racial invectives. My goal here is to demonstrate the casual nature of these kinds of racialized commentaries and interactions, the way that many people openly, unabashedly express these opinions or use racially inflected language in the course of everyday interaction in public, urban contexts in Granada. Most of all, casual racism means that for Muslims and migrants, inhabiting public

space is inherently fraught, as they can expect their perceived social difference to be regularly and explicitly broached by strangers. If being in urban
space automatically means confronting these uncomfortable encounters,
they take on different valences in different city spaces. The following two
examples illustrate the contrast in how casual racism manifests in the
Albayzín and the Polígono.

On a crisp autumn evening, I rode the minibus down from my Arabic
class at a mosque in the *Albayzín* to the city center. The tiny bus, built to
fit through the narrow, winding streets of the medieval quarter, rounded a
corner and jolted to a stop in front of the Arco de Elvira, the historic archway that once marked the entrance to the walled Muslim city of Granada
and today signals the boundary between the *Albayzín* and downtown. As
I rode, I listened to the elderly Andalusian riders, mostly residents of the
Albayzín, banter back and forth about the economy. Through the archway
and down Elvira Street, we could see the edges of the hustle and bustle of
falafel stands, teahouses, a halal butcher shop, and Moroccan lamp shops
that filled the area of the lower *Albayzín*. Several of my bus companions
shook their heads and sighed, and a particularly boisterous man yelled out
in a booming voice, "This region of Spain, those *moros* are going to break
it off and carry it away with them with their balls! [*con sus cojones!*]" A
woman who had been arguing with him laughed and yelled back, "I hope
they and their balls carry you away too, you old *malafollá*!" By calling this
gentleman a *malafollá*, the woman on the bus probably meant something
like "grouch," but her choice of *malafollá* indicates a grouch of a particular
kind, as his orneriness was expressed through an exclusionary attitude
toward Muslim migrants.

Several months later, in the Polígono, I asked Claudia whether she
knew many of the Moroccans now living in this peripheral neighborhood.
She responded,

> They're everywhere! In the grocery store, in the street, on the bus. At the
> park sometimes you sit down on a bench and you see a few people, and
> then a few more come, and then all of a sudden you're surrounded by
> Moroccans! There are just so, so, so many! And I see this, and I think, the
> people here are racist and xenophobic, it's going to be a problem. And you
> know the women from the Najma Association? Well, the other day I was
> walking down the street and it looked like their Arabic classes had just

finished, and they came pouring out of there, such a number of children! And all the women coming out with them, and all with their veils on, and all the children—I mean we're not talking about just a few, it's an impressive mass of people, and if you see this, it affects you. It's not like they're doing anything special, they're just women like any others, and children like any others, but you see this and it startles you!

These Spaniards' reactions to the presence of Muslim migrants in public city spaces are both filled with anxiety, in distinct ways that reflect how Muslim difference and casual racism are configured in conjunction with urban space. In the Polígono, Muslim presence appears alarming because Muslim difference stands out in this neighborhood, historically known for its Roma and working-class Andalusian populations. On the one hand, Claudia asserted that any impending problems related to Moroccans in Granada would be caused by locals' racism, and she acknowledged that there was nothing special about these women and children. Yet her comments reveal that in fact, she saw them as remarkable. She noticed Moroccans' presence in public areas of the Polígono (where non-migrant Spaniards are also, of course, "everywhere") because they *were* special: they wore "veils," they taught their children Arabic, and they seemed to exist en masse. In contrast, my bus companion felt threatened by Moroccans in the *Albayzín* perhaps because they work and socialize in streets that architecturally recall the former, larger Muslim presence in the city, evoking the idea of the *Albayzín* as a former (and possibly present) Muslim space. This gentleman thus feared a Moroccan retaking—even if metaphorical—of Andalusian territory.[3] For Claudia in the Polígono, the simple fact of Muslims' sizable presence naturally "affects" and "startles you" because Muslims are out of place in an area not traditionally associated with Granada's Muslim heritage. In the *Albayzín*, Muslim migrant presence is alarming because migrants *do* seem to be in place, almost too much, in a dangerous way. Next, I take a closer ethnographic look at each of these neighborhoods in turn.

THE *ALBAYZÍN*: MUSLIM DISNEYLAND

The *Albayzín* neighborhood has long been constructed as Granada's most emblematic Muslim space, celebrated by locals as inherently inclusive. In what follows, I complicate that picture by briefly describing the history and social scene of the neighborhood, and then tracing how Islamophilia actually coincides with Islamophobia in the area's main social activities: the Moorish-themed tourism industry, Muslim migrants' community building, and recent urban policing efforts intended to combat neighborhood crime. The tourism sector in the lower *Albayzín* reflects Richard Maddox's observation that within this framework, Muslim social difference must be included and celebrated, but in highly regulated, and ultimately limiting ways (Maddox 2004b; Rogozen-Soltar 2007).

Granadinos of all faiths immediately identify the *Albayzín* with Moorish heritage and contemporary Islam. When I told new acquaintances of my research interests, they often assumed that I lived in the *Albayzín* (I did not), or they would immediately say "Oh, you must go to the *Albayzín*!" Encouraged by the tourism industry, foreign visitors gravitate toward the *Albayzín* to see a living slice of the Moorish past and a quintessential ethnic Moroccan neighborhood in the present. Guidebooks about the city begin with the neighborhood, hotels across the city have maps with directions to the *Albayzín*, tourism companies offer guided tours of the neighborhood, buses to the Alhambra leave from its streets, and boutique hotels sporting Spanish-language signs with Arabic calligraphy-style lettering dot the neighborhood, practically announcing to tourists, "You have arrived in Muslim Spain!" Maddox has called democratic Andalusia's renewed focus on regional difference an example of "cosmopolitan liberalism," characterized by "a highly charged, ambivalent and bipolar view of cultural diversity," in which cross-cultural contact is harnessed for economic and social benefit (2004b, 133).

Geographically, the neighborhood is built into the hillside below the Alhambra and its boundaries roughly correspond to those of the original Moorish-built city. While it is difficult to imagine today, for much of the early twentieth century, the Alhambra was abandoned, seen as an uninteresting relic in disarray. The *Albayzín* followed suit and for many years was primarily home to middle-class and lower-income *Granadinos*. The upper hill sections of the neighborhood were not well connected to the city center, and buses could not (and still cannot) enter many of the narrow, winding medieval streets. Only more recently, as crumbling historic centers across the urban Mediterranean became hip and desirable for new artist, bohemian, and leftist residents (Herzfeld 2009), did the *Albayzín* begin to change, undergoing what some of my research participants fondly call revitalization and others disapprovingly term gentrification (Medina and Pablos 2002). In 1984 the *Albayzín* became a UNESCO World Heritage site and the Alhambra eventually became a top tourist destination. Wealthy northern European expatriates (especially from Britain), speculators, bohemians, and global tourists descended on the neighborhood, in what longtime residents describe as an onslaught. This was the same time that the Andalusian Sufi convert movement was coalescing in Granada, and converts bought properties and established communities in the highest part of the neighborhood. Today, these residents share the upper *Albayzín* with the remaining, now quite elderly, middle-class population. The middle and lower parts of the hilly streets are an eclectic mix of boutique hotels, museums housed in historic buildings, businesses, and abandoned, dilapidated properties in which bohemian youth and radical anarchists have established squatter communities.

This area is adjacent to the three or four streets that house most of the Moorish-themed tourism shops and restaurants where many Moroccans work in the lower (downhill) *Albayzín*, adjacent to the city center. UNESCO recognition and the economic revival of the neighborhood, for which converts often take much credit, spurred the creation of the tourism sector. The lower *Albayzín*'s tourist transformation is recent, unfolding over the past several decades, and incorporating renewed public interest in Islamic heritage since the arrival of democracy, when people began to openly question Catholic historical narratives of Andalusia and Spain. But it also reflects the enduring ethos of the "Spain Is Different" slogan. Coined by Franco's minister of tourism Manuel Fraga, this was the cornerstone of Franco's efforts to sustain the Spanish economy by effectively nationalizing places, cultural forms, and "traditions" associated with Andalusia to "brand" Spain (e.g., Comaroff and Comaroff 2009), marketing it as Europe's exotic playground (Collier 1997; Crain 1997; Kelly 2000; Pack 2006).[4]

Both *convivencia* and *malafollá* are central to the construction of the *Albayzín* as Granada's most emblematic urban space. The word *convivencia* and the phrase "the three cultures" are splashed across the covers of guidebooks, menus, and boutique hotel advertisements for the neighborhood, marking the *Albayzín* as the manifestation of historically rooted multicultural success. At the same time, the city's infamous grouchiness, coded as *malafollá*, has also become a kind of ironic form of urban branding within the tourism industry. It is now possible for tourists in the *Albayzín* to buy *malafollá* T-shirts and mugs at souvenir shops, visit the *malafollá* Facebook page, or taste the *malafollá* label wine from a local Granada vineyard. The term's proliferation among consumer goods in the public sphere stems in part from inside jokes among *Granadinos* who bond over the city's *malafollá* reputation as a form of local sociality, but it also increasingly figures in city residents' efforts to sell an ironic, funny image of the city to outside visitors. The tourism sector located in and around the *Albayzín*, then, traffics in both sanitized and humorous representations of *convivencia* and *malafollá*. Positive invocations of *malafollá* as a persona with which to brand the city often cast it as an exterior gruffness that masks a kind interior and is thus endearing rather than mean-spirited. Nevertheless, tourist-oriented, *malafollá*-themed marketing strategies also subtly index all of the other connotations of *malafollá*, including not only superficial bad moods, but grumpiness that is explicitly oriented toward outsiders.

After a day spent in the lower *Albayzín*, observing sunburned global tourists perusing Moroccan goatskin lamps and teashops while eating falafel, my friend Margarita commented, half joking, that the *Albayzín* was like "Muslim Disneyland." Scholars have made similar observations; in the foreword to an important volume about Spanish historiography and memory of *al-Andalus*, Giles Tremlett uses the term "Moorishland" to refer to a "semifictional version of Spain's past where exotic offerings of orientalism-with-tapas are combined with 'nostalgia' tourism" and in which "Spain's Moorish history is happily raided" to "attract visitors" (2008, xii). Tremlett pinpoints Granada, and particularly the touristy Moroccan shops of the lower *Albayzín*, as the archetypal example of this phenomenon. His witty characterization here certainly points to the economic motivations for the Moorish-themed tourism industry and the resulting, sometimes superficial nature of the forms of Islam and Arabness on display.

Yet overemphasizing economic instrumentality risks setting up an opposition between real or sincere inclusion of Muslims and instrumentalist uses of Islam, implying that inclusion maps onto the former, exclusion onto the latter. In fact, the Islamophilic tourist display in the *Albayzín* is more than an instrumentalist "raiding" of Moorish history. If not, how are we to understand the experiences of Spaniards and other Europeans who attribute their conversions to Islam to time spent in the neighborhood, or the impassioned joy and pride with which Catholic and secular residents of the city, with no money in the tourist game, encouraged me to visit the neighborhood, lauding its beauty and historical meaning?[5] The opposition that implicitly blames economic instrumentality for failures of multicultural inclusion, then, is best avoided. Muslims can find moments of experiencing real belonging in the midst of hokey tourist displays. Conversely, even celebrations of *al-Andalus* in the *Albayzín* that are well intentioned and sincere cannot always stave off Muslims' exclusion and inequality in the neighborhood. Other research on religious and cultural heritage tourism to urban centers in Spain, such as the Christian pilgrimage destination of Santiago de Compostela, suggests that cultural appropriation and commodification can coexist with the achievement of locals' political prerogatives (Roseman and Fife 2008). In Granada, the Disneyland-ish character of the *Albayzín* goes beyond mere instrumentalism to facilitate Muslim inclusion and reinforce stereotypes at the same time.

Inclusion and Exclusion in a Heritage Tourism Site

One reason I do not understand the presence of Islam, Muslims, and Moroccan material goods in the lower *Albayzín's* "Muslim Disneyland" as purely instrumentalist and subordinate to the tourism industry is the importance Muslim migrants themselves attribute to the area as a unique place for belonging and community formation. The proportion of Muslim migrants in the city who work in the *Albayzín* is small and overwhelmingly male, but those who work and hang out there often expressed to me a sense of relief and appreciation in having found a space for Muslim migrant sociality. Many shops in the area are open-air, and employees place stools and chairs up and down the stepped, cobblestone streets and sit outside, talking with one another throughout the day in between attending to customers. This gives the area a distinctly sociable, friendly feel. Many research participants told me the lower *Albayzín* was one of the few places in the city center they felt comfortable speaking Arabic or discussing religion in public. Certainly, in other centrally located or touristy parts of the city,

Moroccans could not comfortably sit outside, breaking the daily Ramadan fast at sidewalk tables, as they did in the lower *Albayzín*. The neighborhood is also a place for men to find support networks for economic success or to learn the scoop on Muslim-friendly housing in the city. Several young men worked at multiple food stands and teahouses in the neighborhood, and several shops were known for coming to one another's rescue with ingredients like pita bread, creating an atmosphere of conviviality. More than once, I arrived in the neighborhood to find men passing job ads and résumés up and down the street between friends and acquaintances and was asked to help edit cover letters.

In addition to functioning as a support network for navigating work, housing, and other migrant issues like visas, the neighborhood's palimpsestic propensity to make Muslims seem "in place" felt empowering to some of my Moroccan interlocutors. Peque, Mehdi, Ziko, and many other Moroccan employees in the *Albayzín* lauded the authenticity they felt the neighborhood gave them, and the contact, albeit limited, it provided them with non-Muslims and non-migrants. In other neighborhoods, these same men were often ignored or dismissed offhand, so selling goods to customers in the *Albayzín* sometimes facilitated longed-for cross-cultural discussions. Customers asked them questions about Islam and Morocco and gave them a chance to share what they wanted. Many research participants told me that working in the *Albayzín* was the only time they were able to make Spanish friends; while most visitors are tourists, some college students frequent bars in and near the area, and Ziko told me proudly one day that he had met a "Spanish girlfriend" and was over the moon about it.

One research participant, Mimo, was glad when tourists would ask about his life in Morocco, so that he could tell them about diversity there and "get rid of stereotypes." He enjoyed describing Muslim religious holidays to people who came into his shop, and he took care to tell them about the Moroccan industries that had produced the imported goods they were buying. Once, I watched him mention an impending trip to Morocco to North American customers (in English), who then asked about his trip, affording him a chance to talk about the *Eid al-Adha* holiday and the importance of being in Morocco to sacrifice a sheep with his family. This prompted a question about the cost of the sacrifice and economic conditions in his hometown. Mimo then spoke freely about poverty in

Morocco. He and other shop workers felt that because they were interacting with Spaniards on "their turf," in a setting understood as Muslim and Moorish space, people were more open to listening to them, apprehending them as "experts" about Morocco. These feelings of inclusion afforded by community-building activities and cross-cultural encounters in the neighborhood cannot be ignored.

The social intimacies formed on these streets nevertheless take place within a tourist attraction that often relies on stereotyped, essentialized images of Moroccans in a display of Granada's Moorish heritage, with migrants figuring as timeless, exotic figures for public consumption. One young man from central Morocco liked to raise his eyebrows periodically and point at passersby munching falafel wraps while scoffing that in Morocco, "people don't even eat that much falafel." His critique never went beyond reiterating this comment, but it pointed to many migrants' awareness that visitors to the *Albayzín* may relish an experience of being in "Little Morocco" without seeing much that corresponds to migrants' memories of Morocco. The prevalence of falafel and belly dance outfits in the *Albayzín* recalls David McMurray's observations about the Moroccan Pavilion at Disney's Epcot Center in Orlando, Florida. Disney hired Moroccan men to come to Florida to "interact with the tourists while wearing sashes and billowy shirts and pants in imitation of a Western dreamscape of the Orient" (2000, 134) but also forced them to shave their mustaches—which were actually commonly worn in Morocco—to comply with facial hair rules in the Disney dress code. In a similar sense, some Moroccan migrants in the *Albayzín* felt forced to enact images of North Africa that would resonate with tourists but felt unfamiliar. While Mimo enjoyed the chance to talk with customers, others felt fatigued by being constantly observed and objectified.

Their sense of the triviality of cross-cultural encounters was produced in the casual racism of daily interactions with tourists and customers who many migrants felt were ignorant and rude. My research participants would make fun of tourists and other customers who fawned over Moroccan imports while crooning wide-eyed over the beauty of Moorish Spain because they found such exuberance hollow. Some also disapproved of certain social practices and styles they noticed among many customers. Young Moroccans who sold falafel at night often bristled at customers' drunkenness, immodest dress, and attempts to buy hashish, offended by the assumption that, as one put it, "all Moroccans sell hashish." Many men were taken aback by the romantic overtures of tourist and college-age Andalusian women, though others were excited by them. Several of my Moroccan shop worker interlocutors understood English and frequently overheard customers talking about them and their goods, unaware that the shop workers could understand them as they discussed Moroccans' supposedly unethical business practices, or penchant for haggling and overpricing knickknacks.

These frustrations also point to the ways in which Muslim migrants' incorporation within the *Albayzín*'s Islamophilic tourism frame sidesteps inclusion of religious difference. Islamophilia takes many forms, and in the *Albayzín*, it seems to sometimes slip into a kind of anesthetized Morocco-philia, or what Fuchs (2009) calls Maurophilia, with the celebratory emphasis on anything deemed "Arab" or "Moorish" *except* Islam. The Moorish tourism sector produces Muslims as particular kinds of interlocutors for visitors to the neighborhood by encouraging consumption of Moorish heritage and Moroccan ethnicity in the form of meals, tea, and imported souvenirs. Emphasizing these dimensions of difference may prevent or at least displace inclusion of Muslims' religiosity. Mayanthi Fernando has written about an Andalusi-inspired, intercultural *iftar* meal in Paris, at which Moorish-themed food, flamenco performance, and pop music entertainment supplanted attention to religious reflection, thus satisfying some participants' desires to enact multicultural tolerance but leaving pious Muslim attendees disappointed (2014). That meal's organizers described their event as a kind of cross-cultural "voyage," but Fernando considers it one "that comforted rather than disrupted the voyager's world by taking her to a faraway place and time. There, the voyager could mingle with fantasy Muslims of *al-Andalus* and feel like a good, tolerant liberal without having to deal in any substantive way with Muslims in the present" (2014, 131).

Although the *Albayzín* pushes visitors into contact with "Muslims in the present," contemporary Moroccans are made to stand in for the past Muslims of *al-Andalus*. Fernando's critique of this past-present tension in remembrance of medieval Spain thus hints at the crux of the problem in the *Albayzín*. While my Muslim interlocutors do not seek out the *Albayzín* as a religiously oriented space in the way a pious Muslim might approach an iftar meal, they are acutely sensitive to the way the neighborhood's tourism sector, which also invites visitors to take a voyage to *al-Andalus*, excludes precisely this "substantive" engagement with what they themselves see as their own cultural, ethnic, and especially religious identities. To be sure, many of my research participants enjoyed spending their days surrounded by Moroccan goods in souvenir shops and were not always concerned with bringing piety publicly into the *Albayzín*. Their concern was that in the context of Catholic-majority Spain, touristy aspects of Morocco—like belly dancing, goatskin lamps, and hookah—should not be the only forms of Moroccan or Muslim identity presented. My Moroccan interlocutors' forms of religiosity were incredibly diverse, but interestingly, this concern about the invisibility of faith came from both self-described pious, devout Muslim migrants and those who described their practice as "secular" or "lax." They all expressed concern about the way the neighborhood facilitated the cohesion and condensation of Islam into folkloric representation in interfaith encounters. Leaving the small, mainly Moroccan-attended mosque in the neighborhood one day with a Muslim friend, we walked by some locals who peered at the building we were exiting and frowned at us with open disgust. My friend turned to me and whispered that the little mosque in the *Albayzín* scared people who knew about it, though most did not even realize it was there. Among all of the beloved teahouses and souvenir shops, this mosque seemed to be the one neighborhood building that left locals and tourists feeling either utterly uninterested, vaguely uneasy, or openly hostile. Religious difference, then, does not successfully make it into the tourism frame.

Through the tourism industry, the *Albayzín* thus becomes a spatialized niche for Moroccan migrant inclusion, facilitating a kind of social safe space for living, working, and socializing as Muslims, Moroccan nationals, and migrants. At the same time, the tourism frame also fosters a particular kind of Muslim inclusion—that is, consumption of ethnic difference (Islam-as-food and Morocco-as-lamps)—and perpetuates racial and ethnic miscommunications and hostilities. These play out in ways that are unique to the neighborhood, made possible and constrained by its Moorish-built architectural landscape, its social history, and its public association with the Moorish legacy.

Crime and Policing: The Forsaken Neighborhood

In addition to tourism, policing in the neighborhood further illustrates how the *Albayzín*'s special status as the city's "Muslim space" creates spatially specific inclusions and exclusions. In recent years, Muslim migrants' place in the lower *Albayzín* has been complicated by a growing sense among city residents that the neighborhood is in decline. While official outlets have not offered evidence for claims of soaring crime rates, the consensus seems to be that petty theft and violent muggings, as well as graffiti, drug trade, public indecency, and squatting are on the rise, along with a range of other illegal activities that have strongly impacted public perception of the neighborhood over the last two decades (Gutiérrez and Bautista 2000). Discussing neighborhood transformations, Catholic and secular residents of the neighborhood described to me a sense of being invaded from "above and below," expressing annoyance with a range of populations bringing change to the neighborhood, including new North African and Middle Eastern migrants, but also wealthy northern European speculators who were driving up rents, and Spanish and European bohemian youth and radical anarchists, "hippies" who in the words of one elderly *Albayzín* resident "maraud" the neighborhood with their dreadlocks and dirty dogs. This diversity also results in an unusually wide income inequality within the small neighborhood, exacerbating social tensions (Medina and Pablos 2002). Public outcry over the degeneration of the *Albayzín* occupies the attention of the city at large, including residents who do not live or shop there, indicating the emblematic nature of the area for Granada's tourism economy, cultural clout, and citywide sense of place.

In the midst of ongoing economic and demographic change, one clear trend is emerging: a tendency to defer local anxieties about a complex range of historical, political, and economic transitions in the neighborhood onto Muslim migrant bodies, which are increasingly dealt with through violence and policing. Specifically, public panic about rising crime in the *Albayzín* has provoked calls for greater police presence to stop what is often considered "migrant crime," reflecting broader national tendencies to criminalize migrants in Spain (Calavita 2003). Ironically, this discourse itself may encourage crimes against migrant residents and shop workers, who are often unable to access police protection because they are undocumented, fear the police, or simply cannot convince the police to show up on their behalf. The way locals' sense of precariousness in a changing neighborhood becomes consolidated into fears of migrant crime is clear in reporting on the neighborhood and the public mobilization of the area's neighborhood association. The Lower *Albayzín* Neighbors Association led a number of street protests and gatherings during my tenure in Granada, most with the aim of denouncing crime and uncivil behavior and demanding police attention. They hung huge banners across well-trafficked areas that read "More Police!" and "No More Robbery!" as well as the occasional economically pointed "Stop Speculators!" slogan.

While their anger was also aimed at Spanish "hippies" and wealthy land grabbers, they were primarily concerned with migrant crime, including from migrant youth. During my fieldwork, a national conversation emerged about the impending "problem" of what to do with second-generation Moroccan children born in Spain, and the growing numbers of unaccompanied, undocumented minors arriving from North Africa (Suárez Navaz 2006). In Granada, a state-run youth home for unaccompanied migrant children—many of them North African—was installed at the edge of the lower *Albayzín* and some locals were outraged. The neighborhood association emphasized the vulnerability of the neighborhood's aging residents and the damage migrant youth crime might cause the tourism industry. As one man explained, the narrowness of the Moorish-built streets meant that much of the neighborhood was necessarily pedestrian, and thus the elderly could not protect themselves by jumping directly from cars to their front doors, so it was not suitable to have undocumented migrant Moroccan children in the neighborhood. When a local paper ran the first of a series of stories covering crime, vandalism, and their effects on residents, commentators wrote in to blame migrants, writing comments like "The first step is to expel all the *sin papeles* [undocumented]" and "The *Albayzín* has been forsaken. Every day there are more *moros*, and more violence" (Vallejo 2009).

Many of my migrant research participants felt that because of this new public anxiety about crime and policing in the neighborhood, the *Albayzín* was slipping from a space of relative safety to a space where migrants were sitting ducks for policing. One day I stopped by the shop where Peque worked, hoping to say hello. When I arrived, Peque's girlfriend explained that their boss, who had residence papers, was running the shop that day. Peque and the others were worried about the police stopping by and discovering their undocumented status, so they were laying low. My interlocutors agreed that the *Albayzín* had been "forsaken" and that violent crime was on the rise, but they balked at the suggestion that they were to blame; instead, as those residents most likely to be working in shops open at night, they felt the most vulnerable, both to crime and to the police being brought in to respond to it.

Khadija: A Disappearance

The story of another shop worker, Khadija, illustrates the central ways Muslim difference is spatially configured by the *Albayzín*. Bringing together both of the previously discussed social patterns shaping the *Albayzín*, Khadija's trajectory illustrates the effects of Muslim migrants' involvement in the simultaneously inclusive and exclusionary heritage tourism industry and the consequences of migrant criminalization taking place in the name of protecting the historic neighborhood.

Khadija was one of my favorite people to visit when I made my rounds through the lower *Albayzín*, stopping to say hello to research participants in falafel shops, souvenir stands, and teahouses. Khadija was a forty-something Moroccan woman from the port city Tangier. Plump, shy but friendly, she wore long black flowing dresses and a red headscarf decorated with a beautiful poppy flower print on most days. Khadija was one of few Moroccan women who work in the *Albayzín* shops, and the only migrant woman I knew who owned and ran her own shop. She told me many times proudly that she was the only Moroccan, male or female, who owned a falafel shop—she said the rest were all Spanish-, Middle Eastern-, or convert-owned with Moroccan staff. I knew that Khadija's business was floundering, but despite tight resources, she invariably heaped a complimentary pile of steaming, freshly made falafel onto a napkin and slid it across the counter toward me when I came through the door, smiling and saying, "For a friend." Khadija did not have many friends. The first time we met, as I was introducing myself, a Moroccan man who worked in a nearby shop popped through the door, said hello in Arabic, broke a huge piece of chocolate off the bar he was munching and handed it to Khadija, grinning, before leaving to go back to work. Khadija did not touch the chocolate. "Is he a friend?" I asked. Khadija shook her head. "No. I don't have a friend, no husband, no boyfriend, no friend. Just a lot of problems."

When we met in 2008, Khadija had been living in Spain for five years. She had moved there with her husband and their teenaged daughter with the hope of running a small business. They opened the falafel shop together, but her husband passed away from heart disease one year after their arrival. Migrating to Spain was exciting at first, but once she was left widowed, a single mother in a still-new country, things went rapidly downhill. Business was slow—the sharp talons of the economic crisis were beginning to sink painfully into Spain—and Khadija was behind on tax payments for her business. This meant that while she had possessed legal residence papers and a permit for her shop since arriving in Spain, she could not go to the local police station to renew her now-expired papers. She was nervous about falling into undocumented status, and particularly upset because her legality woes meant that she could not go visit family in Morocco; without papers she would be unable to reenter Spain legally. Despite the difficulties she faced and the depression they engendered, Khadija kept working to provide for her daughter, Houda, now a young adult studying in college while also working at her mother's shop. While Khadija was often in low spirits, her face would light up with pride whenever Houda came by, or when she showed me pictures of her daughter, which she liked to pull out whenever I visited.

I often visited Khadija informally, but I also conducted a series of taped interviews with her. One day I arrived at Khadija's falafel shop at a pre-arranged time for an interview, but the shop was closed. I called her but got no answer. I had learned that interviewees did not always show up at scheduled times and places—some had a different sense of time than this type A, always prompt North American, and others had to cancel when issues related to work, childcare, or transport arose. I figured Khadija just needed to reschedule. A few days later, I stopped by and she explained that the night before our interview, she had been mugged on the way home from work, after closing the shop. The muggers had taken her wallet and phone, so she could not get in touch to cancel. I asked if she had gone to the police and she said no, that it would just add more complications. There was a group, she said, that had been robbing at least one shawarma or souvenir shop per night in the lower *Albayzín*, and she guessed her muggers might be connected to them. But, she said, "the police don't care because we're all foreigners around here."

Several weeks later, Khadija's shop was targeted by the group of young men she said were harassing local businesses. Sometime during Houda's shift, several obviously drunk Spanish young men came in and ordered chicken shawarma sandwiches. While public drunkenness was a constant source of annoyance for Muslim migrants working in the *Albayzín*, it did not usually elicit fear; most drunk customers were harmless college students or tourists. But when Houda had finished preparing their order, these men refused to pay and told her in aggressive tones to fork over the food. After trying unsuccessfully to negotiate with them, Houda declined to give them the sandwiches, tossing them in the trash. Filling me in the next day, Khadija said, "They shouted at her, '*hijo de puta, puta mora!*'" ("Son of a bitch/prostitute, Moor bitch/prostitute!") Khadija often had a kind of resigned attitude about the inevitability of such incidents, but this time she was shaken by the fact that her daughter had been the object of hostility.

After a short visit to the United States midway through my fieldwork, one of my first stops upon returning to Granada was Khadija's shop. It was closed, with the metal grate pulled all the way down over the doors. I came back the next day, and the next, and it was still closed. Khadija did not answer her phone. I asked around the *Albayzín*, and no one seemed to know where she had gone, but one man told me she had closed her business for good and he did not seem to think she was in Granada anymore. Khadija had been constantly fretting about her residence status and her business finances. I never managed to reestablish contact with her and I always wondered if she had gone out of business and given up on Spain, or if she might have been deported. By the time I returned to the neighborhood in the summer of 2014, another shop had replaced Khadija's, and no tourist was the wiser.

Khadija's experiences illustrate how casual racism is specifically, spatially fashioned in the *Albayzín*. First, the crime she and her daughter suffered in the mugging and subsequent encounter with racially hostile sandwich thieves emerged from neighborhood dynamics of crime and policing, which have clear racial, economic, and even legal consequences for migrant Muslims. The rising presence of police, a result of citywide demands to protect the Moorish treasure of the *Albayzín*, resulted in policing that did not protect Khadija but instead caused her to fear fines, incarceration, or deportation. In their efforts to save the neighborhood, locals' anxieties about a range of neighborhood changes were deferred onto Muslim migrants, who came to embody the very vulnerability they were thought to create as supposed criminals. Here, casual racism and structural racism worked in tandem as a feedback loop that marginalized Khadija and others.

Second, Khadija's and Houda's encounters in their falafel shop, paired with the life experiences Khadija shared with me in our conversations, show how encounters that take place within the Moorish tourism framework exclude attention to what might be called migrants' backstories. Just as celebration of food and souvenirs can foreclose recognition of the religious dimensions of Muslims' identities, the range of migration-related predicaments Khadija experienced are invisible in *Albayzín* tourist encounters with Moroccans. Visitors to her falafel shop were not privy to the common spiral created by migration policy, in which economic woes jeopardize migrants' ability to maintain legal paperwork, which in turn cuts off their mobility to Morocco. This resulted in Khadija's case, in ongoing depression and an undocumented status that prevented her from seeking out police protection after incidents where the casual racism of public space became wholesale violence and theft. While the omission of individuals' life stories is common in business transactions in many contexts (few Spaniards know the personal situation of their bankers, for instance), they are particularly vexing here. Because the *Albayzín* is explicitly set up as a place where Muslim salespeople come to stand for Islamic Spain, it becomes especially important that common experiences of Muslim migration—like undocumented status, economic disenfranchisement, or the inability to protect oneself from crime—are not included or visible in interactions that are otherwise taken as straightforwardly representative of who Muslims are and what they are like for tourist consumers.

Overall, Khadija, Mimo, and the rest of my research participants in the *Albayzín* illustrate how the neighborhood transforms casual racism into policing of Muslim migrants and neglect of their safety. Because of its centrality to the tourism industry and its place in public historical memory of *al-Andalus*, the neighborhood incorporates Muslim migrants as part of the city's proud self-representation. Yet the hyperpublicity of the *Albayzín* also puts Muslims on display, not just for tourists who are encouraged to consume ethnic difference without acknowledging Moroccans' religious difference or migrant struggles, but also for neighbors and police whose surveillance endangers migrants' place-based community formation in the neighborhood.

THE POLÍGONO: A MOROCCAN DANGER ZONE

Just as non-Muslim Andalusians, European expatriate residents, convert Muslims, and even other researchers assumed my interests should naturally lead me to the *Albayzín*, Muslim migrants often shepherded me toward the Polígono, instructing me to go there when I told them about my project, or inviting me to their homes and social events in the neighborhood. The Polígono could not be more different from the *Albayzín*.[6] Situated on the geographic margins of the city, rather than near its urban center, this neighborhood is not related to romantic historical memories of medieval Muslim Granada or linked in any way to city pride. Quite the opposite, the neighborhood has been historically known as a ghetto for Roma and the working poor. Moroccans are increasingly being slotted into this zone of urban remoteness as a newly emerging resident population of the Polígono. Because of lower rents and more migrant-friendly landlords, Moroccans have found the area easier to rent in than other neighborhoods, and many now live there. Given the powerful social meanings attached to neighborhoods, what does it mean for Moroccan migrants to increasingly reside in—and be publicly imagined as residents of—the Polígono?

As Moroccans become more associated with the urban disenfranchisement of the Polígono in the wider city imaginary, their racialized marginalization becomes more concrete. Being included into Granada as residents of the Polígono means gaining recognition as belonging to a local place, but in a process that spatializes Moroccans *as marginal*. In turn, the Polígono increasingly becomes seen as a Muslim migrant space, but one without the tourist trappings of the *Albayzín*. The "Muslimness" of the Polígono is largely understood in terms of migration, racial alterity, and political exclusion. The neighborhood becomes a kind of "Moroccan danger zone" in two ways—for the dangers of exclusion (political, socio-economic, psychological) it poses to new Moroccan residents and for the way Moroccan presence solidifies citywide views of the Polígono as a dangerous space where migrant crime and potential Muslim fundamentalism might loom. In the following sections, I introduce the neighborhood and then trace the effects of living there on new Moroccan residents, including individuals who lived there and members of the Moroccan women's association, Najma.

The Polígono, as well as its adjacent neighborhood, *Almanjáyer,* sits on the northeastern edge of Granada, its outer boundaries seeping into the rural province and small satellite commuter towns.[7] Construction in the neighborhood began in the 1960s (Egea Jiménez et al. 2009), and today it boasts large blocks of uniform, residential low-income housing. In the popular imagination of many city residents, this neighborhood has always been home to Granada's working-class and Roma residents, the most marginalized members of society. In fact, the neighborhood, like many outskirts of urban sprawl, has grown dramatically since the 1980s due to the influx of migrants and rural Andalusians looking for city work. The Polígono and its inhabitants are notorious for their supposed crime, unemployment, and poor manners. News reports on the neighborhood focus almost exclusively on crime, detailing violence, drug rings, and very occasionally, police investigation into supposed radicalism. The area has featured several times on the TV show *Callejeros,* a nationally broadcast, documentary serial in which journalists tour marginal neighborhoods, interviewing drug dealers and users, prostitutes, and other archetypes of urban disenfranchisement, offering up a spectacle of urban underbelly for an implied audience of middle-class viewers. Images of the Polígono's social marginality are compounded by its dilapidated built landscape. Some homes lack basic city infrastructure like consistently functioning electricity, running water, or gas, and some families, particularly on the outskirts, have incorporated elements of rural subsistence life into their urban properties, with the occasional horse, donkey, or chickens in the backyard or patio. These markers of rurality confirm for residents of the city center and upscale neighborhoods the down-and-out, less urbane nature of Polígono residents.

The Polígono's stark contrast to the *Albayzín* was readily apparent to me every time I went there. On one of my first visits, I went to meet up with Clara, the convert Muslim introduced in chapter 2. We decided to conduct our interview over tea or coffee, but the Polígono is one of very few areas of Granada that are almost purely residential. When I asked Clara where we could find a good cup of coffee, she said the Polígono was too desolate, pointing out how odd it is to find a neighborhood so devoid of businesses in a country that prides itself on having more bars and restaurants per capita and per street than anywhere else in Europe! We walked for about a half hour before arriving at the edge of a more central neighborhood where we found an open café. The abundance of *cafeterías* is one of the signature characteristics of urban life in Granada, and their relative absence from the Polígono marks the neighborhood as alien to *Granadino* city life.

Hajar: Polígono Isolation

One of my Polígono research participants, Hajar, often expressed sadness about her life in the neighborhood, which she described as lonely, insecure, and immobile—she felt stuck. Her dismay over her new neighborhood contrasted sharply with her memories of strong family networks and social connections back "home" in Morocco, which had facilitated her sense of safety and easy mobility in her natal city. I met Hajar at Najma, the Moroccan women's association located in the Polígono. After we got to know each other a bit, I asked if I could interview her. Hajar was shy about it, saying quietly, "Well, you should know that I don't even know how to read or write." After I explained that this wasn't necessary for an interview, she agreed and invited me to her apartment, which was located in a fairly rough area of the Polígono. Hajar surprised me by meeting me at the corner bus stop because she was concerned about my safety. As we walked up six flights of stairs to her apartment, I told her I felt badly that she had come down to meet me—she was six months pregnant and the stairs clearly tired her—but she said she could use the exercise as she was cooped up too much at home. As we climbed the stairs, she periodically turned around to whisper to me which apartments were home to neighborhood drug dealers. The building was painted schoolhouse white with lime green accents, and the bars over everyone's windows and doors made it feel more like a prison than an apartment building. Inside, though,

Hajar's apartment was modest but comfortable. We sat down next to her television, which was blaring news from Morocco, Egypt, and Syria in Arabic. Hajar changed the channels back and forth between Arabic news and Spanish-language *telenovelas* as we talked.

Hajar found living in the Polígono difficult. It was the only place she and her husband could afford and where they could find landlords willing to rent to Moroccans. Hajar's young son had a severe brain disease and has required several expensive surgeries, leaving the family in a financially precarious situation. Her husband, like the husbands of many Moroccan women I worked with, had a job as a bricklayer. He liked his work and felt his boss was fair and kind, but he did not earn enough for them to rent or buy in a better neighborhood. Hajar appreciated having Moroccan neighbors in the Polígono—she and a fellow Moroccan woman who lived two floors down took turns baking a weekly supply of Moroccan cookies for both households on alternate weeks. But she was frightened of her other neighbors and hesitant to let her children play outside because "there are too many Gypsies, and bad boys." Hajar had clearly internalized *Granadino* stereotypes about the danger of highly stigmatized Roma people. She was also reacting to a real sense of insecurity that pervades parts of the neighborhood, fed by years of political and economic disenfranchisement and a lack of basic services like law enforcement to provide the neighborhood with safe public space. She used to take the kids to a community center next door to their apartment building, but they stopped going because they saw drug dealing there.

After that, Hajar mainly stayed at home. She came once or twice a week to Najma for Spanish classes and for her children to take Arabic and Qur'an classes, but other than that, she rarely ventured out except for errands. Hajar saw isolation as necessary to protect her family from neighborhood influences. She was dismayed to see that some of her Moroccan "countrymen" seemed to have joined into what she considered "Gypsy" activities like selling and using drugs. "It's fine for the Gypsies or the Spaniards to do it, but the Moroccans? Who are coming here to give their children better opportunities, to make their lives better? That seems really bad to me—it's really bad." With two small children, one of whom was ill, and a baby on the way, it was difficult for Hajar to manage trips into the city center or other safer neighborhoods with parks where the children might play. Fiercely protective of her children, she would not risk them socializing with neighborhood "bad kids." She missed her family and friends in Morocco and hoped her husband would be willing to move back in the near future. My conversations with Hajar profoundly brought home for me the way inclusion into the city via residence in the Polígono engendered new subjectivities for migrant women who experienced a strong, place-based sense of immobility, insecurity, and outsider status, inflected by racial, socioeconomic, and migratory difference.

After my first interview with Hajar, I walked back to the corner bus stop and sat on a bench; the bus comes to the neighborhood infrequently, so I knew I had a long wait ahead of me. A group of teenaged boys eyed me from a dirt lot across the street. Eventually, they came and sat down on the bench next to me and burst into what seemed an exaggerated, almost farcical flamenco improvisation, all the while staring at me intently. Though the thought made me feel a bit narcissistic, I could not help but interpret their song as performative and directed at me—they seemed to be performing the social difference they knew was expected of them as Roma "*Gitano*" boys from the Polígono. Whether the boys were trying to poke fun at me as an outsider to the neighborhood, to entertain, or to agitate, their performance struck me as indicating a clearly internalized sense of otherness-in-place.[8] I wondered if these were the same "bad boys" Hajar was afraid of, what they thought of their new Moroccan neighbors, and whether Moroccans and Roma in the Polígono would develop cooperative community relationships or if hostilities would grow. Hajar and other Moroccan mothers in the Polígono clearly felt that the neighborhood's characteristics were forcing their families into a process of exclusion, the result of which they saw embodied in their Roma neighbors. Would Hajar's children grow up feeling marginalized by the spatialized alienation of the Polígono in the way these boys likely did?

The Najma Association: Inclusion into a Zone of Exclusion

Najma, mentioned earlier as one of the few Polígono locations Hajar felt safe attending, was one of my main field sites in the neighborhood. The association is a prime example of how Moroccans are collectively included into a zone of exclusion by virtue of living in the Polígono. The main goal of the organization's cofounder and president, Soukaina, was to "get

women involved" and "drag women out of their homes into the neighborhood" and into "city life." Teaching, learning, and socializing at the
association helped women become active citizens of the neighborhood,
as Soukaina put it. But the neighborhood they were joining was a decidedly marginalized space. The association's location, the materiality of its
grounds, and routine interactions with neighbors and custodial staff all
communicated the message to participants that being part of the Polígono
meant marginalization.

While open to all migrants, Najma is essentially a Moroccan women's
and children's organization, offering Spanish-language classes for newly
arrived migrants and Arabic and Qur'an classes for children of migrant
parents. Najma is also a social space, and at least half of every afternoon
session is spent at "recess," during which children play outside on the
large patio and mothers chat—gossiping about the neighborhood, venting about life in Spain, and strategizing for careers or planning birthday
parties. In fact, most mothers I spoke with whose children participated in
the free classes Najma offered told me they had enrolled them in part for
the religious education, in part so they would have strong enough Arabic
skills to communicate well with grandparents on summer return visits to
Morocco, and in part because the kids' classes served as free childcare,
offering mothers a chance to socialize with one another. Fathers and teenaged boys are present as occasional Spanish-language students, or when
they drop off and pick up their wives and children; otherwise, Najma is
a women-only space, save a few Spanish men who periodically volunteer
as language tutors.

The location and grounds underscore how life in the Polígono intro-
duces migrants to their marginal place in the city. The association is located on the grounds of a former public school, near the intersection of
two wide, nondescript boulevards with cracked pavement. The old school,
closed after being deemed unfit for Spanish schoolchildren, is surrounded
by a sizable patio with rusted-out play structures and a tall, green iron
fence on all sides. On my first visit, one of the women explained to me that
the school buildings were crumbling, but the regional government had
allotted the small campus to the association and one small migrant social
services agency because "it's good enough for us." On the same long city
block are a gun shop and a huge barracks complex for the local Guardia

Civil (Spain's military police), which means that Moroccan women who come on foot, including undocumented members, have to parade their families past the gun shop and police on their way to and from the association. Attending classes and events at Najma also brings Moroccan women into contact with other Polígono residents and visitors, including the many Roma and working-class Andalusian neighbors who socialize on the adjacent streets and frequently watch Najma attendees come in and out the gate. Often, I arrived early because of the bus schedule and stood on the steps in front of the locked gate, which custodial staff usually opened for us a few minutes after our classes were supposed to begin. As we congregated outside, local children would gawk at us, sometimes shyly approaching to ask soft-spoken questions about headscarves or Allah, and other times yelling things from a safe distance.

If Moroccan women at Najma felt observed and scrutinized by their neighbors, it was certainly a two-way street. Moroccan and Roma mutual racialized antagonisms around Najma reveal the way Moroccan presence in the Polígono incorporates migrants into a zone of spatial, political, and socioeconomic marginality already occupied by local Roma. While Roma and other working-class Andalusian Polígono residents are curious about the new Moroccan residents in the area, Moroccans are nervous about Roma both because of the sense of urban precariousness they represent in Granada and because of their own racialized attitudes and fears of "Gypsies." Along with Hajar, Jihan, the woman who had been trapped on her balcony, would constantly scold me, saying "Mikaela, don't forget to grab your purse; you never know, there could be Gypsies around." She also lamented frequently that around the edges of the Polígono, approaching downtown, people would sometimes point to her headscarf, saying, "Why is that on your head, are you a Muslim or a Gypsy?" These comments slotted her into a stigmatized category of which she wanted no part.

Najma provided a space for Moroccan women's sociality and networking, but one that solidified their sense of political, economic, and geographic exclusion as residents of the Polígono. Nearly every day, conversations began with commentary on the children and wound up on the topic of economic woes and job hunting. Many women had worked, in either professional or blue-collar jobs, in Morocco and had a hard time breaking into the job market in Granada. Others had never worked outside the home before, preferring to be stay-at-home mothers who ran their households. But in Granada, with Moroccan men facing unemployment and underemployment, many women felt they needed to start working, even if job seeking sometimes undercut normative gender roles in their marriages, a common way in which migration reconfigures gender and family (Boehm 2012). While the women at Najma came from varying socioeconomic backgrounds and ethnicities (some identified as Amazigh, some as Arab), in Granada, a sense of downward mobility affected all, and during Najma social hours, ethnic and economic divisions that might have held more sway in Morocco seemed to dissolve as women identified with one another as Moroccan migrant Muslims. This was clear when they turned to me one day, saying I needed to really understand the employment predicament of Moroccan migrant women. Lina was a woman with an advanced degree. She said, "Even with my advanced studies, I can't work here, except as a cleaner. It's the only thing you can do with a headscarf—they don't care if you have a scarf on while you're cleaning." Imane added, "It's really hard if you've studied in your own country, and the only thing you can do here is . . . whooosh!" She made a sweeping, downward gesture with her palm facing the ground to indicate downward mobility. "It's difficult." Other women joined in, asking about how to find cleaning jobs, how much pay to expect, and what employers were like. Just as the *Albayzín* provided a space for sociality and a support network for some Moroccan men to grapple with residence papers and employment issues, Najma occupied a similar role for Moroccan women.

The materiality of the facilities housing Najma also fostered and communicated casual racism and spatial disenfranchisement to the participating women and children. The fact that Muslim migrants were being housed in a facility deemed not good enough for a public school was not lost on Najma participants, who often complained bitterly of jagged, rusty iron jutting out of window frames, the smell of mildew, and the dripping rain that seemed to seep in everywhere during winter. Sometimes women at Najma would laugh dryly while referring to "our palace" or "our castle," particularly on days when things like doorknobs broke. Compounding the sense of exclusion women read from the decaying building itself was the sense of disrespect from the state-employed custodial staff who controlled the grounds. One of my activities at Najma two afternoons a week was to teach the Arabic alphabet to a class of toddlers. Our pedagogical supplies consisted of a few alphabet coloring books that the children shared. One day, as we colored in pictures of animals while learning the Arabic letters in their names, I asked if anyone had a pet. A four-year-old named Salma mischievously said, "Yes, my family has a pink hippopotamus," and seemed pleased with the giggles that followed. Catching onto the joke, Karim jested with glee, "I have a pet. My family has a bicycle!" which was met with uproarious laughter. I noticed, however, that a quiet boy named Omar was not laughing. It turned out Omar desperately needed to use the restroom but was holding out on asking to go, because the bathroom was always very dirty and often locked. I persuaded everyone to go on a field trip to the bathroom down the hall, but as usual, it was in fact locked. Sighing, I recalled how often while the kids played outside, their mothers and I wondered aloud what we would do if someone locked the front gates to the compound while we were all inside—would we have to climb out over the fences? Herding the children with me, I went off in search of Boris, the Russian-Spanish migrant janitor with the keys to the bathroom. He did not want to open it, suggesting these Moroccan kids would make a mess and that they use a bucket, only opening the bathroom door after much insisting.

The women at Najma concluded strong lessons about their social place in the city from their experiences of these material conditions and treatment. Women understood the dilapidated school and unsavory treatment by the custodial staff as specific to the Polígono neighborhood and indicative of Spaniards' disdain for Moroccan migrants. After incidents like the bathroom episode, my Najma interlocutors would often make conjectural comments about how things like this probably never happened in nicer parts of the city or in civic associations not run by and for Moroccans. Through daily use of the crumbling building and in daily interactions with neighbors and custodians, women came to understand themselves as excluded Polígono residents. Moroccan migrant children can become strikingly aware of their own marginality as migrants and Muslims at early ages (Colectivo IOÉ 1996; García Sànchez 2014), and it is safe to assume that the children at Najma were also likely taking in these lessons about their place in the city.

Later the same day as the bathroom run-in with Boris, Jihan and I had combined the toddlers with slightly older children and we were desperately trying to play a tape of children's songs on a stereo that refused to work. Eventually, we wondered if something was wrong with the electricity rather than the stereo itself. The lights were off in the room—southern Spanish sunlight poured through the large, scruffy windows, so we had no need of artificial light. I switched the lights on to test our electricity theory, and they stayed off. It was an electrical problem after all. Jihan threw her hands up in the air and said sarcastically, "Now why would *that* be?" as if to imply that she knew precisely why. Confused by her tone, I suggested a fuse had blown, pointing to the fuse box located high on a wall above us. Jihan reached up, flipped a fuse switch, and the lights came on. Then she looked at me, hands on hips, eyebrows raised, and said, leaning over, as if conspiratorially, "Very interesting, eh?" Still not grasping her meaning, I responded that given the age of the buildings in Granada, fuses were likely to blow. Jihan ignored me and said purposefully, "Well, or maybe the *Spaniards* did it!" "You think Spaniards blew the lights out?" I asked. Jihan nodded meaningfully. "It could be. Maybe the Spaniards came in and put out the fuses so we wouldn't have any lights. There's no other explanation. I mean, *they* can't reach up that high!" she surmised, emphatically gesturing toward the children who sat perplexed, watching us.

The fuse box mystery reflects the interplay between spatial, structural, and casual racisms in Granada. Jihan's assumption of anti-Moroccan sabotage was likely a misplaced but perfectly understandable assessment of the situation, informed by a backdrop of having absorbed daily tensions that cohered into a powerful framing narrative for her experiences in the neighborhood. Jihan was primed to expect the worst from "the Spaniards" because of daily microaggressions. The dilapidated material conditions and the peripheral geographic setting of the old schoolhouse contributed to her sense of marginality, and routine objectifying curiosity and hostilities from Polígono residents and the school's custodial staff during her visits to Najma engendered her pervasive sense of being watched. Unlike most of the Najma participants, Jihan did not actually live in the Polígono, and she was especially frustrated that activities for Moroccans seemed limited to this particular neighborhood.

Hajar, Soukaina, Jihan, and the other women and children who participate at Najma all individually and collectively negotiate the inclusionary-exclusionary social logic of the gradual consolidation of Moroccans as part of the Polígono world. Here, far away from the celebrated Moorish monuments of *al-Andalus*, Moroccan migrants are incorporated into Granada as part of its most marginal place. In view of the broader city, Moroccans are at once ignored, cast out into a neighborhood central city residents fear, and yet visible as a growing part of the urban periphery, increasingly naturalized as marginal and frightening because of their status as dangerous Polígono residents. Within the neighborhood itself, a kind of double exclusion exists, as Moroccans become objects of racial and religious scrutiny and sometimes hostility, while also themselves internalizing antipathy toward Roma and working-class Polígono residents, attempting to distance themselves from *"Gitanos"* and the disenfranchised futures they seem to herald for Moroccans and their families.

CONSOLIDATING MUSLIM NEIGHBORHOODS: (IM)MOBILITY AND RACIALIZED SPACE

The ways in which the more centrally located *Albayzín* and the more peripheral Polígono are differently being consolidated as Muslim space are clear in variously positioned *Granadinos'* tendencies to identify one or the other as more authentically Muslim. Although the *Albayzín* is in many ways central to the city of Granada—geographically, economically, and in terms of city pride and self-representation to the world—the neighborhood is also remote in one important respect. Precisely because it has been so successfully constructed as Moorish or Muslim space, the *Albayzín* today is primarily visited by Spanish and foreign tourists, rather than non-Muslim locals. Mohammed, a Moroccan migrant in his twenties who worked at a souvenir shop and lived in one of the less expensive apartments in the lower part of the neighborhood, explained this to me: "Granada is really touristy. Very few *Granadinos* actually come here, so I have very little contact with people from here. If they come to the neighborhood, it's only to show it off to out-of-town guests who are visiting Granada." Gloria, a Catholic social services NGO employee in the Polígono, reiterated this to me in an interview in which she made a case for the Polígono as the "real" Muslim neighborhood of Granada. I was asking her how much employment the Moorish-themed tourism industry brought to the Muslim community as a whole, and she said that while the *Albayzín* is popularly known as a Muslim area, it really only employs a small fraction of Muslim migrants. More importantly for her, the *Albayzín* cannot function as a true space of inclusion because in her view, "The racist grandmothers just don't go there," so the neighborhood does not really foster interactions between Muslim migrants and non-Muslim *Granadinos*.

According to Gloria, the Polígono was a more authentic place to learn about Islam and interfaith relations in Granada. At first I was surprised to hear her describe the Polígono as more important than the *Albayzín*— most people I knew who lived in more central neighborhoods never went there, and while they also rarely went to the *Albayzín* it was very much on their radar; they talked about it, lauded it, and encouraged visitors to go there. No one encouraged visits to the Polígono. But for Gloria, the absence of tourists combined with the presence of a long-standing population of locals meant that the Polígono was a more real space of authentic interaction between *Granadinos*—albeit marginal ones—and migrants. This neighborhood *was* full of "racist grandmothers." Many of my Moroccan research participants agreed with Gloria, identifying the Polígono, rather than the *Albayzín*, as Granada's "Muslim neighborhood" or "Moroccan neighborhood." Ultimately, both neighborhoods are becoming understood as Granada's quintessentially Muslim spaces, but by residents with very different perspectives.

The way city residents read racial and religious difference into physical movements between neighborhoods also reveals how the *Albayzín* and Polígono are becoming solidified as different kinds of Muslim-associated space. Urban segregation is often especially palpable in the kinds of anxiety minority presence provokes in different spaces, and in reactions to the movement of different kinds of people between neighborhoods. As discussed earlier, tourist maps and bus routes institutionalized movement to the *Albayzín* from many parts of the city. The sociospatial "remoteness" (Ardener 2012) of the Polígono does the opposite. The first time I went to the neighborhood, I documented the experience in my field notes, excerpted here:

> I took the bus to the Polígono/Almanjáyer to interview Fatima today. Everyone told me not to go. My housemates, Mariela's boyfriend who was

over. At the bus stop downtown I was looking at the route map and I asked someone about stops in the Polígono. All the strangers at the stop told me not to go there. Even the bus driver seemed worried. As we rounded the corner into Fatima's smaller neighborhood within the Polígono, there was a group of young men in velour sweat suits surrounding two small dogs that looked like pit bulls. Someone on the bus said in this area there is a lot of illegal dogfighting. It is amazing how different this feels, not more than 20 minutes from the bullfighting ring!

Because I was perceived as middle class and respectable, my travel into the Polígono provoked concern for my safety.

Movement by differently viewed actors, in the opposite direction, awakens other responses. I noticed this the day I went to the Polígono to interview Clara and we had to return to the city center just to find a coffee shop. Clara was one of the few converts I knew who socialized primarily with migrants, and because she wore a Moroccan-style headscarf, she was often perceived as Moroccan. It was she who suggested we meet up in the Polígono. We met outside the large discount grocery store and stopped in so Clara could pick up a few things. Inside, we ran into a recently arrived Moroccan migrant, Wafae, along with her husband and their new baby. They seemed excited to see me, as it was our first meeting outside of Najma classes. As we left the store, they waved, and Clara smiled and waved at a few other friendly acquaintances. As we walked toward downtown, the friendly waves of the Polígono turned into concerned and even hostile stares. I wondered if I was imagining things, but Clara interrupted my thoughts to point out that now that we were closer to the city center, everyone was noticing her headscarf. She said this always happened when she came downtown.

The spatialized social anxieties provoked by my movement *to* the Polígono and Clara's movement *out* of the neighborhood reflect how the spatialization of racial, religious, and migrant identities can create the kind of stuckness of which Hajar complained. Such immobility is a feature of migrant life across urban Europe. In France, anthropologists have documented how Muslim French movement from ghettoized *banlieus* where many reside (Selby 2012) to the city center on Paris's RER trains invites public scrutiny and violent policing (Silverstein 2000; Ticktin 2011, 37). In Spain's North African territory of Ceuta, black African migrants are held in CETIs (semi-detention-like, temporary residence centers for the undocumented) located on the outskirts of the city. Ruben Andersson notes how in their peripherally located neighborhood, CETI residents are seen as benevolent victims, racialized and infantilized with the Spanish diminutive form as "*negritos*" (little blacks). But when these same Africans venture into Ceuta's public square to protest their indefinite holding in the CETIs, they are differently racialized, now as dangerous "*negros*" (2014). In Paris, Granada, or Ceuta, there is no city space that is fully safe, where migrants are not racialized or otherwise marked as minorities. The fact of their designation as different remains, but the register, contours, and implications of their othering for politics and sociality are spatially configured.

Nevertheless, Soukaina, the president of Najma, enjoyed and fiercely defended an uncommon mobility across city space. I rarely if ever saw many of the Moroccan women I knew in the Polígono outside the neighborhood, but Soukaina went all over the place. As she moved between the Polígono and many other parts of the city, she articulated her spatial mobility as a challenge to the racialized designation of Muslim and non-Muslim spaces. Soukaina; her husband, Hamza; and their seven-year-old daughter and three-year-old son also lived in the Polígono, but in a slightly nicer area than most Najma women, closer to the city center, which they afforded thanks to Hamza's IT job at an Internet café. Soukaina resented having to live in the Polígono—they had tried to rent elsewhere but could not find prices or landlords as amenable to Moroccans as in the Polígono. Like Hajar, Soukaina worried about negative neighborhood influences on her children. She wanted them to grow up as healthy, pious Muslims who studied hard. But she also had a stronger sense of entitlement than the less educationally and economically privileged Hajar. While Hajar felt stuck in the Polígono, Soukaina felt empowered to struggle against the neighborhood's limits. She was an advanced PhD candidate in the sciences at the University of Granada and in addition to cofounding and running Najma, she served as a translator and chaperone for Moroccan women at clinic and hospital appointments throughout the city, especially for prenatal care.

Soukaina often spoke to me about her life in distinctly spatialized terms, with each respective space—home (Morocco), Granada, and the

Polígono—indexing different degrees of racial and religious inequality that she had to manage. Seated in Soukaina's living room late one evening, after sharing dinner with her family, we looked at photo albums of her family life in Morocco, periodically interrupted by her toddler son. Despite Soukaina's stern warnings, Nawfal repeatedly crept out of bed to serenade us with toy bongo drums, grinning mischievously in his green footie pajamas. Soukaina explained that in Morocco, on annual vacations they were able to take thanks to their legal residence papers, she was "treated like a queen." She was from a large, solidly middle-class family, and her sisters helped take care of her children. They spent every summer at the beach, where she could truly relax. In Granada, in contrast, there was "no rest." While people from all walks of life might make similar distinctions, associating everyday life with stress and vacation with relaxation, there is an especially pronounced dimension of this distinction for Moroccan migrant women, whose lives in Europe are often marked by a distinct lack of the female, family social networks that facilitated sociality, work, and the smooth running of households and childcare prior to migration. Annual visits home remind North African migrants of new configurations of gender and family life in the diaspora (Ben-Yehoyada 2011; Salih 2003), and Soukaina and many others spatially mapped the transition from social support to isolation onto the move from Morocco to Spain.

Within Spain, Soukaina associated each city space in Granada with particular kinds of stresses. In the Polígono, she was constantly busy tending to her hyper children without the help of her sisters, working to be sure they got a "good education" despite the neighborhood's shortcomings. She spent evenings trying to catch up on Spanish news "to be an informed citizen of Spain" while also catching up on political and family news in Morocco via TV, Skype, and phone. When she left the neighborhood to attend university classes and work in her lab on campus, she became exhausted from having to "prove" that she was intelligent despite her headscarf.

Between her studies, motherhood, and association responsibilities, Soukaina rode her *moto* (small motorbike) all over the place, and she self-consciously spoke up against the spatialized racialization of Muslim migrants as she did so. One way Soukaina accomplished this was by accompanying other Moroccan women on prenatal care visits to hospitals in central neighborhoods. On these visits, she had a knack for making

racially charged jokes meant to put both Spanish hospital staff and ex-
pecting Moroccan mothers at ease. Discussing these visits with me and a
group of Moroccan women at Najma, she laughed about the anxiety their
presence outside the Polígono provoked, saying, "Well, I just say [to the
doctors], 'Yeah, yeah, it's me again, with another *mora*!'" This prompted
giggles and a discussion of what exactly *moro* and the feminine *mora* mean.
Soukaina summarized authoritatively, "*Moro* is an abbreviation for Muslim. Well, it's a bad translation in Spanish for Muslim, but that's what it
means. Of course, here they use it in a negative way. But I don't, I always
say it as a joke. That's why when I get here [to Najma], I always say, 'Hey!
All you *moras*! What are you doing?'"

Soukaina's joking uses of the term invoke the spatial dimensions of
Moroccans' racialized exclusion at multiple scales—those of nation and
city. They are marked as migrants—and thus Moroccans out of place—
within Spain at large, and as *moras* out of place within Granada's central
neighborhoods. Soukaina knows that Moroccan women are often stereotyped in Spain for having too many children, an image that contributes
to ideas of Moroccans as "traditional" and stokes fears of a slow Muslim
retaking of Spain through demography, with Moroccan babies as a kind of
population "Trojan horse" (Dietz 2004, 1092). Aware that hospital doctors
in Granada engage pregnant Moroccan migrants through this lens, viewing them as a suspect presence in Spain in general and in non-Polígono
areas of Granada in particular, she tries to call them out on their prejudice
while also "breaking the ice" with her racial humor. In announcing her arrival with "more *moras*" she refers to both the patients' arrivals in hospital
waiting rooms and to the impending arrival of more Moroccan children
in the Spanish population. She also knows that Muslims' presence in the
Polígono, while becoming normalized, still garners attention; her joke
about asking what all the women are doing congregating at Najma reveals
awareness of the concerns of neighbors, like Claudia, whose comments
earlier in this chapter express a taken-aback sense of surprise at the "mass"
of Moroccan women and children coming and going at the association.
By gathering women at Najma in the Polígono and by bringing pregnant
Moroccan women to clinics outside the neighborhood to receive what
she considers good care, Soukaina attempts to assert Moroccans' right to
presence in the city by inserting Moroccan women into institutions and

city spaces. All the while, she eases the tensions this produces for Moroccan migrant women and native *Granadinos* alike by jokingly revoicing what she imagines doctors and neighbors are thinking—that she and her friends are *moras* out of place.

CONCLUSION

In the *Albayzín*, Moorish architecture fosters tourism and community formation among Moroccan shop workers. Yet the neighborhood also places them on awkward display for tourist consumption and leaves them vulnerable to policing efforts that defer conversations about neighborhood change onto criminalized and victimized Muslim, migrant bodies. In the Polígono, racialization of Muslim migrants funnels Moroccans who cannot rent apartments elsewhere into the neighborhood, where their designation as Polígono residents then further cements their incorporation into the city as part of the racially and religiously marginalized, socioeconomic underclass. Once ensconced in the Polígono, neighbors' scrutiny and a sense of material dilapidation and social insecurity also shape their quality of life in relation to neighborhood placement. While Soukaina struggles against racial and spatial marginalization, many Polígono residents do not have the university connections or financial resources that help her to do so.

My goal in this chapter has been to present ethnography that moves between areas of the city to highlight how racialization of Muslim migrants' religious and migratory difference becomes enshrined in the urban landscape, both fostering and responding to spatialized social divides. In Granada, the *Albayzín* can become so strongly associated with the Moorish past and Islamophilic celebration that it obscures the processes of Muslim migrant exclusion that unfold there and the existence of far more Muslim migrants in other parts of the city like the Polígono. Interrogating the place of Islam in Granada along religiously or historically oriented lines focused on Islam or *al-Andalus* often leads exclusively to the *Albayzín* (e.g., Rosón Lorente 2008), ignoring peripheral neighborhoods in Granada that are not historically constructed as emblematic of Moorish history. In contrast, analyses fixed along axes of race and migration might lead scholars toward the Polígono alone, missing how migrants in Europe create economic and social networks smack in the middle of central places like the touristy *Albayzín*, or among African migrants at the Gare du Nord train station in Paris (Kleinman 2014), not just in peripheral ghettoes. Ethnographically, focusing on the *Albayzín* and the Polígono together demonstrates the spatial differentiation of casual (and structural) racism as it shapes urban public life in Granada, as well as the way casual racism combines racial, religious, migratory, class, and gender difference. In learning about how convert Muslims, migrant Muslims, and non-Muslims interpret the place of Islam in the city, I was drawn back and forth between these neighborhoods by different research participants, leading to a city-wide picture of how racial and religious difference becomes spatialized, and the different possibilities for inclusion and exclusion in the touristy *Albayzín* and the disenfranchised Polígono, each now becoming "Muslim space" in profoundly distinct ways.

NOTES

1. For more on the spatialized processes through which national, regional, and class identities are produced and politicized in Spain, see Roseman and Parkhurst 2008.

2. This complex of concerns about Islam and migration does, however, shape occasional far right political actions. In Granada, the annual *Toma* festival commemorating the Muslim city's 1492 defeat by the Catholic Kings regularly draws crowds of neo-fascists and neo-Nazis with anti-Muslim and antimigrant placards. Many Muslims I know stay home on this day to avoid the risk of street violence.

3. In Andalusian colloquial Spanish, to say that someone performs a task with his *cojones* can imply both a gritty determination to succeed at all costs and a perceived low-class crudeness. His comment thus played on Moroccans' marginal class position and cast them as dangerously determined to take over the region.

4. Such national harnessing of Andalusianness while stigmatizing Andalusians reflects a long history in which the region has been marked both as different and as metonymic of the Spanish nation-state (Fernandez 1988).

5. In *Exotic Nation: Maurophilia and the Construction of Early Modern Spain*, Barbara Fuchs reveals through historical and literary analysis that Spanish engagements with Moorishness in material culture have always gone beyond instrumentality. She suggests that Moorishness has a "habitual presence in Iberian culture" (2009, 3), creating a kind of "Moorish habitus" that pervades material culture in Spain, making Moorishness always already somehow included, despite what she calls Spanish attempts to "quarantine Moorish influence" (143).

6. In Spanish, the word *Polígono* can sometimes refer to an office park or industrial campus, but in dense urban contexts it often refers to peripheral urban outskirts with large, uniform, low-income housing developments that may be funded through government programs and/or private development companies.

7. Most of my research participants used the term *Polígono* to refer to the official districts and subneighborhoods of Almanjáyer, *Polígono de Cartuja, Cartuja, Rey Badis, La Paz,* and parts of *La Chana.*

8. Derek Pardue, in a different Mediterranean context, has traced similar patterns in which musical performances by migrants and racial minorities become expressions of urban emplacement in peripheral housing projects in Lisbon (2014).

4

❖

A RELUCTANT *CONVIVENCIA*
Minority Representation and Unequal Multiculturalism

Muslims in Granada consistently answered my questions about their relationships with *non*-Muslims by broaching the issue of differences *within* the Muslim community.[1] This was especially the case when Muslims discussed their efforts to represent Islam positively in Spain. When I asked Lara, a young Spanish Muslim from Granada's convert community, to tell me about relationships between Muslims and non-Muslims in Granada, she compared past and present, saying:

> Before, people might have laughed and been like, "Oh, there go the Muslims," but they were respectful. . . . We [converts] have always lived in the old quarter, in the *Albayzín*, in the upper part. And people used to yell "*Moro!*" at my mother, but in general they respected us. But now I see a lot more confusion. On a global level, there's all this media imagery of terrorists, and now people think of Muslims as terrorists. These days in Granada you hear of really bad things, even acts of violence. It could be because there are so many Moroccans here now, and people think they're taking their jobs.

When Lara was born in the 1980s, most of Granada's Muslims were Spanish and European converts like her parents. Today, Muslim migrants from Morocco vastly outnumber convert Muslims in the city. Although in these comments Lara ostensibly blamed rising racism on heightened global antipathy toward Muslims, she also subtly faulted the growing Moroccan population, nostalgically invoking a past in which European converts monopolized the image of Muslims in Granada. Latifa, a Moroccan migrant roughly Lara's age, answered the same question about relationships with non-Muslims by insisting that the first thing I needed to know was that "the Muslim community is divided" between European converts and Muslim migrants.

Anxiety over public opinion about Islam, Muslims' responsibility for representing Islam to their largely Catholic and secular neighbors, and the attendant risks and challenges of this work were constant themes of conversation during my fieldwork. Lara's and Latifa's comments hint at the central argument of this chapter: that Muslims in Granada experience their efforts to represent Islam to wider Spanish publics as hinging on their ability to manage tensions within the city's diverse Muslim population. These tensions reflect converts' and migrants' vastly different access to social and political resources, a disparity produced by the different ways convert and migrant Muslims are incorporated as minority subjects in Granada. The previous two chapters have shown how converts are more able to successfully tap into romantic, public, historical imaginaries of Islam to claim rootedness in Granada, while migrant Muslims are more likely to bear the brunt of spatially configured casual and structural racism in the city. Building on the theme of unequal multiculturalism, in this chapter I trace how converts' and migrants' different social positions within Spain stem from and sustain distinct strategies for minority representation and experiences of the moral and political stakes of managing how their communities figure in Spanish imaginaries of Islam. This is most powerfully expressed in the ways convert and migrant Muslims disassociate from one another. Converts often claim to practice a "culture-free" Islam, which they contrast to Moroccans' "traditions." This discourse cloaks convert religiosity within an unmarked category of "European" and marks migrant Muslims as outsiders. Migrants, on the other hand, largely accuse converts of exclusionary social practices and religious inauthenticity. Both groups worry about the other's potential contribution to public perceptions of Muslim extremism.

By examining how Muslims manage widely circulating discourses about Islam in urban social encounters, this chapter reveals the inequalities and tensions among Granada's Muslims that shape their differentiated experiences of minority representation. Muslims' representational efforts in Granada, widely described by my research participants simply as "giving a good impression of Islam," are in fact a complex set of diverse representational practices. Converts and migrants explicitly engage both with one another's and with non-Muslims' ideas about Islam in their efforts to conceptualize and practice "Muslim representation." This chapter moves the discussion of representation out of the media, courtrooms, museums, or social services offices more commonly studied in scholarship on minority representation (e.g., Dávila 2001; Henkel 2006; Naficy 2001; Shryock 2004b), and into the minutiae of everyday life in less institutionalized urban spaces that are equally important to the larger processes determining where and how Muslims may (or may not) fit into Europe. I analyze both Muslims' encounters with non-Muslims and contentious conversations between convert and migrant Muslims about how best to represent themselves to others. My goal is to shed light on "the delicate representational politics that determine how Otherness is acknowledged and suppressed in the act of showing" (Shryock 2004b, 16).

THE IMPERATIVE TO REPRESENT ISLAM

In Granada's context of regional ambivalence about Islam, how did converts and migrants go about trying to represent Islam? Why did they spend so much time thinking and talking about representation with me in the first place? During my fieldwork, a central current in Muslims' representational efforts was the difficulty of reconciling their competing desires for positive publicity on the one hand, and for the protective benefits of privacy on the other hand. Given Muslims' visibility as a marked social group, the centrality of Islam to debates about regional identity, and the growth of hostilities toward Muslims in Granada, public attention to Islam was inevitable, and managing self-presentation took on particular urgency. Yet this visibility also instilled in many a defensive desire to shield themselves from unwanted scrutiny by observers ranging from neighbors to tourists to state agencies. Such scrutiny is part and parcel of Muslim minorities' increased visibility in many contexts since September 11, 2001, and the spread of the global war on terror, in which Muslims have become objects of study, investment, sympathy, anger, alarm, and regulation by governmental and nongovernmental agencies (Abu-Lughod

2002; Bowen 2008, 2010; Howell and Shryock 2003; Jamal and Naber 2008; Özyürek 2009).

Global anxieties about Islam also mean that individual Muslim communities are often charged with the responsibility for explaining, defending, or, more often, denouncing the actions of self-identified "Muslim extremists" halfway around the world after widely publicized acts of violence, lest they be grouped together under the broad banner of "Muslim terrorists." The globalized and undifferentiating nature of such public demands for Muslim explanations places a huge burden of representation on Muslims worldwide, but perhaps especially on those living in Western spaces. This burden was acutely observable in the ways my research participants had been conditioned to defend themselves from associations with so-called Islamic terrorism. When I first introduced my research interests in Islam to new Muslim research participants, or initiated first interviews with new interlocutors, many would begin our conversations with unsolicited comments about terrorism. Either they would preface our interaction by directly or casually asserting that Muslims in Spain are "moderate" and "not terrorists," or they would commend me for doing research that could help expose Muslims' terrorist image as false. A few people even expressed pleasant surprise when they realized I was not going to ask them about this topic. These interactions all revealed Muslims' expectations regarding non-Muslim North American assumptions about Islam. The persistence with which my interlocutors addressed terrorism or initially expected me to do so reveal the degree to which a learned expectation of surveillance and suspicion from intrusive observers shaped their ways of seeing non-Muslims. When I asked one woman why she had expected me to want to talk about terrorism, she explained that this was the only topic non-Muslims, and sometimes researchers, seemed to broach. She relayed being approached one day by an undergraduate political science student from the local university who had shown up outside her mosque to distribute a survey that included questions such as "Do you support political violence?" and "Were you in favor of the Madrid train bombings?"

My Muslim interlocutors often articulated their keen interest in representation by citing the growing visibility of Islam-as-terrorism and Islam-as-foreign in national media and political discourse. Many complained about "the media," sensing that the daily barrage of images of clandestine migration from Morocco (often of capsized boats and drowned or rescued migrants) and (often sensationalist) reports on suspected terror cells in national news reinforced stereotypes of Muslims as faceless victims drawing away national resources or as faceless, foreign threats to security (Beck 2012; Granados 2004). Jihan told me as we sat in her living room one day, with a TV news program buzzing in the background,

> I can kind of see how people are racist. I'm not saying they're right—it's wrong—but it's what they see on TV, in the media, that's all they hear about us. And whenever there's a terrorist attack involving Muslims they say "Muslims" or "Islamists" did it, but when ETA makes an attack, they just say ETA did it, not "ETA, the Catholics" or whatever religion they are. I wish they would also just say "Hamas" or "Al-Qaeda," not "Hamas, the Muslim group."

ETA, the terrorist organization that fought for Basque independence during much of the past century, for years eclipsed Islam in the public imagination of terrorist threats in Spain. But since the March 2004 Madrid train bombings, attributed initially to ETA but ultimately to Al-Qaeda, public discussions of terror threats in Spain have shifted from fears of regionalist Basque ETA campaigns to worries about "Muslim extremism" that resonate within the broader context of the global war on terror.

Jihan and many others lamented an increasingly hyperbolic tone in public discourse about Islam. For example, when Muslim groups demanded an apology after an anti-Islamic speech by Pope Benedict XVI in 2006, Jose María Aznar, former Spanish president and then leader of Spain's conservative party, countered that the pope need not apologize, because "No Muslim has ever apologized to me for conquering Spain and being here for eight centuries. The West didn't attack Islam, they attacked us" (Agencias 2006). Aznar's public comments gained notoriety for the way in which they conflated medieval and present-day Muslims and positioned both as terrorists and/or invaders, using the oppositional language of a clash of civilizations. Many Muslims spoke to me about this and other highly publicized political commentary about Islam as examples of the government's hostility toward Islam and the media bias that presented Muslims as inherently dangerous and foreign.

My research participants were often either unaware of or skeptical of state-level Muslim associations' abilities to counter the anti-Islamic official narratives of media and political discourse. The Spanish federal government, patterning its efforts to engage with Muslims on its history of relations with the Catholic Church, has "demanded a single interlocutor" with which to interact on behalf of all Muslims (Díez De Velasco 2010, 247). In response, since the 1980s a few Muslim associations, often led by converts hoping to serve as "brokers" between "Islam" and "the West" (Leman et al. 2010), have emerged to jockey for primacy as liaisons with the state. But these associations are largely unsupported by Muslims in Spain, who often consider them undemocratic and utterly divorced from the lives of Spain's Muslim residents (Arigita 2006).

Muslims' sense that they themselves bore responsibility for representing Islam stemmed from their appraisal of these national issues but also from Granada's union of Islamophilic and Islamophobic discourses. My interlocutors sensed a general saturation of the city with reminders of Islam as a public presence, and this context helped produce their own experiences of public visibility. They cited things like Muslim- and Arab-related imagery in signage on businesses, street names, Moorish architecture, and even regional Andalusian colloquialisms that highlighted the centrality of Islam in a negative way, like my landlord's use of the expletive phrase "I shit on the Moors!" As a result, many considered active work to improve public opinion of Islam a personal and communal duty. Two examples—the construction of converts' public-oriented mosque and a Middle Eastern migrant woman's experience of being called upon by a stranger to answer for Islam—are instructive. They demonstrate both how Muslims in Granada arrived at a strong imperative to represent Islam and the uneven ways this burden of representation arose for different Muslims.

The *Mezquita Mayor de Granada* is a beautiful, whitewashed mosque high in the hills of the touristy, Moorish-built *Albayzín* neighborhood.[2] The mosque's name translates as "The Great Mosque of Granada" and its opening in 2003 made international news.[3] The mosque enjoys a stunning view of the Alhambra, for many the culmination of Moorish architecture in Spain, which sits nestled in the foothills of the snow-capped Sierra Nevada mountain range across a narrow valley. The mosque is adjacent to the *Mirador de San Nicolás*, the public square and lookout point that is perhaps the most-visited spot in the city (and in Spain) for its unrivaled view of the Alhambra. The Mezquita Mayor's location on one side of the square thus places it in the geographic center of Granada's public representation on a world stage.

Despite financing from the United Arab Emirate of Sharjah and a Moroccan imam, the foundation leaders and the majority of regular congregants are converts, and Muslims in Granada often refer to it as "the convert mosque" or "the one up there," referring to the upper *Albayzín*.[4] The Mezquita Mayor is the most publicly recognized mosque in Granada, and the one that non-Muslims are most likely to encounter, given its privileged location on the main *Albayzín* tourist route. The general public can meander through the gardens, take organized tours, purchase souvenirs, peruse literature about Islam, chat with the "greeters" (young men stationed at the gate), or take Arabic courses. Occasionally, convert women sell homemade baked goods to passersby at folding tables that are set up outside, facing the San Nicolás square. The Mezquita Mayor operates in stark contrast to the main mosques attended by Muslim migrants, which tend to be out of the public eye. Many are converted garages or other formerly domestic or commercial spaces rather than structures built originally as mosques, and many are located in peripheral neighborhoods not frequented by nonresidents. Unlike the Mezquita Mayor, other mosques I was familiar with during fieldwork became visible to wider publics only when they were victimized by theft or discriminatory vandalism that received local news coverage.

The unique public orientation and representational work of the Mezquita Mayor result from a combination of the mosque's geographic location, converts' own theological motivations for openness, and demands made by local skeptics of Islam during the roughly twenty-year struggle to build the mosque (Rosón Lorente 2008). Many converts, especially members of the Murabitun community, felt strongly about the Islamic concept of dawa, which they understood primarily as the spreading of Islam to new converts. They aimed to create a welcoming and informative environment at the mosque to accomplish this. Converts' dawa outreach, however, was also conditioned by their concerns with Islam's negative public image. This was clear when Belén startled me one day after the Friday *khutbah* (sermon) by turning to me to say, "See, Mikaela, it's not like what you might think. You might think in the mosque they talk about terrorism, or who knows what, you know, fanatical stuff. But, see? It's just about, you know, 'Be virtuous!' and nothing more."

Belén's reflexive defensiveness was also informed by efforts from local non-Muslims to prevent the construction of a mosque in the city's treasured *Albayzín*. Many converts bitterly recounted the twenty-year struggle to obtain final permission for the mosque construction, which was impeded by Catholic and secular neighbors' complaints, a mandated archaeological excavation of the plot, difficulties obtaining permits, and other obstacles one convert woman considered "government-stalling tactics." When I first lived in Granada in 2001, I asked a man who worked at an adjacent, touristy restaurant about what was then a gaping hole, surrounded by piles of plywood and tarps, that sat next to the San Nicolás square. He told me that local Muslims wanted to build a mosque, but that for now, it was just an archaeological site, and that the neighborhood would probably not let them construct a mosque there. According to my research participants' memories of the "mosque controversy," the mosque foundation's leaders, among other compromises, finally promised to make the minaret shorter than the bell tower of a nearby historic church, to avoid placing windows in walls facing a nearby convent, and to keep the mosque open to tourists and the local public for part of each day to make sure the building did not disrupt the flow of tourism in the area. Only then were they allowed to build the mosque. The prolonged resistance to the mosque certainly indicates a level of local trepidation about converts. On the other hand, their ultimate success in opening the mosque in Granada's prized tourism neighborhood also reflects their ability to satisfy local demands for certain kinds of openness and self-representation.

Muslim migrants also experienced a strong imperative to constantly display, explain, and otherwise represent Islam (and immigration). Yet they developed their preoccupation with representation differently. Muslim migrants by and large were not motivated by dawa. Without the theological impetus to spread Islam, or the institutionalized means of representation that were both forced upon and sought by converts at the Mezquita Mayor, many migrants found the responsibility to represent Muslimness thrust upon them as individuals in unofficial public settings. Such encounters were persistent, often gendered, anxiety-producing events. Hana, an Arab woman from the Gulf region who had lived in

Spain for nearly twenty years when I met her, still feared these kinds of situations in public, explaining that they had increased since she began wearing a headscarf five years ago. One afternoon, following a public talk about the Israel-Palestine conflict held at a civic association, Hana told me that a non-Muslim woman near her in the audience "took advantage of the fact that I'm a Muslim to ask me about Islam. She asked me if it was true that in the Qur'an, it says a man is allowed to hit a woman." Hana recalled that she had hesitated before saying that as far as she knew, the Qur'an did indeed give men this permission, but that one must also take into account the various interpretations of the Qur'an, and the fact that such violence is not necessarily practiced just because it is textually permitted. Hana agonized at length about her response. Had it been accurate? Had she made herself or her religion look bad? While she appreciated the Spanish woman's desire to learn about Islam, Hana found it troubling that she had asked *her* to explain Islam's position on violence toward women, since she was not a religious scholar and was not sure of her own position on the issue.

Hana's experience illustrates how strangers hold Muslim migrants responsible to account for a wide variety of questions related (or thought to be related) to Islam, regardless of their relevance to the original reason for a given encounter. Her story was not an isolated case. Many Muslim research participants, usually migrant women, told me stories about being approached abruptly in offices and stores, or on buses and sidewalks by strangers with (occasionally violent) commentary about their headscarves. Such calls to representation are clearly gendered. Headscarves have become such a strong signifier of Muslim difference that they can serve as a metonym for Muslimness in general, and some non-Muslims feel comfortable asking women in headscarves to explain and defend all manner of topics about which they are curious. Further, Spain increasingly resembles the rest of Europe in that calls for gender equality and denunciations of Islam, especially practices like veiling, go hand in hand (Auslander 2000; Bowen 2008; Fernando 2010; Partridge 2012; Scott 2007). In Granada, I found that Muslim migrant women were approached because of their physical visibility and interrogated because of their supposedly subordinate status in Islam, creating a constant source of stress surrounding public spaces. Their experiences differed from those of converts, who were not perceived as minority subjects in the same way. These divergent ways in which representational imperatives arose for convert and migrant Muslims engendered distinct practices of representation.

CONVERTS' REPRESENTATIONAL
PRACTICES: MOSQUE MEDIATION

My convert interlocutors' representational efforts revolved around their mosque and reflected attempts to reconcile their competing desires for positive publicity on the one hand and for privacy on the other. My encounter with a convert named Muna exemplifies this tension. I met Muna one of the first times I attended a lunch at the Islamic Studies Center, adjacent to the Mezquita Mayor. When I entered the women's hall, the floor dotted with ornate rugs and communal bowls of couscous topped by heaping piles of roasted vegetables, Belén steered me away from Muna, saying, "Uh-oh, we don't want to sit by *her*." As I followed Belén to a group of women seated in a circle, sharing couscous safely at the other end of the room, I silently wondered why we were avoiding Muna. Later, when she noticed Muna glaring in our direction, Belén went reluctantly over to her and soon returned, flustered, whispering that Muna was angry I had been brought to the mosque. According to Belén, Muna had admonished her for bringing an American outsider to the mosque "to criticize us!" Concerned that my presence might be disruptive or intrusive, I asked Belén if it was wise for me to be there. Another woman eating with us overheard and said wryly, "Muna is fanatical and should be ignored." This prompted a discussion among the women at our rug, who took turns condemning Muna's inhospitality and extolling "moderation." They insisted that I was welcome and should come every Friday.

Muna and the women who sat with me that day took opposing approaches to dealing with an outsider. Sure that as an American, I was there to criticize, Muna reacted with anger and an attempt to avoid visibility, while the other women made an effort to be conspicuously welcoming and to dispel any possible interpretation of their community as "extremist" or hostile. Despite the apparent contrast, these reactions reflected a shared hypervigilance of outsiders' encounters with their community, and the Mezquita Mayor's balancing act between public outreach efforts and protecting private space for Muslim worship and sociality. Granada's Moorish-themed tourism industry, the impositions of neighbors, and converts' own missionizing motives brought a steady public that ranged in composition from local schoolchildren to dreadlocked hippies from Madrid to elderly German and Japanese tourists. This resulted in encounters between Muslims and non-Muslims that included curious passersby observing Muslims praying, solicitations of potential converts to "see the light," and uncomfortable glances between unsuspecting tourists taken aback by the sudden appearance of headscarves when stopping at the door to ask directions to the nearest bar, or between disgruntled Muslims whose sense of religious calm was interrupted by drunk or unruly Andalusian teens.

Convert women I spoke with about the mosque's openness offered differing analyses of this hypervisibility. Some were enthusiastic that the mosque's public facet improved Muslims' reputation in Granada. One of the Islamic Studies Center's couscous cooks described how tourists routinely stopped by the kitchen door, which she left propped open, to say that it smelled good, giving her an opportunity to be friendly and show that Muslims were in her words, "good people." The work involved in welcoming newcomers was tiring for some women, but others described the annoyances of such publicity as a necessary trade-off. As one woman reflected, "Well . . . it is a bit strange to be praying and then see people looking in that window. But it's good in a way too because it helps to spread Islam because people see that we're not terrorists." Recall from chapter 2 that converts' main modes of claiming rootedness in Spain were to insist on Islam's compatibility with Andalusianness and Spanishness or to tie conversion to Islam to rosy public images of *al-Andalus, convivencia,* and cosmopolitanism. Describing how converts had tried to justify their mosque project, one woman suggested that it was these values that made the mosque great for the city as a whole, not just converts. Arguing that refusals to permit mosque construction reflected an exclusionary, unmodern, Catholic provincialism, she said it was good for Granada and for Spain to have this mosque as a testament to Spain's reputation for tolerance. In this way, she cast the mosque as doing a service to the city and the state rather than just the Muslim community, exemplifying how converts figure adoption of Islam and Muslim inclusion as both the revival of Spain's lost cosmopolitanism and a pathway forward toward modern European multiculturalism.

The mosque's openness also afforded converts an opportunity to engage newcomers in discussions about becoming Muslim. Lubab saw dawa as central to the mosque's mission and told me that holding visiting hours and welcoming tour groups were vital. "It can't be an ordinary mosque if we want to do dawa." Nearly every time I attended the mosque, at least one person would stop me to talk about the benefits of entering Islam, and women who were particularly hopeful that I would convert often invited me to help sell brownies at their bake sales. Thus, most of my convert interlocutors acknowledged feeling a certain discomfort with the mosque's public outreach activities, but most concluded that these were necessary for improving Muslims' public image and growing the Muslim community.

MIGRANTS' REPRESENTATIONAL
PRACTICES: PERSONAL PRESSURES

Converts' institutionalized visibility at their mosque contrasted with migrants' disproportionate visibility as easily recognized and racialized outsiders in other spaces. As chapter 3 illustrated, Islam is often racialized in Andalusia, such that Muslims are interpreted as racially different, and in turn, those who are seen as Arab or North African (based on public perceptions of skin color, dress, and language use) are often assumed to be Muslim. Like Hana, other migrants I worked with were frequently thrown into public encounters with curious or hostile non-Muslims in stores, on the streets, or at work. Migrants understood representing Muslimness in terms of constant vigilance to avoid, prepare for, and manage such encounters. This involved small choices about interactions but reflected serious forethought and calculated, disciplined self-sacrifice to "make a good impression," as many put it. For example, a Senegalese Muslim man named Matar explained how he and all other Matars he knew had changed their names in Spain, since this common Senegalese name is also the Spanish infinitive form of the verb "to kill." Chuckling and shaking his head, he said he had changed his name because as a black, male, Muslim migrant he simply could not go around introducing himself as "Murder" (here using *asasinar*, a Spanish synonym for *matar*) because it "doesn't work out too well."

In addition to accommodations like name changes, many Muslim migrants refrained from responding to what they saw as racist, impolite, or unfair behavior on the part of non-Muslims. Over mugs of strong mint tea, Shaíma, a twenty-four-year-old mother of two from Morocco's Rif Mountains, recounted her two-year strategy of biting her tongue in interactions with her neighbor, an elderly Spanish woman she called a "real racist" who hated Muslims and migrants. This neighbor lived in the apartment below Shaíma's and had taken to cutting off the bottoms of Shaíma's hanging window plants in the shared interior patio of their building. Explaining why she never asked the woman to stop chopping her plants, Shaíma stated emphatically, "Because! We are so criticized, and we are not in our country! We have to make a good impression. Because if I responded or got angry I would be giving a bad representation, a bad image of my culture!" Shaíma's representational strategy and her sense of a strong imperative to represent "her culture" in the first place were thus mediated by her identification not only as a Muslim but also as a migrant. Such interactional anxieties also underscore how the demands for rights made by Moroccan migrant and national Muslim associations through official channels have a long ways to go in changing the nature of casual racism in urban encounters where migrants do not feel safe standing up to discrimination.

Many Moroccans channeled anxieties about representation by facilitating outsiders into particular kinds of encounters with Muslim migrants and away from others. Shaíma, for instance, went to great lengths to make sure that I met "rich Arabs" in Granada. I had initially met Shaíma through our mutual participation at Najma, where most women were working-class Arab and Amazigh migrants from northern Morocco who lived in the Polígono. In contrast, along with Jihan, Shaíma was one of the few Najma participants who lived in a centrally located, mostly middle-class neighborhood. She invited me to help teach Arabic on Saturdays to the children of a few Syrian, Jordanian, and Moroccan migrant families who lived there.

During class, Shaíma talked at length about the pupils' wealth, inter-rupting the lesson periodically to point out the children's nice clothing and dignified comportment:

> See how well behaved and well dressed these children are? It's not like
> in the other association. The women there, from where the classes are
> located, to how they dress, to how those kids behave; you can tell they
> are poor people, really very poor. But in this class it's different. . . . Their
> fathers are not laborers and working-class people. The majority are doctors
> and wealthy people.

Shaíma's closest friends in Granada were the women from the "very poor" association; these were the women with whom she drank tea, reminisced about Morocco, and communally cared for children. She genuinely loved her friends. Yet she was equally determined that they not be the primary Muslim migrants with whom I interacted, despite the fact that they vastly outnumbered the "wealthy Arabs" in her neighborhood. Shaíma's desire to disrupt class-based stereotypes of Muslim migrants reflects both the internal diversity of Granada's migrant Muslim community, and the fact that concerns about class and ethnicity always crosscut efforts to represent Islam in Granada.

Like convert Muslims, Moroccans and other migrants expressed varying degrees of optimism, pessimism, resentment, and begrudging acceptance of the pressures of minority representation. Soukaina, the Najma president, echoed convert women's discussion of the awkwardness of tourists' visits to their mosque, telling me that answering questions about Muslims and Moroccans is part of her responsibility as a migrant who cares about improving her community's local status. After a week in which two undergraduates from the local university had come to the association to interview her for research projects, followed by a visit from a government researcher studying publicly funded NGOs, and then an impromptu interview on the association's steps with local neighborhood Roma women inquiring about Islam and Muslim women's lives, I began to understand why one of the other women at the association had once referred to the women there as "*bichos* [bugs] under a microscope."

Feeling concerned about this, and not wanting to wear out my own welcome, I asked Soukaina if she was tired of explaining Islam all the time, on top of her daily duties as a doctoral candidate in the sciences, a mother, a wife, a teacher, and an association president. She replied, shrugging, "Noooooo, no way. It doesn't bother me. Here, we're very open. We're not closed off. We're interested in people studying us because if they interview us about the situation of migrants, then that improves it, so it helps us too." Later Soukaina added,

> I can't complain. No. Because it's my responsibility. And if you believe something is your responsibility you never get tired of it. I don't get tired. I'll never get tired, *insha'Allah* [God willing]. Because I feel it's my responsibility to "the other," to help ["the other"] get to know me, to get to know the reality of Muslims.

Here I should note that Soukaina's and others' discussions with me *about* representing Islam to non-Muslim publics were themselves acts of representation to a non-Muslim. I spent many hours with Soukaina over the course of two years, and she was often quite frank with me. I believe she meant her comments here, and they befitted her tireless, energetic personality. However, they also reflect certain burdens placed on Muslims, who feel they must make a conscious effort to conspicuously show their willingness to integrate into mainstream social life.

I read Soukaina's comments as having at least three degrees of meaning. She had used the words *abierta* (open) and *encerrada* (closed off or locked up, related to *cerrado*, discussed in chapter 3). Given the prevalence of these words in *Granadino* descriptions of likeable and unlikeable personalities, respectively, using these terms to express Moroccan women's "openness" was likely in part a way of situating Moroccans within local norms of good social practice and likeability, as contributors to urban *convivencia* rather than the unsociable *malafollá*. But these ideas also have broader significance for questions of Muslim integration in European cities. Soukaina was well aware of fears that Muslim migrants are purposely "closed off," dangerous, separatist outsiders in religious and ethnic enclaves that may be more loyal to an imagined global Muslim leadership than to the state or society. These are common anxieties about Muslims in Europe, where policy makers, pundits, and newscasters often assume a risk of migrant "ghettoization" associated with criminality and radicalism (Andersen and Biseth 2013; Silverstein 2000; Terrio 2009). Finally, the adjective *encerrada* has a particular gendered significance. Spanish feminist critiques of Islam often use that term to describe Muslim women as secluded at home, and Moroccan women I worked with often took care to point out that they were not *"encerrada"* as a way of combating gendered stereotypes. By distancing Moroccan migrant women from the term, Soukaina was also working against broad assumptions of Moroccan women's gendered subjugation. Soukaina's reiterations of a responsibility and willingness to engage with outsiders must be understood in relation to these representational pressures.

Not everyone coincided with Soukaina's and others' emphasis on making small steps toward improving Muslims' status through careful attention to self-presentation in everyday interpersonal encounters. Mehdi, Ziko, Peque, and others who worked in the lower *Albayzín* expressed frustration over the daily indignities faced by undocumented migrants in the area, like missing work when they had to hide from police, and feeling that Spanish and international tourist customers stereotyped them, as discussed in chapter 3. They argued that I should use my research experience to change minds about Muslims in *"Amreeka"* (Arabic for America), but that Spain was a "lost cause" with respect to public impressions of Islam.

In contrast to both Soukaina's cautious determination and these young men's sense of utter defeat, Nigel, a middle-aged Senegalese Muslim man, expressed an unmeasured optimism. I met Nigel in the context of an NGO meeting during which staff were scrambling to figure out how to find and fund a living arrangement for him and his family, as they struggled with finances and residence permits. We chitchatted while the staff dealt with paperwork, and he told me that his mission in Spain was to improve the image people had of Islam. In the midst of a seemingly desperate situation, he engaged me in a cheerful conversation about Islam, informing me that he was very hopeful about the possibility for Muslim inclusion in Spain. He was particularly confident after seeing then king Juan Carlos's annual Christmas address to the nation, in which he claimed the king had exhorted native Spaniards to be tolerant of migrants and non-Christians. He asked me to help him find out the king's official address, because he wanted to write this "good, intelligent king" a personal letter of gratitude and encouragement. These contrasting examples of Soukaina, the defeated Moroccan young men, and Nigel illustrate the range of emotions and opinions migrants held regarding the future of Islam in Spain, from

nihilism to unbridled optimism. Such diversity reflects the range of experiences within Granada's heterogeneous Muslim migrant population.

Despite such diversity among migrants, on the whole, my migrant interlocutors' experiences of representing Islam in Granada differed significantly from those of converts. The discrepancies proceeded primarily
from the racial and socioeconomic inequalities governing how migrant
and convert Muslims are incorporated into Andalusia as religious minorities, what values motivated their practices of representation, and what
resources and avenues for representation were available to them.

REPRESENTATION AND MUSLIM TENSIONS

The disparities traced thus far between migrant and convert representation produce and reflect disagreements between and among converts
and migrants about representation, religion, and minority politics. These
tensions recall Michael Herzfeld's useful definition of cultural intimacy
as the anxieties of identity formation and representation that stem from
group insiders' belief that cultural practices stigmatized or harshly judged
by outsiders may be precisely those that "provide insiders with their assurance of common sociality" (2005, 3). My research participants represent
an interesting twist on this formulation. For Muslims in Granada, the representational practices of fellow Muslims were deemed embarrassing or
vexing, often precisely because they did not provide an "assurance of common sociality." Instead, they revealed the uncomfortable distances among
Granada's Muslims, highlighting a stressful dynamic between Muslims'
sometimes fierce deliberations over how to present Muslim identities to
the wider non-Muslim community, on the one hand, and their related
deliberations over just what constitutes Muslim identity in the first place,
on the other hand.

While debates over representation involve a great deal of picking and
choosing what to show and how to act in encounters with non-Muslims,
this does not mean that there exists an agreed-upon "backstage" Muslim
identity to which Granada's Muslims subscribe when non-Muslims are
not looking. Through quarrels over what should be shown, how, and by
whom, Muslims confront discrepancies both in their representational

strategies and in their definitions of Muslim identity, authenticity, and authority. These debates are the ramifications of their differently raced, classed, and gendered experiences in Granada. The myriad tensions between converts and migrants highlight the difficulty of forging a politics of Muslim solidarity in a place where social and political identifications are highly situational and structured by inequalities.

One day I conducted a joint interview with two young Muslim migrant women who were close friends. Karima identified as Senegalese-British, and Rana was Moroccan. Both were university students, and Rana also worked for Spanish employers as a domestic worker. We ate ice cream in a downtown café and discussed their experiences living in Granada. Perhaps prompted by our interview's location in a place frequented primarily by locally born *Granadinos*, I asked them how they would characterize their interactions with native Spaniards at school and at work. Echoing Lara and Latifa from this chapter's opening, Karima immediately answered, "People here always talk about '*convivencia*,' but I can tell you that there is no *convivencia* in Granada." Rana chimed in, "How can there ever be *convivencia* in Granada between religions when there isn't even *convivencia* among just the Muslims?" By skeptically referencing *convivencia*, the supposed interfaith harmony rooted in the history of Muslim Spain, Karima and Rana evoked what I found to be a widespread understanding among Muslims in Granada that, as Rana said, "the community is divided." Some converts and migrants are friends, spouses, and in-laws, but many regard one another with either indifference, resignation, or hostility, and interact only infrequently.

Even in the absence of many face-to-face encounters, the different groups of Muslims in Granada are aware of and opinionated about one another, and they construct their own identities in relation to their notions of what other Muslims in Granada think, do, or are like. In particular, Moroccan migrants and Spanish and other European converts, as the largest groups, display a high degree of ambivalence about one another, each expressing both admiration and trepidation about the other. Converts more explicitly and self-reflexively create their own senses of Muslim selfhood in relation to their notions of Moroccanness. Because being Muslim is newer to them, often chosen at some point during adolescence or adulthood, they are sometimes more self-consciously vocal about the process of constructing Muslim identities. In contrast, Moroccans' views of their own Muslimness vis-à-vis that of converts become apparent in more subtle ways. Converts' and Moroccans' assessments of and reactions to one another illuminate the complexity of self-representation by demonstrating how actors' shifting prioritization of various audiences' views shape practices of self-display. Converts and migrants thus navigate a kind of reluctant *convivencia,* oscillating between attending to and ignoring the other's opinions and views, and between expressing like and dislike for the other.

Moroccan Ambivalence about Converts

Among Moroccans, I encountered both celebration of conversion as a quasi miracle and disparagement of converts as racist religious imposters. For some, the existence of European conversions to Islam signaled a potential for Muslims' acceptance in Spain, and some Moroccans had positive encounters with converts. One young Moroccan woman, who had been the subject of a highly publicized headscarf controversy at her school during her early teen years, recalled with gratitude the unsolicited help of local converts. She had lived in central Spain at the time, and converts there had stepped in to offer her family their linguistic and social resources for handling an overwhelming onslaught of media attention. For many other Moroccans, however, converts remained an unknown, slightly suspicious entity. While they anticipated discrimination from Catholic or secular Spaniards, many Moroccans initially expected the convert community to share a religiously based solidarity. They were thus surprised, and especially dismayed, to experience tensions with converts, whom they had imagined would be their European allies, in contrast to non-Muslims, from whom they more often expected Islamophobic attitudes.

Many Moroccans' stories of the encounters that led them to dislike converts involved the converts' mosque and converts' representational styles. Mohammed, a Moroccan in his early twenties, had come to Granada to join his older siblings who had migrated previously. He hoped to study at the University of Granada, as many Moroccan students do, but found himself working in a Moroccan-themed shop in the *Albayzín* selling goatskin lamps and hookahs to make ends meet. Sitting together one day on low stools near the doorway of the shop where he worked, I asked Mohammed if he knew many convert Muslims. "Yes, actually I have a lot of contact with them," he said, waving his arm toward the street, alluding to the close proximity of convert-owned shops. Mohammed said he had been pleasantly surprised to learn of the convert community upon arriving in Spain. Then he frowned, whispering, "But the truth is, I don't like most of them," and shared the following story.

One evening at dusk, Mohammed had gone up to the "convert mosque" with a female friend, also a Muslim migrant. They had heard it was an impressive building and wanted to check it out. When they arrived, some people were already inside the mosque for the evening prayer, but many were milling about on the patio, talking, laughing, and enjoying the view of the Alhambra. The gate was shut, and when Mohammed waved the man he referred to as a "guard" over to open it, this man refused, acting as though they were tourists. Wondering how the "guard" could confuse them with non-Muslim tourists (particularly because his friend wore a headscarf), Mohammed explained, "We're Muslims, and we want to see the mosque." The convert man replied that visiting hours were over, that they could come in to pray if they wanted to, but not just to see the patio. This angered Mohammed, because he could see that many converts were chatting on the patio, rather than praying inside. Recalling this in our interview, Mohammed shouted, "They wouldn't let me in! To a *mosque*! Which to me, as a Muslim, is a sacred place!" Throwing his hands in the air and raising his eyebrows with incredulity, he continued, "I felt *rejected*, and by other *Muslims*!" Mohammed felt certain that he was denied entry because he was a Moroccan, and thus not considered part of the mosque community.

Mohammed's incensed reaction to being excluded from the Mezquita Mayor was echoed in many other Moroccans' complaints about the mosque and about converts' religious and representational practices more broadly. These complaints reflected Moroccans' concerns about Muslim representation, as well as deeply felt aesthetic, religious, and political misgivings about converts. For instance, some Moroccans felt converts practiced an overly "strict" Islam that reflected a failure to be authentically Muslim.[5] For Mohammed, converts' strict mosque greeters/guards and their inability to recognize that all Muslims ought to be welcome at a mosque was proof of their lack of fluency in both Islamic theology and social norms. At the same time, Mohammed's friend Youssef scoffed at orthodoxy as something only those new to Islam, or insecure in their religiosity, would emphasize. He combined concerns about religious practice and representation, worrying that converts' "overly strict" religious observance gave the impression that Muslims in Spain were "extremists, like we're all Wahabis or something." Given media attention to Wahabism as a form of Islam supposedly prone to "extremism," Muslims in Spain often worried about being perceived as "radical" Islamists, a term that substantively meant little to them beyond its ramifications for public perception and its consequences for treatment of Muslims.

If sometimes united in their shared frustration with converts, Moroccans' varied criticisms were motivated by multiple, often opposing concerns, revealing the diversity of this community. In contrast to Mohammed's and Youssef's complaints of convert strictness, some pious Moroccans articulated precisely the opposite critique of converts, instead linking suspicions about converts' representational agenda with their own concerns about proper Islamic comportment. They worried that converts' interest in spreading Islam led them to downplay the importance of the Islamic pillars of faith and engage in unorthodox practices, sacrificing piety to appeal to Catholic or secular sensibilities. Rana criticized convert women at the Mezquita Mayor along these lines. Her comments illustrate how complex, politicized grievances about representation and religiosity become entangled:

> They have different practices, ones that make you feel uncomfortable, like they wear makeup, and strong perfume, and a different kind of headscarf. You just don't feel at ease praying there. The women are too focused on appearances, and not on the prayer. . . . It's an adaptation of Islam to the West. They wear those kinds of headscarves to avoid scaring people so much. I mean, the work they're doing, making people aware of Islam in the West and getting rid of the image of Islam as something closed off is good and important, but you also can't just deceive people.

Here, Rana was referencing a distinction between the styles of headscarves worn by many (though not all) Moroccan and convert women in Granada. While Moroccan women who wore headscarves tended to wear hijab in a style reminiscent of home (a scarf covering their hair, ears, and often neck and upper forehead), many convert women wore loosely wrapped scarves in the shape of a small turban that covered most of their hair (usually done up in a bun) behind the head, leaving the front of the hairline, ears, and neck uncovered. Rana explained that she liked the architecture of the converts' mosque because it reminded her of beautiful mosques in Morocco, but that she no longer prayed there because she felt distracted by convert women's choices regarding modesty.

In addition to competing religious sensibilities and concerns about representation, critiques of converts were often profoundly political. My Moroccan interlocutors' commentaries reveal discontent with converts' perceived role in cementing a politics of multiculturalism that enshrined inequalities among Granada's Muslims. Rana, for instance, could not share convert women's efforts to "avoid scaring people so much," in part because convert-style headscarves violated her convictions regarding proper embodiment of Islamic womanhood, and in part because Moroccan women's more rigid racialization denied them converts' ability to flexibly identify both as Muslim and as Spanish or European. Moroccans expressed resentment that while converts worked to spread Islam, migrants faced issues of police violence, discrimination, and restrictive migration laws. Those like Youssef, who thought converts portrayed Muslims as "all Wahabis or something," feared the potential of perceived convert extremism to reverberate in public discrimination toward migrant Muslims. This was a particular concern for migrants who took issue with converts' claims of ownership over Islam in Granada. Some of my interlocutors inferred a certain smugness in the mosque's name, the Great Mosque of Granada, translated for English-speaking visitors on signage as simply the Mosque of Granada, as though it were *the* singular mosque rather than one among many. For Moroccans, this nomenclature emphasized supremacy rather than acknowledgment of converts' membership in a broader religious community. Moroccans' criticisms of converts thus revealed representational anxieties that were also shaped by religious and political concerns born of Granada's unequal multiculturalism.

Convert Ambivalence about Moroccans

Convert Muslims in Granada often created their new Muslim identities in relation to their ideas of Moroccanness in a way that both placed Moroccans on a pedestal as "authentically Muslim" and disparaged Moroccans as racial or ethnic others who mistook "culture" and "tradition" for "real Islam." Those who saw Moroccans and other migrant Muslims as potential Muslim role models often expressed a taken-for-granted belief in the authenticity of Muslims born into Muslim families in Muslim-majority societies. A middle-aged convert named Jasmina, for instance, expressed a strong desire for migrant Muslims' recognition of her own membership in the Muslim faith. She recalled an argument she had had with a Moroccan woman at a bus stop. Like Clara, who also resented being presumed an immigrant, Jasmina wears a headscarf in a manner more similar to Moroccans than to the style of many convert women. The Moroccan woman at the bus stop had seen Jasmina's hijab, mistaken her for a fellow Moroccan, and begun speaking to her in Arabic. When Jasmina made clear that she was Spanish-born and couldn't understand Arabic, the woman, according to Jasmina, began shouting at her, "How can you be Spanish? You're wearing a veil [*velo*]!'" Riled by her memory of the incident, Jasmina told me that eventually she had convinced the Moroccan woman that she was in fact a Muslim Spaniard by showing the woman her Spanish ID card, which had prompted an apology. Jasmina concluded her story saying, "This woman said some horrible things to me, screaming at me that I thought I was better than her. The thing is, the Moroccans know that Islam is merely a religion [and not a nationality], but they still sometimes don't realize that Spaniards can be Muslim."

While Jasmina sought recognition from Muslim migrants, Belén tried to emulate them. I first visited Belén's apartment within a year of her conversion, when she was still newly creating a sense of Muslim selfhood. She and Ahmet had just moved into a new apartment, which she was in the process of decorating. She proudly showed me her Moroccan tea set and the cushions she had arranged to emulate a Middle Eastern sitting room, saying, "Now that I'm Muslim, and living with an Arab man as his wife, I always try to have snacks around and make tea whenever anyone comes over, because it's very important to Arabs and Muslims to be hospitable." The socially prominent role of hospitality in some Arab, Muslim, Mediterranean societies (Herzfeld 1987) has become a widely circulating stereotype, and Belén had picked up on it and incorporated it into her new Muslim lifestyle and self-understanding. I encountered similar comments and practices even among convert women who had no social contact with Arabs or other migrant Muslims. Self-conscious transformation in bodily practices and uses of domestic space are common ways of inculcating desired religious, social, and affective states among new Muslims (Ahmad 2010; van Nieuwkerk 2006) as well as born Muslim women involved in piety movements (Mahmood 2005; Meneley 2007). Purchasing Moroccan-style clothing and cooking Moroccan foods allowed convert women in Granada to fashion new Muslim selfhoods in tangible ways. Such practices also index the extent to which in Granada, imaginaries of Islam are intricately bound up in ideas about Morocco, with Moroccans and Morocco-associated objects and practices implicitly recognized as models for constructing authentic Muslim lives.

Yet other convert women explicitly rejected these practices. As one woman put it, "dressing up as Arabs" was counterproductive to the goals of establishing a European Islam and making Islam accepted in Granada. These women sometimes politely, sometimes bluntly, distanced themselves from Moroccans. In the words of Farida, a *Granadina* convert:

> A lot of people confuse me with Moroccans, and once they think I'm a Moroccan, then they think, "Oh, [she's] stupid!" They think I can barely read and write, and this really bothers me. Because, I mean, the fact that I wear a headscarf doesn't have anything to do with being Moroccan, and besides, the Moroccans, I mean, maybe they're a little lacking in the intellect department but they're still people, and they work really hard.

Farida's comments recall those of Jasmina earlier. Like Jasmina, Farida was upset by the general public's failure to recognize that "Spaniards can be Muslim." But unlike Jasmina, who sought Moroccans' recognition of her Muslimness and membership in their religious community, Farida was more concerned with non-Muslims' perceptions, and she feared being seen as Moroccan. Though intended as an antiessentialist argument about the diversity of kinds of Muslims, and perhaps meant to defend Moroccans, Farida's words also clearly reflect her assumptions about Moroccans' racial difference.

This desire to emphasize that being Muslim need not be linked to a particular ethnicity or nationality was further apparent in many converts' insistence that they practiced a "pure" Islam, untainted by "culture," "tradition," or "backwardness." Many converts used these less overtly racializing—yet still othering—terms to describe Islam as practiced by

Moroccans and other non-European Muslims. A British expatriate explained to me over couscous at a lunch following Friday prayer at the Mezquita Mayor that migrants "really bring their own culture and traditions, so it's not necessarily really Islam, you know? We like it here because it's not culture or tradition, it's the purest Islam." The irony of her comment is that couscous is a Moroccan dish that most Spaniards I know do not regularly eat, yet it features every Friday at the convert mosque, its consumption indicative of how converts' practices are influenced by Moroccan cultural norms. This woman was a close friend of Nahlah, the Swiss woman who had also moved to Granada to join the convert movement, and who celebrated its "outrageousness" in chapter 2. Nahlah elaborated on what was special about having a community of European-born Muslims in Granada, saying of converts, "We have the same culture . . . so this is my place." Such assertions, while often purportedly about religious practice, ultimately revealed converts' racial, class-based, and cultural anxieties about their fellow Muslims.

When my convert interlocutors paired accusations of migrants' cultural misunderstandings of Islam with explicit claims of European ownership over religious purity, authenticity, and authority, I was struck by an apparent contradiction. How could converts simultaneously claim a bond based on their specific European cultural identities *and* claim that their brand of Islam was pure, unmoored to any particular cultural or historical corruptions? By mapping cultural contamination onto Muslim migrants and claiming culture-free Islam as their own, they subtly constructed "European" as an unmarked social category, from which difference was understood as deviance. Through their discourse of culture-free Islam, converts made an argument not just about religious practice or authority, but also about racial and cultural value. These opinions shaped some converts' decisions to avoid friendships with migrant Muslims, to encourage their children not to date or marry migrants, and their general denunciations of migrants' presence in the city.

Such discursive sifting of "true" or "pure" Islamic beliefs and practices from supposedly culturally based "traditions" is not unique to Granada's converts. Similar distinctions are common to much of the heterogeneous yet globally reaching Islamic revival, in which Muslims involved in piety and reformist movements increasingly participate in the active study of Islamic texts and theological debates, often in search of the "truest" forms of Islam and their role in creating ethical lives and communities (Hirschkind 2006; Mahmood 2005). My convert interlocutors' distinction between "pure" Islam and "tradition" particularly recalls the process Lara Deeb (2006), termed "authentication" among pious Lebanese Shia women, in reference to these women's emphasis on practicing both "true" Islam and "cultural authenticity." Religion-culture distinctions have also characterized the arguments of "second-generation" Muslims born to migrant parents in Europe and the United States, who seek to purify Islamic practice from the traditions of older generations and countries of origin from which they may feel disconnected (Bowen 2010; Ramadan 2004). Similarly, in Bulgaria Kristen Ghodsee finds that young Muslims returning to religion in the postsocialist period embrace a new form of "orthodox" Islam and repudiate earlier generations' "traditional" presocialist Islamic practices (2009).

What is unique and somewhat startling among Granada's converts is the exceptional degree to which this distinction maps onto and bolsters ideologies about the racial, ethnic, and gendered difference of Muslim migrants. Narratives of purity distance converts from migrant Muslims, in part by relegating the latter's practices to a realm of impurity, but also through a subtly shifting use of temporality. Islamic reformists' disavowals of "tradition" often imply a strong break with the past. While Deeb's interlocutors and others in Islamic reformist movements sometimes articulate their goals as the renewal of or return to a set of long-lost pious and ethical practices, they also position their own reformed piety in opposition to recent pasts. The authenticating discourse of Deeb's interlocutors in Lebanon, for instance, entailed "people's sense of a clear-cut difference between 'now' and 'then'" (2006, 22) that relied on contrasting "modern" versus "backward" or "traditional" Islamic practices. In Granada, my convert interlocutors articulated no such rupture with an immediate or recent past. Instead, they positioned their Islamic practice as ahistorical and/or as a continuation or renewal of Granada's medieval Muslim past that would replace Spanish Catholicism, rather than a poorly practiced Spanish Islam. This small difference had significant consequences, as it allowed converts to claim both religious authority and local belonging in ways that migrants could not.

First, converts staked their religious authority in the claim that they had no cultural baggage in need of abjuration. Brand-new to Islam, they had a clean slate and direct access to religious authenticity. The implication was decidedly political, as this claim allowed converts to sidestep criticisms of Islam as an unmodern, even terrorist religion, attributing such problems to other Muslims' "ethnic" Islam. Their assertions also resonated, then, with liberal modern discourses about Islamic fundamentalism, in which an imagined "culture-religion" dichotomy has permeated attempts to discern good or better "kinds" of Islam, or Muslims that may be more compatible with Western values (Shryock 2004b, 2010). Yet, consonant with their emphasis on a European identity, my convert interlocutors also consistently emphasized their conversion as a return to the religion and culture of *al-Andalus*, as describe in chapter 2. These conflicting impulses—claiming a fresh, ahistorical Islam *and* a historically rooted, Spanish Islam—were actually quite consistent with more general *Granadino* ambivalence about Muslims in Andalusia; these claims appealed to both local fears of and nostalgia about the place of Islam in the region.

Further, some converts in Granada, particularly older members of the Murabitun community, eschewed what they called "European ideals" but nevertheless articulated their differentiation from migrants through a language of Europeanness. A conversation I had with Widad, an elderly convert woman in Granada, illustrates how converts often disassociated themselves from migrants to situate their own Islamic practice within liberal European social norms that they themselves also found wanting. Over two years, I had many conversations with Widad and her friends in which they offered vociferous critiques of "European values." Like many Murabitun, Widad advocated withdrawal from the global capitalist economy and often critiqued what she felt was a Spanish obsession with individual freedoms at the expense of social and communal values.

However, this was not always the case. Over tea in her restored historic home in the *Albayzín*, Widad broached with me the issue of tensions with Moroccans, charging that unlike converts, Moroccans practiced "tradition" and "not Islam." Using these comments as a springboard for a gendered critique of Moroccan and Arab Islam, she said that she aimed to emulate the first Muslim women, who were dynamic and emancipated. In contrast, she lamented that today,

> the Wahabis want to put the women in the black sack. I wouldn't want to live in Saudi Arabia or any of these countries where the women are treated that way. I'm, we're, you know, we are Europeans; we're not Moroccan or Tunisian. You know, we're not Arabs! And we've taken on Islam, so we dress discreetly, and we're Muslims. We don't take after—we don't go around in djellabas, and we don't go around in chadors. We're living in Spain!

Here, in the context of discussing Muslim migration, Widad slipped easily from asserting that it is possible to be both Spanish and Muslim, to asserting that *only* Spanish and European Muslims lay claim to Muslim authenticity, to finally implying European cultural superiority through the idiom of gender equality. In the process, she lumped together a range of nationalities, schools of Islamic thought, and various styles of modest dress as non-European Islam marked by gender oppression.

Widad's decision to frame her comparison of European Islam versus Moroccan or Arab Islam in terms of gender is just one example of how converts asserted a cultural superiority over migrants. She established a strong distinction between connected triads of, on the one hand, European converts; pure or real Islam; and cultural superiority (as evidenced by gender equality), and, on the other hand, Moroccan or Arab-born Muslims; tradition, culture, or "impure" Islam; and cultural inferiority (expressed as gender inequality). This discourse of gender equality as a cornerstone of European identity is often used to disparage Widad's own religion, and it has become central to dominant European liberal discourses of modernity with which she herself is uncomfortable. Her decision to employ this widely circulating discourse of gender equality to distance herself from migrant and Arab Muslims is thus especially striking.

Widad's alignment with Spanish normative gender values here illustrates clearly how the politics of minority vulnerability—in this case, vulnerability associated with public perceptions of gender inequality as integral to Islam—color Muslims' interactions and disassociations from one another. Widad's comments demonstrate that to understand forces

like Islamophobia, scholars need to recognize and research how they pervade even Muslims' own constructions of religious and cultural difference (cf. Shryock 2010). In a recent book about German converts to Islam,
Esra Özyürek sees German converts' occasional efforts to distance themselves from Turkish Muslims as a product of a new process of racialization
of Muslims in Germany and in Europe at large (2014). German converts'
desire for space from migrant Muslims is a response to a wider Islamphobic
social context in which converts unsuspectingly find themselves marginalized because of their new association with a racialized minority religion. In
Granada, converts' negative views of migrant Muslims' racial and cultural
difference respond to similar social processes. Tensions between converts
and migrants are not a natural reflection of their social difference or exclusively related to unequal multiculturalism; they also reflect and are exacer-
bated by the wider context of Islamophobia in Spain and Europe. Converts'
disavowal of migrants (and Moroccan and Roma residents' mutual antagonism in the Polígono) are examples of smaller communities' self-protective
responses to a larger social milieu in which they are all stigmatized and
victimized. Yet in Granada, these antipathies seem to stem not only from
converts' experience of Islamophobia but also from their internalization of
race-based prejudice against Moroccans and other migrants.

CONCLUSION

In Granada, both apprehension about and celebration of Islam contribute to Muslims' visibility, and many Muslims feel compelled to represent
themselves and their religion to Andalusian, Spanish, and global publics.
Yet European converts' and migrant Muslims' unique experiences of the
burdens of minority representation create pervasive tensions that map
onto—and reinscribe—racial and cultural hierarchies in the city. Even
seemingly inclusive gestures, such as Europeans' conversions to Islam,
are structured and contained by normative ideas about race, religion,
gender, and migratory mobility, and thus entail their own limitations
and exclusions. In particular, converts' means of distancing themselves
from migrants demonstrate how widely circulating ideas of Europe as
an unmarked, non-Muslim space, of Andalusia as Catholic, and of

Islam as racially marked and foreign exert enormous power over Muslims' own forms of self-identification and representational politics, limiting the degree to which European conversion movements can truly produce space for all kinds of Muslim difference. Meanwhile, migrants' critiques of converts reveal impatience with modes of Muslim inclusion that do not include foreign-born Muslims. Converts' and migrants' tensions over Islam and representation illustrate that it is not sufficient, analytically or politically, to point to Spain as a further example of European Islamophobia or as an antidote to this specter. Both perspectives flatten the complexity of multicultural politics. To simply decry Andalusia and Spain as racist or to celebrate *convivencia* presupposes religious uniformity and solidarity among Spain's Muslims, a move that occludes the inequalities that *both* phobic and philic discourses about Islam produce within the so-called Muslim community.

This chapter has focused on the tensions crosscutting the diverse Muslim communities with whom I worked, because in Granada, and surely in other zones of encounter, these internal dynamics make the political identifications, representational strategies, and other social practices of some members of minority groups more flexible or successful, and of others, more fixed or circumscribed. Chapter 5 takes up this question in the realm of debates about gender and Islam in Granada, examining how Muslim migrant and convert women are differently drawn into complex negotiations between gendered aspirations of piety, public expectations about normative gender roles in Granada, and Andalusians' growing anxieties about Muslims' bodily practices.

NOTES

1. Parts of this chapter appeared in Rogozen-Soltar 2012b, "Managing Muslim Visibility: Conversion, Immigration, and Spanish Imaginaries of Islam" in *American Anthropologist*.

2. For a glimpse of this mosque's self-presentation, including interviews and media appearances by the director, see the official website www.mezquitadegranada.com.

3. In global news media, the Mezquita Mayor was billed as the first mosque built in Spain since the Inquisition, though this was not actually the case. The mosque probably garnered enthusiastic media attention because of several factors. It was the first mosque

constructed in modern Andalusia by and for Spanish and other European converts to Islam, rather than foreign-born migrant Muslims from the global south. It was also a new construction, whereas other mosques in Andalusia at the time were often located in pre-viously built structures—apartments, garages, and community centers—that had been converted into use for Muslim worship by small groups of Muslim migrants. Finally, the mosque's symbolic location in the touristy, Moorish-built *Albayzín* neighborhood, directly across from the Alhambra, evoked discussions of Islam's rootedness in Andalusia in a way that Muslim migrant prayer spaces may not have done.

4. Moroccans, Senegalese, and other migrant Muslim men and women do attend the Mezquita Mayor occasionally, particularly if they live or work nearby. This may be espe-cially true on the men's side. However, converts were the majority, and among both my migrant and convert interlocutors, the mosque was understood as a predominantly con-vert space.

5. Religious practices and perspectives were hugely varied among both converts and migrants, and their range of pieties is not the focus of this book. However, one broad difference was the prevalence of Sufism among converts. Although many non-Murabitun converts did not identify with or practice Sufism, the public visibility of the Murabitun meant that migrant Muslims often believed all converts were Sufis. Despite the historical prevalence of Sufism in Morocco, my Moroccan interlocutors were far less likely than converts to identify with Sufism, or to participate in activities common to Islamic revival movements such as attending classes about Islam, teaching about Islam, or engaging in in-depth discussions of Islamic texts or websites on a regular basis. I did not meet any mi-grants who identified as Murabitun.

5

EMBODIED ENCOUNTERS

Gender, Islam, and Public Space

Criticism of Muslims' gender roles and relationships has become a primary mode of talking about Muslim difference in Europe, and of justifying the exclusion of Muslims in the process of claiming European openness and tolerance. This was the case for Jose, a Spanish man who was proud of his multicultural open-mindedness. Over drinks, Jose went to great lengths to assure me that he unconditionally accepted and respected all minorities in Spain, with one exception: Muslims. He explained,

> For example, there's a *moro* doorman at my building, and every time he opens the door for me I've always said, 'Thanks' and 'How are you.' I have had no problem with him. Except, one day I saw him walking in the street with his wife, and she was covered, you know, head to toe! And she was carrying their grocery bags, and he wasn't carrying anything. So now I don't like him anymore. I can respect all kinds of cultural difference, but that's my limit, man. I mean, if he wants people to think he's a good person he should treat his wife with respect. That's how I know I'm a good person, because I behave appropriately with my family, my friends, my girlfriends. So that's why I don't like *los moros*, because they're so *machista* like that. And I'm a modern man, so I can't tolerate that. So now I don't talk to him anymore when I go in and out of my building, because why should I have to put up with or respect a *moro* like that, who doesn't even respect his wife?

Jose's logic reflects several intertwined assertions that are becoming increasingly commonplace in discussions of Islam and gender in European societies (Auslander 2000; Ewing 2008; Fernando 2014; Tarlo and Moors

2015). The first is that Muslim men oppress Muslim women and that this is antithetical to modern European culture, understood as committed to gender equality. The second is that one can spot Muslims' categorically problematic gender relations in their dress, especially in Muslim women's practices of sartorial modesty (Scott 2007). The third is that this gender abnormality makes Muslims so uniquely different that it disqualifies them as recipients of the otherwise indefatigable liberal tolerance often seen as central to modern, progressive European identities. Denouncing and excluding Muslims, then, becomes a central way of demonstrating one's tolerant European sensibilities (Van der Veer 2006). This is why, as Soukaina put it, "Nowadays, if Europeans want to criticize Islam, *van directamente a 'la mujer!'*" (They go right to "the woman").

The idea that pervasive gender oppression marks Muslims as unfit for democratic citizenship reflects pan-European, even globally circulating notions of modern subjectivity that morally and politically privilege the capacity for agency, conceptualized as self-realization, emancipation, and freedom from social or material constraint (Asad 2003; Keane 2007; Mahmood 2005).[1] Within this framework, headscarves are understood as indexing nonagentive subjectivities, as is clear in Jose's comments.[2] This tendency to presume and denounce Muslims' gender inequality is gaining a foothold in Spain. In Granada, it is reconfigured by locally salient anxieties about demonstrating the region's modernity and Europeanness through professions of gender equality, and these anxieties have different ramifications for convert and migrant Muslims. Non-Muslims often see convert Muslim women as traitors to feminism, as either dupes or defectors throwing away Spanish feminists' hard-earned gains since the Franco era. In contrast, they often see Muslim migrant women as backward and in need of saving, presuming that contact with emancipated Spanish women will naturally educate Muslim migrant women, who will then adopt normative Spanish gendered subjectivities and practices (cf. Abu-Lughod 2002). I refer to this cluster of assumptions and expectations in Granada as the "liberation narrative."

In this chapter, I argue that as gender inequality becomes solidified as a key signifier of Muslims' inassimilable nature, vociferous critiques of Muslim patriarchy consistently obscure two important phenomena. The first is the role of non-Muslim Andalusians' own embodied cultural norms in constructing a public sociality that systematically excludes Muslims. My Andalusian interlocutors often implicitly understood Andalusianness in terms of imperative bodily practices such as socializing in public spaces, consuming pork and wine, and participating in a form of public sexuality. Catholic and secular *Granadinos* often saw these practices as neutral manifestations of normal sociality despite their cultural specificity and inaccessibility to Muslims, especially pious women. The normativity of such practices produces a particularly invidious exclusion, as it marginalizes Muslims while placing the responsibility for navigating religious difference entirely onto them.

The second process obscured by the liberation narrative is the complex and diverse ethical reasoning that goes into Muslim women's decisions about pious practices. Many converts have been raised in European contexts where gender equality and personal choice—understood specifically as a Western secular norm—are important social values. Their conversions prompted careful reevaluations and constructions of feminine selfhood and practice that drew on Islamic traditions, as well as their socialization as Spaniards or northern Europeans. Migrant women came from a variety of pious and secular communities and actively reworked how to be Muslim women in Granada, where they newly experienced life as religious minorities. My research participants did not identify as wholly nonliberal subjects in complete opposition to normative Andalusian gender ideologies, and they also balked at the assumption that they were fully liberal subjects "underneath," just waiting to be rescued or uncovered. Yet public discourse reduced Muslim women's complex discourses about gender and piety to a story about convert women who abandon feminism and migrant women waiting to be rescued by it. This chapter explores the consequences of these erasures through ethnography of interfaith encounters in public space that are marked by the liberation narrative.[3] Because I worked more with women, their stories appear more here, but gendered ideas about Islam in Granada create gendered exclusions of men as well. In particular, notions of Muslim and migrant men as *"machista"* resulted in widespread surveillance, criminalization, and policing in public space, as well as refusals of aid from NGO workers who tended to see Moroccan men in particular as perpetrators rather than people in need of help (Rogozen-Soltar 2012a).

As I researched debates about Islam and gender in the city, I came to see Granada as a particularly useful place to think about discourses of Islam's gendered difference in Europe. While other studies have focused on national debates in contexts where legislation regulates Muslim women's dress, the encounters around gender and bodily practices that I saw in Granada showed how even in regions with permissive legislation toward religious minorities and no headscarf ban, city life can still be structured by anxieties about headscarves and about gender, Islam, and bodily practices more broadly. Recent anthropological work has dislodged the idea that Muslims' practices are "the problem" for integration by training a critical ethnographic lens on the norms of European host societies (e.g., Bowen 2008). Much of this work is about France, where, for instance, Mayanthi Fernando (2014) expertly traces how the inchoate but nevertheless powerfully disciplining tradition of French *laïcité* (secularism) disrupts (and excludes) Muslims and Muslim religiosity, all the while casting Muslims themselves as a disruption to French identity and security. The ethnography in this chapter follows a similar line of inquiry, asking how these issues unfold on the Catholic periphery of secular Europe. In Andalusia, locally particular ways of being in public space have been historically shaped by the region's own Catholic difference from secular Europe, and this motivates the particular social construction of Muslims' gendered difference as *too much difference* in Granada.

WHY GENDER MATTERS

How is it that Muslims' supposed gendered abnormality, indexed by bodily practices, comes to be understood as "the problem" for their inclusion in the first place? Anxieties about Andalusians' own reputation for gender inequality as a marker of Moorishness and non-Europeanness shapes locals' concerns about gender among the growing Muslim population. On the one hand, many of my Andalusian interlocutors subscribed to the liberation narrative, deeply influenced by broader European conversations about Islam. On the other hand, in Spain, and especially Andalusia, the imagined division between locals as European secular people characterized by gender equality and Muslims as outsiders characterized by Islamic gender oppression is not so starkly drawn. My interlocutors saw both secularism and gender equality as crucial, but new and tenuous markers of a still-solidifying Spanish democracy. Because of Andalusia's historical image as a fervently, sometimes gratuitously Catholic society marked by obsession with religious zeal, death, gory passion plays, and overwrought religious festivals—an image to which anthropologists contributed in no small way (e.g., Harris 2000; Mintz 1997; Mitchell 1990)— Andalusians are sensitive about being considered insufficiently secular. Since the transition to democracy, then, emphasizing gender equality in self-understandings and self-presentation has become a common way for people to assert their modernity and Europeanness, though these are seen as only nascent achievements. As Jane Collier showed in a longitudinal study about social change in Andalusia during and after the democratic transition, new trumpeting of gender equality in Andalusia may have less to do with concrete changes in women's lives and status with respect to men than it has to do with an increase in regional perceptions of women's equality as an index of modernity and democracy (1997).

Katherine Ewing (2008) suggests that Europeans' insistence on enforcing what they perceive as European secular gender norms among minority populations stems from a conflation of local cultural values and practices related to gender, family, and public life with purportedly pan-European or even universal ideals of human rights, democracy, freedom, and secularism. Thus, non-Muslims see Muslims' difference from local cultural norms as exemplary of civilizational conflict, even when their own practices do not align with imagined European norms. In Granada, Andalusians did not seem to mistake their local practices for actualizations of idealized European norms. Instead, they constantly worried about not being secular or European enough, all too aware of discrepancies between local practice and imagined European norms to which they may aspire. Thus, Muslims' perceived gender difference did not simply secure Andalusians' sense of a European "us" versus a Muslim "them." Instead, it also further impeded Andalusia's and Spain's ability to close the gap between local or national practices and an imagined European civilizational ideal.

At the national level, since the transition to democracy, the Spanish government has focused legislative attention and publicity on promoting gender equality as a mark of Spain's modern, democratic status. More than any other arena of antidiscrimination policy, the early socialist-leaning governments of newly democratic Spain foregrounded gender, enacting gender parity requirements in electoral politics, policies upholding gender equality in the workplace, gay rights initiatives (including legalization of same-sex marriage), abortion rights laws, and programs to address sexual violence (Bustelo and Ortbals 2007).[4] Accompanying the celebration of gender equality laws is a daily media blitz demonstrating how far Spain has yet to come, by detailing statistics on domestic abuse and other violence toward women. Regions or social sectors seen as lagging on standards of gender equality come under criticism, particularly Andalusia, where gender inequality and gender violence are common news topics and foci of government institutions like the Andalusian Institute of Women.

Ideas about gendered backwardness have been central to historical constructions of Andalusia as a region "behind" or marginal to the rest of Spain and are often indexically linked to ideas of Moorishness. In spite of local governments' efforts to institutionalize gender equality, Andalusians have been accused of maintaining a *"machista"* society (Calvo and Mart 2009; Ortbals 2008, 2009; Threlfall 1998; 2007).[5] The prevalent stereotypes of Andalusians' *"machista"* gender roles came across clearly in my fieldwork conversations with central and northern Spaniards. When I asked a northern Spanish interviewee about what, if anything, sets Andalusia apart, she immediately brought up gender, saying, "Unlike the northern women, Andalusian women don't really have much relevance in society, because of *machismo*. They tend to have large families. Historically, Andalusian families are like clans, all living together." She thus implied that Andalusians had not yet caught on to the changes in gender relations that heralded the rest of Spain's entrance into modern democratic life.

The view of Andalusian women as stuck at home with large families, barred from public life, mirrors Spanish depictions of Muslim Arab patriarchy. Sometimes these parallel constructions converge, as when Eva, a woman originally from Madrid, told me that she did not care for men in Granada. She explained that Andalusian men today were like other Spanish men from older generations that had lived under Franco. "They're too *machista*, they're so Arab [*son tan Árabes*], they order their wives to do all the housework." Using "Arab" as an adjective for supposedly sexist Andalusian men expresses a number of linked anxieties about gender,

Islam, local belonging, and regional identity. Eva's casting of *"machista"* *Granadino* men as "Arab" maligned Arabs in contrast to Spaniards, and Andalusians in contrast to other Spaniards by invoking the region's Arab legacy.

Gendered criteria for appraisals of Andalusians as *"Árabe"* often oscillated between casting Andalusian and Muslim Arab men as one of two static stereotypes, either dangerously virile or pathetically effeminate. Spanish descriptions of *Granadino* men, both past and present, enact this dynamic. I commonly heard northern Spanish friends living in Granada joke that local men's accents "sound gay," even as they suggested that men in Granada were especially machista and that the region had more problems with domestic violence than northern Spain. Further, Spanish depictions of medieval Muslim men emphasize the brutality and potency of an unstoppable army, often trafficking in highly sexualized imagery of Moorish invasion-as-penetration of Spain, while nevertheless casting the Muslims of *al-Andalus* as having feminine qualities (Soto Bermant 2007). This dual discourse of "Arab" masculinity, used to describe both North Africans and non-Muslim Spaniards, clearly invokes European imperial legacies. Historically, depictions of Arab, Muslim, and other non-European men as weak and effeminate have been central to orientalist discourses about colonized subjects in a range of contexts (Said 1978; Stoler 1995), even as Arab and Muslim men have also been cast as oppressors of women in justifications for European and American interventions on behalf of Muslim women in colonial and neocolonial projects (Abu-Lughod 2002; Ahmed 1992; Hirschkind and Mahmood 2002; Puar and Rai 2002; Spivak 1994).

In Granada, such gendered discourse is central to depictions of the city's slippery position between European and North African identification. The most often repeated story of medieval Muslims' exit from Spain is the refrain that Boabdil (Spanish for *Abu Abdullah*, the last Muslim ruler of Granada), "wept like a woman for what he could not defend like a man" upon handing over the city's keys to the conquering Catholic Kings. This phrase is written in pamphlets for tourists, and is retold frequently. I have heard it many times in organized contexts (like tours) and as a popular anecdote in locals' historical narratives of the city. The final Catholic triumph over Moorish Spain is thus glossed as a gendered one

that turns powerful, masculine, Moorish military "invaders" into emascu-
lated, conquered victims who are later to be colonized during the Spanish
nation-state's ventures in northern Morocco.

Gendered stereotypes about Andalusian, Arab, and Muslim men today reflect the gendered dimension of the *moro* as a palimpsestic and
chronotopic figure in Andalusia. Inmaculada García Sánchez (2014) uses
these terms to refer to the easy and frequent slippage between historical
imaginaries of medieval Moors and present-day Muslim migrants from
Morocco in particular. I suggest that her insight is easily extended to Andalusians as well, whose suspect gender relations aid conflations between
them and "*moros*" past and present. When Andalusians are understood
as Arab or Muslim-influenced, they are cast as oppressive of women.
When Andalusians are seen as more prone to gender violence and sexism
than other Spaniards, they are cast as *medio moros*, or half-Moors. Non-
Muslim Andalusians are aware that both secularism and gender equality are suspect in their region—land of Spain's Muslim heritage, major
public Catholic celebrations, and the renowned machista—and have a
strong stake in publicly criticizing and distancing themselves from the
perceived gender inequality of Muslim resident communities. In this
context, gendered difference becomes a go-to discourse for explaining
Muslim difference.

PUBLIC SOCIALITY AND OBJECTIFIED PIETY

Public discussions of multiculturalism focus on Muslim women's gendered practices, but embodied norms of Andalusianness that go unnoticed
by many locals help to create an exclusionary public sociality. In this section, I show how Andalusian embodied norms of sociality create obstacles
for Muslim women's inclusion, tracing how Muslim women manage and
engage with these obstacles. The ethnography of these processes reveals
both Muslim women's complex reasoning around questions of gender
equality, freedom, and piety, and the way this reasoning is excluded from
and illegible in public space, especially in interfaith encounters, which
are framed by the liberation narrative. I start with the importance of

socializing in public space and then turn to practices of consumption and gendered and sexualized dress and interactional styles.

Socializing in public is one of the ubiquitous but unremarked-upon practices that is most central to normative understandings of Andalusian-ness and local belonging. The largest cities and tiniest mountain villages of Granada are designed around an abundance of public space. Homes are reserved for socializing among families or occasionally the closest of friends, and one of the first things foreigners learn when living in Andalu-sia is the degree to which most social life happens in public places—parks, public squares, streets, and bars and restaurants (most of which boast *terrazas,* patio areas that spill out onto sidewalks and squares). Special events like birthday parties and mundane daily chats with friends are all far more likely to happen in public space than in someone's home. The social relations that make life friendly, good, happy, healthy, moral, and normal happen "in the street," meaning in public space. Many interlocu-tors repeated the phrases *"Vivimos en la calle"* (We live in the street) and *"Somos muy callejeros"* (We're very much street people). These phrases of self-presentation often go hand-in-hand with claims of Granada's suc-cessful *convivencia.* Social life "in the street" is supposed to facilitate and reflect urban *convivencia,* with only the worst *malafollá* refusing to engage in life *"en la calle."*

Many *Granadinos* I worked with explicitly contrasted their brand of so-ciality to the supposedly more homebound people of northern Spain and northern Europe, referring to them as "taciturn," "overly reserved," and in the words of one *Granadina,* "cold, boring people" who "stay at home." Their strong identification with public sociality, with its emphasis on the goodness of socializing "in the street," is often a rebuttal to national Span-ish and global tourist imaginaries of Andalusia as the lazy land of play and parties. Andrea, a forty-year old Andalusian woman raised by *Granadino* emigrant parents in France, had moved to her parents' natal Granada as a college student. She remarked that the key difference between her French city and Granada was that in the latter, social life takes place in public space. She said:

> In France, teenagers just go to school, classes, and home, very little more than that. Here, how can I explain it to you, people get together so much

in the street, the young people are way more mature. They're more used to stepping out, the Spaniards, well actually no, it's really the Andalusians, the *Granadinos*. And I wouldn't change a thing. I don't know if you know this, but in Spain, they have a concept of Andalusians that we don't like to work, because they always see us out *in the street*. But this doesn't mean we don't work. We work as much as anyone else, but we know better here how to enjoy life. It's not just work, work, work, it's going out, getting together with friends, meeting up, in bars, *in the street*. I like it more.

Andrea's comments—in which she repeats "in the street" three times—reveal the importance of reputational anxiety in Andalusian identity narratives that foreground socializing in public spaces. Defensiveness about their global reputation for laziness and parties feeds into a prideful re-working of these tropes in a discourse of public sociality as a marker of goodness.

Granadinos I worked and lived with were happy to educate me and other foreigners, including northern Spaniards, on the values and practices of public sociality. When I was living in Spain for the first time, *Granadino* youth frequently dragged me to public parties, proud of the city's reputation for having some of the largest crowds in the nation for *botellón* (massive, open-air, youth drinking gatherings in public spaces) despite its small population.[6] Many years later, while I was conducting fieldwork for this book, friends and colleagues invoked the more "mature" version of this—insisting on meeting for nightly evening drinks after work hours, so I could be a "real Andalusian" rather than someone who "goes home" at the end of the day.

While my Andalusian interlocutors described their regional mode of sociality with the phrase *"Vivimos en la calle"* (We live in the street), my Muslim interlocutors often used the contrasting refrain *"Somos de casa"* or *"Somos gente de casa"* (We are homebodies). For some converts, especially Murabitun, becoming a "homebody" was part of a conscious effort to refashion gendered bodily practices and gendered spatial relations. Some convert women, including Lubab, Nahlah, Muna, and eventually Yassmin, decided to stop working outside the home and to move their social activities into domestic spaces and a convert Muslim women's center. Their purposeful avoidance of public spaces they had once frequented helped them create new gendered subjectivities in line with their interpretations of Muslim practice.

Migrant women from Morocco also referred to themselves at times as "homebodies." Jihan, Soukaina, and others sometimes explained this as a product of their histories of socialization in Morocco, where their active social lives with wide family-and-friend networks often centered on domestic spaces. But many also described becoming *"gente de casa"* (homebodies) as a product of their arrival in Spain, a response to feeling unwelcome or insecure in restaurants, public parks, or neighborhood spaces, like in the cases of Khadija and Hajar, who felt unsafe in the *Albayzín* and Polígono, respectively. While for many lifelong *Granadinos* public conviviality and a willingness to live one's life in the company of strangers can seem central to normative participation in civic *convivencia*, for some Muslims, engaging in the *convivencia* of a public park, bar, or promenade also opens one up to negative public encounters with those who embody the infamous *malafollá* through their hostility to outsiders. Clara, the convert woman who was often mistaken for a migrant because of her residence in the Polígono and her choice to wear a Moroccan-style headscarf, articulated a strong sense of dread and frustration about public space. She had a keen self-awareness about how she was objectified in public space, as well as the way power differentials in public encounters made it difficult for her to counter those who treated her as *"un mero objeto"* (a mere object).

Clara felt constantly called out directly, or talked about in dehumanizing ways in public space. Because she felt that casual racism could easily slip into violence, she was hesitant to defend herself or respond in any way to strangers who made comments about her headscarf or otherwise engaged her about Islam in public. Recalling a time when a man had come up to her on the street, spit at her feet, and threatened to pull her headscarf off, yelling "What a disgusting Moor!," she said, "I used to respond by simply talking to the person. But since there are aggressive people, the truth is, I get scared. If it's a man, maybe he'll hit me, you never know. So I don't say anything because I'm afraid." To illustrate how this fear led to her remaining silent in the face of any kind of public commentary on Islam, she told me a story about an uncomfortable bus ride. "The other day I got on the bus, and I sat down near an elderly couple. The woman was saying to the husband, 'Get off the bus and buy bread,' and he says, 'No. No, you hush up, and be submissive, like this girl,' pointing to me." Here, Clara imitated the man grinning in jest, to show that he had meant his comments to his wife as a flirtatious joke at Clara's expense. Clara continued, "He meant that she should be submissive to him, just like this Muslim girl who's locked up in her house and does whatever her husband says, and is quiet! I felt paralyzed because I wanted to tell him that I'm free, but who knows what he would do, and besides, I was so surprised that I was kind of in shock. And his wife just laughed at me!"

Clara was stunned and humiliated by this exchange, and her pale cheeks flushed as she recounted it to me. Even though the man on the bus did not say out loud that Clara was "locked up" or "quiet," or followed her husband's orders, Clara confidently inferred these meanings from his use of the word *submissive*; she was sure that his joke was about gendered stereotypes of Islam. Besides, she said, she had experienced so many similar encounters that she felt certain of the range of nonagentive attributes and activities encoded in his use of the word *submissive*. In addition to Clara's feeling like an unprotected target for objectification, the crux of her frustration was the way this man misinterpreted her own understanding of herself as a pious Muslim, and, crucially, the power imbalance that left her unable to confront him.

It was important to Clara that I know how wrong this man was about her. Rather than simply being blindly "submissive," Clara had spent much time carefully thinking through what it meant to be a pious Muslim Spanish woman living in Granada. Like many women with whom I worked, and like many Muslim Europeans (Jouili 2015; Fernando 2014; Özyürek 2014), Clara carefully drew on dominant Spanish discourses of women's freedom and on the importance of submission in pious practice. She neither wholly embraced personal liberation from imposed structures of obligation nor entirely jettisoned personal will from her vision of ideal Islamic practice. While explaining this to me during a long conversation about her conversion process, she also discussed some of her fellow converts' positions on these questions. In carefully parsing out her differences from them, she highlighted the diversity of thought among Muslim convert women in Granada. While acknowledging that some convert women actively critique Spanish norms of gender equality that emphasize women's personal freedoms, Clara initially seemed to embrace normative Spanish ideals of women's freedom and choice:

I'll tell you what I've heard from other convert women, but it's not what I feel. I know a woman who married a Syrian, and entered into Islam, and she talked a lot about freedom, and how before, she'd been so addicted to fashion, and material things, and how becoming Muslim allowed her to leave all that behind and gave her a sense of freedom from it. [long pause] But not me. I was never a slave to material things. And I wasn't unfree before. And I still wear makeup sometimes, if I want to. But my freedom is interior. I'm very happy because I feel free. This is important [motions for me to continue writing what she says in my notebook], because lots of people think that if you become Muslim, it's because they made you [te obligaron]. But no. I'm very free.

Here, in her emphasis on individual choice and freedom, Clara seemed to subscribe to a "freedom" that sounds like the Spanish idea of libertad, individual freedom from constraint, coercion, or outside pressure. Unlike some convert women, Clara did not see Islamic values as a critique of Spanish women's false consciousness about gendered freedoms. Conversion for her had not been about rejecting Spanish concepts of freedom.

But as she continued, it became clear that her view of freedom, especially in relation to religious piety, was not so straightforward. Clara complained about her fellow Spaniards' tendency to assume that she had been coerced into conversion by a Muslim spouse. She went on to highlight the distinction between choosing to convert to Islam because of spousal pressure and doing so because of one's own religious conviction and choice, placing special emphasis on how the latter better facilitates submission to God, saying:

And this is important because there are women who convert because of their husbands, and then if the relationship ends, they leave Islam because they had only converted for a man, it wasn't a free entry. And that's really bad, because someone who doesn't truly feel the Islamic religion, how is that person going to cumplir [fulfill] all the prayers, Ramadan, all the obligations that you have to do?"

As it turns out, Clara's rationale for the importance of self-possessed decisions was not the idea of individual agency-as-freedom as an end itself, but rather her sense that freely choosing Islamic beliefs and practices is a requirement to be able to truly, fully submit oneself to God and to successfully fulfill all of the obligations that "you have to do" to be a good, pious Muslim. The stranger's joke on the bus reduced all of this to Clara's supposed "submissiveness," intuited from seeing her headscarf. The frequency of such encounters made public space frightening at worst, uncomfortable at best, for Clara and many other women.

PORK, WINE, AND SEX

Public sociality in Granada is also deeply shaped by particular norms of consumption, dress, and comportment between genders, what might be dubbed the trifecta of "pork, wine, and sex." In addition to the kind of objectification Clara described, this trifecta becomes a source of anxiety when Muslims try to (or for employment purposes, need to) engage in Andalusian public sociality. Most of the difficulties my research participants articulated had to do with consumption of pork and wine and engaging in premarital sexual relationships or in nonsexual physical contact with men outside their families. Converts often described these norms as challenges to their efforts to refashion their bodies, gendered subjectivities, and gendered social roles. They had been socialized into these norms and, after lifetimes of embodying them, worked to transition into lives marked by pious practices that departed from them. Migrants spoke of these norms as shaping their experience of learning the "culture" of their new host society, and of learning about how to be Muslims in a non-Muslim majority country.

Yassmin, the Senegalese-German-Spanish convert teenager from chapter 2, struggled to cultivate piety within Andalusian public sociality. In our many conversations, Yassmin often focused on her struggle to figure out what kind of Muslim woman she wanted to be and how to achieve her goals. She often characterized expectations of public sociality as obstacles to achieving full social inclusion and developing piety at the same time. Yassmin articulated her struggle in terms of the fraught relationships between bodily practices, religious subjectivity, and social inclusion.

Yassmin's mother was very involved in convert women's dawa activities. Her mother wanted me to convert to Islam, and I often got the sense that Yassmin had been instructed to help with that effort. About half the times I saw Yassmin, we were at the Mezquita Mayor mosque, a convert women's center downtown, or teahouses with other convert women. In these contexts, Yassmin always wore a headscarf (in the turban style of most convert women) and long, loose tunics. In these settings, she often guided our conversations toward religion, offering lengthy soliloquies on Islam, gender, and Islamic marriage, and suggesting that she could teach me some of the prayers, washing rituals, and other bodily practices that would help me understand "what Islam is like." However, many of my interactions with Yassmin were social events with her and her housemates or school friends. Yassmin had graduated from secondary school but had not yet begun university. She had recently moved into an apartment with two non-Muslim young women when I met her. When we hung out with these friends, Yassmin often wore fashionable, close-fitting T-shirts and only sometimes wore her headscarf when we met for Coca-Colas or walked through the city on leisurely afternoons. In these settings, she rarely talked about Islam and even seemed shy when her friends or I asked questions about religion.

According to Yassmin, her non-Muslim friends saw her headscarf as "a limitation." Though most were generally accepting of her religious difference, their questions about the headscarf centered on how it limited her. About a year after we met, Yassmin became engaged to a man she met through her mother's Murabitun connections in Sub-Saharan Africa. Yassmin did not identify as Murabitun or even necessarily as Sufi but had been raised in the Murabitun fold. One afternoon shortly after the engagement, she mentioned that since becoming engaged, she was wearing the headscarf more often. I asked how she felt about it and she described the hijab as a central node in a cycle of self-making in which bodily practices and one's inner state of spirituality are mutually reinforced. She framed her comments in relation to the imagined, ubiquitous Spanish critic of headscarves and her friends' view of the scarf as a limitation. Yassmin at once acknowledged and rejected their understandings of the headscarf as a bodily imposition, saying "Even I, who understand the meaning and importance of the scarf, even I sometimes when I wear it, I feel overwhelmed. It's like getting used to wearing glasses, you know? At first your body isn't used to it and so you don't like it."

But she went on to say how useful the headscarf is once the body becomes accustomed to it.

But it's also true that when you wear the headscarf—well, it's not just
wearing the headscarf, because when you wear it, you're always conscious
of being Muslim, and when I wear it there are things I wouldn't do, you
know? I mean now I don't do the things I did before, like when I would
drink, or now I would never go to a nightclub. I used to go.

Here, Yassmin changed revealingly to the present tense as she continued,
"I go once in a while, not a lot, just to dance and let loose and de-stress. Just
to um, you know, try things out, see what it's like." Now Yassmin mum-
bled something only partially audible about dancing with boys, turned
bright red, and then stopped talking for a moment, before concluding
her thought: "I know it's not the most appropriate thing, and with the
headscarf on, I would never go. So the headscarf really protects you a lot."

Central to Yassmin's discussion of wearing the hijab is how she found
it difficult to continue participating in normative youthful public sociality while doing so. She glossed this as positive in one respect—the hijab protected her from engaging in behavior she saw as non-Islamic and
immoral—but she also expressed regret at having to leave public sociality
behind to cultivate an ethical, pious life.

Even though she seemed to describe piety as incompatible with Andalusian public sociality, Yassmin did not face a simple "clash of civilizations"
or values. She felt committed to and shaped as a person by both the values
of her Andalusian social world and her growing piety and engagement
with the Islamic community, both locally and globally. Yassmin continued
talking, moving back and forth between using the past tense and present
tense to discuss participation in public youth sociality—going to bars
and botellón gatherings and hanging out with boys. She was struggling to
fashion a life in which she wore a headscarf, abstained from public parties,
and stopped "wearing strappy tank tops," but she also lamented that her
non-Muslim friends could not understand these changes. For Yassmin,
transforming her bodily practices was crucial to preparing for marriage
and the degree of piety she felt should accompany this major life step. But
she also said she would be very happy to continue her social life "en la calle"
if doing so did not always entail judgment of her headscarf as a negative
limitation and if public sociality did not have to revolve around activities
that were inappropriate for her.

Pork and Wine

The pervasiveness of pork and alcohol in Andalusian public social spaces is difficult to overstate. *Cafeterías* (cafés) are usually combined bars and coffeehouses, which means that most establishments serving tea and coffee also serve alcohol.[7] The tapas culture of Granada compounds this. While Spain is internationally known for its tapas (small plates), tapas are especially common in Andalusia, and Granada and the neighboring province of Jaén are the only provinces in Spain where more elaborate tapas (i.e., something more than a small plate of olives, chips, or nuts) are served for free and automatically with every beverage purchased. While fish, eggs, cheese, and vegetables are common elements of tapas and *pintxos* (a northern version of tapas) elsewhere in Spain, tapas in Andalusia sometimes include these ingredients but are especially likely to be pork-based. While traditionally served with alcoholic beverages, most establishments in Granada now serve a tapa with any kind of beverage. This means a Muslim who orders a soda or tea in a bar-coffee shop is very likely to be handed a plate that includes pork. Consumption of alcohol and pork is thus inextricably linked to normative use of public space.

My Muslim research participants commented on this frequently, and I experienced the pervasiveness of pork as a vegetarian. When I first lived in Spain, I quickly learned to ask for "no meat," because to order a "vegetarian" item simply meant ham products *with* vegetables added. Today, vegetarianism is far more common in Spain, but when I politely refuse pork I am usually met with comments explicitly noting the links between pork and Andalusianness or Spanishness. I have been told by friendly waiters: "You must try the ham, it is the pride of Spain"; "We Spaniards all love our ham"; and "Spain isn't Spain without ham!" I have also been jokingly asked by well-meaning servers, "But you aren't a Muslim, are you?!" My refusals of pork are treated as humorous or annoying at worst, but for Muslims, these comments can become what locals call social *"roces,"* small, irritating scratches, or microaggressions that become a nuisance over time, and some Muslims felt these roces made socializing in public space unworth the trouble.

Conceptual links between the consumption of wine and pork and local or national (implicitly Catholic) identities have a long social history in Andalusia and Spain, which is mostly outside the scope of this book. However, even a cursory review of the role of pork products and alcohol as long ago as the Inquisition reveals a strong historical precedent for linking pork and wine consumption to Catholic national belonging constructed in opposition to Islam. During this period, state and public discussions of Muslims' nonbelonging in Spain emerged as inextricably linked to a host of familial and bodily practices, including cooking, food sharing, and consumption. A central way the incipient Spanish nation-state identified Muslims and "crypto-Muslim" Catholics was by enforcing consumption of pork and alcohol products. Early in the Inquisitorial process, Muslims and Jews were encouraged to convert to Catholicism, but eventually conversion stopped working for the state as a solution to the problem of religious difference, because converts' sincerity came under suspicion. To ascertain whether converts had really, truly adopted Catholicism or were still secretly Muslim or Jewish "underneath," the general public was encouraged through official edicts to report on anyone seen observing Muslim or Jewish food practices (Kamen 1985, 162). In a similar vein, failing to conspicuously observe Catholic practices of consumption was considered proof of heresy. Inquisitorial trial documents are filled with quotations from defendants who based their claims of Christianity on what they fed their families. "We have pork and wine in our house" became a testimony to religious (and national) legitimacy in trials (Root 1988, 126).

The idea that pork and wine consumption are inherently Andalusian or Spanish is thus traceable back to the very inception of the nation-state, where love of these products was constructed as Spanish because it was understood as Catholic and *not Muslim*. I certainly would not draw a straight line from the way the Inquisitorial state disciplined citizens' bodily practices through surveillance of pork and wine consumption to the contemporary emphasis on these products in embodied Andalusian identity. In the intervening centuries, Andalusian cuisine has surely developed in response to any number of factors, from locally available resources, economic shifts, and political interventions into the food economy, to the exigencies of the global tourism industry. Yet the role of pork and wine in Inquisitorial prosecution of suspected "crypto-Muslims" provides some historical context for the fact that pork and wine consumption, far from being meaningless or trivial preferences, are deeply rooted bodily practices in Granada, forming a kind of culinary habitus that during the Inquisition was created in opposition to Islam.

Many of my Muslim research participants brought up the pervasive presence of pork and wine, sometimes in arguments about the city's Catholic ambience, but often in casual remarks about how they never went to restaurants or cafés, or how they did not enjoy these venues. When migrants talked with me about not having Spanish friends, they invariably brought up pork and wine to explain why they did not go to many social events with Andalusians. When converts talked about losing touch with their preconversion friends, they often said they felt uncomfortable attending the usual daily or weekly tapas evenings because they felt awkward constantly having to ask for pork-free offerings and lamented the fact that alcohol was always freely flowing.

Belén was the most outspoken of my research participants on this topic. Recall that Belén saw Islam and Andalusianness or Spanishness as perfectly compatible. In keeping with that framing, she frequently brought up the question of different expectations of bodily practices among Muslim and non-Muslim social circles. She usually concluded that when convincing people that Muslim bodily practices were normal was not possible or likely, the best thing to do was to jettison pious bodily practices, or hide them, in the hopes of avoiding conflict with critics of Islam. Belén made an effort to *cumplir* (fulfill the religious obligation), avoiding pork and alcohol whenever possible, but she aimed to do so in unnoticed fashion. She chose dissimulation as her method, in a strategy that could not help but evoke medieval Spanish converts to Catholicism professing their pork consumption in court. Because Belén's family was unaware that she had become Muslim, and because she was sure they would figure it out if they realized that she no longer consumed pork or alcohol, she decided to pretend that she still consumed them. When she visited family members, Belén took fake sips from her wineglass, or swished wine in her mouth and then spit it back into the glass when no one was looking. She busily cut up slices of *jamón serrano* at family holiday gatherings, and messed up the porky contents of her plate to make them appear half-eaten. Belén no longer saw pork and wine as constitutive of Spanish selfhood, but she still recognized the powerful social significance of abstention from these "Spanish foods."

Belén delighted in recounting a funny story about compulsory ham consumption involving her elderly neighbors' interactions with her Muslim migrant husband. Her devout, Catholic neighbors had invited her and Ahmet to dinner over the Christmas holiday one year after she and Ahmet were married but before Belén had converted. They offered Belén and Ahmet the standard Christmas ham at the table. Ahmet explained apologetically that as a Muslim, he could not eat jamón. Their hostess nodded, seeming to understand, saying, "Oh, I see," and then disappeared into the kitchen. Moments later, she returned to the table bearing a new plate of jamón, but this time it was slices of the very expensive *jamón ibérico de bellota*, made from wild roaming pigs who graze on acorns in oak forests, widely considered the premium variety. The woman proudly placed the new plate in front of Ahmet, saying, "And how about some of the *good* stuff?" For Belén, this story epitomized the naturalized ubiquity of jamón, and it indicates just how unthinkable it is for many *Granadinos* that someone would forgo pork products. Rather than taking seriously Ahmet's initial decline of the offered ham, the elderly and generous neighbor could only imagine that he just wanted fancier stuff. While many Muslim women expressed frustration, or sheer exhaustion, at having to constantly find polite ways of refusing ham, Belén found this story hilarious. She told me about it one morning at the NGO where she worked and I volunteered, and every time she passed me that afternoon she would repeat the punch line, "How about some of the *good* stuff?!," hooting with laughter. Her ability to find humor in the situation reflects a combination of her general temperament, her particular views of pious practice (which emphasized accommodation to Spanish norms), and also her privilege, as a Spanish woman facing less risk of exclusion as a Muslim than migrants.

In the last several years, several companies have begun to offer what they call "halal jamón" in Spain. Faysal Dali is the proprietor of one of the largest operations, based in Andalusia. He makes halal "jamón" by curing primarily lamb with the spices associated with traditional pork products. In an interview with American National Public Radio in 2014, Dali connected his burgeoning halal jamón business to the idea of *convivencia*, saying "I'm living and making my product in a region where Muslims, Jews, and Christians have a history of living—and eating—together" (Frayer

2014). As of 2014, most of Dali's products were marketed to global Muslim tourists to Spain, and restaurants and cafés near the Alhambra in Granada were some of his largest clients. On the one hand, the introduction of halal jamón, however oxymoronic the phrase may sound, seems to portend a gastronomic inclusion of Muslims, making a national culinary tradition available to them in a way that could facilitate the welcoming of Muslims in public spaces like bars and cafés. On the other hand, this trend also illustrates just how important jamón consumption is for participation in Andalusian public space in the first place. So far, none of my research participants have expressed much awareness of or interest in consuming halal jamón; time will tell whether its existence changes the way Muslims may engage in *tapeo* (bar crawling), the cornerstone of public sociality in Granada.

Miniskirts and Public Affection

Andalusian efforts to demonstrate regional modernity by adopting a self-conscious politics of gender equality involve discarding what are now considered the puritanical mores of the Franco era in favor of openness about sexuality and male-female affection in public interaction and dress codes. When I was a college student studying abroad in Spain years ago, a unit of my program's "cultural orientation" afternoon included local professors explaining to the foreign students that Spanish youth are far more prone to public displays of affection than Americans and other nationalities. That this kind of broad generalization was included in a lesson about Spanish culture reveals how important public physical and sexual affection have become in self-representations of modern Spanish culture. Public displays of romantic affection are common and may also be related to the fact that so much of social life takes place in the street; it is far more common for romantic partners to meet up in public than in their homes. This is especially the case for young people still living with their parents, and many Andalusians live at home until their late thirties or marriage, whichever comes first. Muslim interlocutors commented on the tendency toward public displays of affection. One woman complained that teenagers were always making out on the benches at her favorite park. Beyond public displays of affection, though, what most of my Muslim research participants noticed about gendered physicality in the public sphere were the practice of exchanging two kisses upon hellos and good-byes, and a general fashion trend toward revealing clothing for women.[8]

In Granada, dress and the gendered and sexual moralities clothing creates and indexes reveal that differences between Muslim and non-Muslim circles can be stark. In postsocialist Bulgaria, another context shaped by the resurgence of Islam during a time of political and social transition, Kristen Ghodsee (2009) found a similar dynamic. Muslim women involved in piety movements during the revival of Islam in postsocialist public life aimed to remake themselves in part by adopting more pious dress, while non-Muslim women hoping to embody a postsocialist modernity used sexually revealing clothing to mark themselves as modern. In Granada, many of my Catholic and secular research participants saw revealing clothing as part of modern fashion trends, and while some were too young to see their clothing as related to Spanish democracy, others self-consciously contrasted their outfits from Zara and Mango to the buttoned-up style required by their parents under Franco.

During the fieldwork for this book, I often divided my days between different groups of research participants. Sometimes the considerable contrasts in their attitudes about clothing were made especially clear as I moved back and forth between social groups. I frequently spent the morning with a group of Muslim women who would critique what they saw as non-Muslim *Granadina* women's self-objectification and scandalous, sexualized clothing. They believed that women's revealing outfits encouraged men to objectify them and led to immoral sexual practices. One morning, I interviewed a Muslim convert entrepreneur who spoke at length about her hijab and long skirt. They served as public protection for her dignity and professionalism, she said, because men could not judge her legs the way they do with women who wear *minifaldas* (miniskirts). She referred, as many Murabitun did, to the demands of fashion on non-Muslim women as a "form of gender slavery," both because of the need to constantly buy new clothes as trends changed and because of pressures on women to attain unnatural thinness and other expectations of bodily perfection.

Later that day, I was preparing to go out for an evening of tapas with two Catholic women, my friend Elena and her out-of-town guest, Petra. I came into the living room of my apartment to find Petra wearing precisely one of these minifaldas, which she excitedly said was new, from a local boutique considered very fashion-forward. The skirt was covered in print, and as I got closer to her, I realized it was decorated with English-language words and phrases, all sexual in nature and quite graphic. I wondered if Petra understood their meaning. Covering clothing and accessories with English is a common way of marking them as stylish, so I was used to my interlocutors asking me what the English phrases on their purses and sweatshirts meant. Not wanting to embarrass Petra, I gingerly asked if she spoke English. She said no, and asked me to translate her skirt. Tentatively, I read her some of the words and phrases scattered across it, which included "Cock," "Suck," and "Bitch, I know you like pussy cams." I assumed that Petra would be dismayed and likely want to change clothes. Instead, she was delighted: Petra and Elena decided the skirt was even more fashionable than they had realized.

Not all Muslim women I knew were opposed to revealing or sexually provocative clothing, and not all non-Muslim women embraced Petra's style; some would have been mortified by her skirt. But the fact that Elena and Petra saw the skirt as fashionable and did not give a second thought to wearing it typifies a common position regarding the modern desirability of revealing or sexually explicit dress among young, fashion-forward non-Muslims in Granada, and it illustrates a clear contrast between the sensibilities of my morning and evening companions. While Elena and Petra saw the skirt as unremarkable, or as cool and fashionable, they routinely noticed and pointed out women in headscarves on the street. Only a few days before, I had admonished them in embarrassment as we walked through the city when Elena pointed conspicuously to several women in headscarves across the street and said loudly, "Hey, Mikaela, look, there go some of your women!"

Belén talked extensively with me about the sexualized nature of clothing norms and about physicality between men and women. Her approach to handling the unfashionable nature of modest clothing and the pervasiveness of "los besos" (the kisses people exchange upon meeting or taking leave) was similar to her method for dealing with pork and wine. Sitting in the NGO office one day, she was talking about how frequently she went to the mosque, and how she was incorporating Muslim practices into her daily life in general. She pointed to a scarf folded up in her chic purse, explaining that she put the headscarf on only to pray at the mosque, out of respect, but did not see it as necessary elsewhere. She did not interpret the headscarf as an important component of women's piety, and she also saw it as too cumbersome for her social life, because people would "always be asking about it" or "judging me." After discussing how often she prayed at the mosque, she stopped talking for a moment and then said:

> I'm not a very extreme person, and because of that, there are things I just can't *cumplir* [fulfill, as in an obligation]. For example, a Muslim woman shouldn't be giving men kisses all the time. I try to greet men with a handshake. But of course, when you live in a society where everyone gives kisses to everyone all the time, what can you do? You can't do anything! It would be a *lucha constante* [a constant battle or struggle]! And of course, I don't want anyone to think I'm unfriendly, or crazy, or rude. No, I want people to see me as normal. I mean, I'm not going to walk into a public official's office and when he tries to kiss me, say, "No, stop!" and stick out my hand, and create a kind of physical barrier between us, no way.

Belén often had me accompany her to government offices, where her schmoozing with officials was likely to bring us success in the many grant applications we submitted for NGO funding. She saw her ability to move easily in such circles as paramount, and she felt strongly about the work she did at the NGO combating racism and discrimination. This fed into her decisions about when to cumplir—and when not to as well.

Unlike Belén, a convert named Mounira actually relished the struggle Belén had dismissed as untenable, the *lucha constante* (constant battle or struggle) of finding ways to fulfill religious obligations in Granada, especially with respect to bodily practices. The struggle oriented her postconversion daily life, providing a constant touchstone. Explaining her decision to pay close attention to what she called "the rules" of Islam, she said, "I was like, if I'm really practicing Islam, I don't want to do it half-assed. I wanted to convert to Islam because I really wanted to change my life." Mounira frequently brought up two *luchas* (struggles) in particular—her desire to change the physical nature of her relationship to her boyfriend and to men in general and her desire to wear a headscarf. She wanted to practice Islam "fully" and without giving up her standing as a "good feminist" among non-Muslim Spanish women, which she found difficult. While she could talk as much as she wanted to about her careful deliberations to an anthropologist who was a happy listener, Mounira had a harder time conveying the complexity of her religious choices in public encounters where, like Clara on the bus, she felt her capacity for fulfilling both Islamic "rules" and Spanish norms of female liberation was invisible.

For example, over morning muffins at a convert women's center downtown, Mounira described her encounter with a middle-aged Spanish fruit seller nearby:

> As I was buying fruit, she was saying to me that I didn't have to wear the headscarf, because, you know, back in the Franco period a lot of women wore scarves. That her generation of feminists fought for women so that we could wear pants and do all sorts of things men can do. So, I always try to let her generation know that what they did was important. But Gloria Steinem, I read something just yesterday where she said that the feminist movement is not defined by whether a woman has the right to work, but that all women are treated justly. So that's all I want.

Mounira recalled that when she shared the Gloria Steinem quote with the feminist fruit seller, the latter seemed impressed that she had read it, and relieved to know that Mounira was familiar with this canonical Western feminist public intellectual.

In conversations with me, Mounira discussed wearing a headscarf (which she wore in the turban style of many converts) in two main ways— as a "liberating" relief, and as a welcome form of "discipline." While these might sound contradictory, they reflect her complex combination of local Andalusian modes of thinking about choice and liberation on the one hand, and Islamic piety on the other, placing them in conversation rather than opposition. Mounira saw her donning of hijab as the apex of her process of becoming a fully Muslim woman, and she relished the spiritual, bodily, and social transformations it helped produce. In contrast to Belén, who does not mind greeting and farewell kisses, for example, Mounira was happy that her headscarf deterred men from trying to kiss her or shake hands as they said hello or good-bye, and she said the headscarf emboldened her to scold them if they did try. She also felt that wearing it helped her remember her faith and kept her from making "bad decisions" like sleeping with her boyfriend, something she had been trying to stop since becoming Muslim. In all of these ways, the headscarf had a desired disciplining effect, but one that Mounira also saw as liberating. When

Mounira started wearing the headscarf, she was clearly elated, and I asked if she could explain what made her so happy about it. She replied:

> Before, I felt like a closeted religious person. So now I feel this part of me is being liberated to say, "I am very religious and disciplined in my religion," and [this is] how I'm choosing to practice it. I feel like for six or seven years I've been admiring Muslim women who wear the hijab, and now I get to just let out that inner Muslim woman that I have had for so long. She is just like, "Aaaahhhh, finally!" You know, and I just get to wear the hijab and be who I am and I find it very liberating. Because it symbolizes that I'm living as much as I can under the discipline of my faith, and discipline in and of itself, when practiced in a healthy manner, discipline is a way of being liberated.

She added that in wearing the headscarf, she is using its discipline to re-create herself as a more pious, spiritual person so that eventually, her soul can reach eternity. Thus, as much as wearing the hijab is a liberation of her previously "closeted" religious self, it is also a strategy for changing and improving upon that self through the cultivation of piety.

Mounira's comments echo the concept of Western liberal personhood that took root in Andalusia during the democratic transition, in which liberal, modern persons came to be understood as those whose outward actions freely expressed their interior desires and beliefs (Collier 1997). From Mounira's point of view, wearing hijab liberated her from the outer constraints placed on her by an Islamophobic social context that initially made her hesitant to convert. Now she was free to express her internally felt religiosity. But the disciplining nature of pious bodily practice was equally important to her, and fundamentally constitutive of her inner spiritual state, oriented toward God and the ultimate liberation of her soul for eternity. For Mounira, "liberation" begot pious discipline and vice versa; they were not exactly the same, but neither were they separate or in conflict.

However, in her encounter with the fruit seller, Mounira's complex engagement with discourses of liberation and piety was reduced to an assertion of having read Gloria Steinem. As a result, Mounira lamented that Andalusian feminists had so little understanding of Islam, and she expressed frustration with having to constantly explain herself to women like the fruit seller who had lectured her on not throwing away feminist gains since the arrival of democracy. Mounira and Belén both had complex engagements with Islamic piety and with local discourses about gender and bodily norms, which they had thought about at length and clearly articulated to me in our conversations. Belén's goal was to adopt her new religion while departing from Andalusian norms of public sociality as little as possible, or with as little visibility as possible. In contrast, Mounira relished the difficult process of developing new bodily practices in her cultivation of Muslim piety. Despite their differences, both women shared the experience of confronting compulsory bodily norms that signify belonging and public sociality in Granada, while making pious Muslim women's inclusion difficult. In their careful thought and deliberate practices, Belén and Mounira demonstrated the diversity and complexity of Muslim women's engagements with ideas of piety and liberation or freedom, as well as the exclusion of their careful reasoning from interfaith encounters in which they had to either acquiesce to norms of public sociality or face social exclusion.

Even as Mounira felt marginalized in public space, the remainder of her conversation with the fruit seller reveals the uneven way exhortations to respect feminism impact convert and migrant women. Mounira was solidly middle class and college-educated, which helped give her access to her Gloria Steinem rejoinder as well as the confidence to respond to critics of Islam with less fear of the consequences. She also clearly positioned herself as a fellow European to back her defense of Islam with an air of authority. She continued describing the fruit seller's response to her Gloria Steinem comment: "She was very open about her racism, saying that she hates *moros*. So the whole thing with the hijab is grounded in a lot of racism toward Moroccans. So I told her that that's not Islam. It's a question of [the] development of that country." Mounira felt relatively successful in having changed this woman's perspective and went on to say that changing other Spaniards' minds about Islam's faulty gender roles was empowering. However, in this encounter, she seemed to have done so by excepting Moroccans from her counternarrative of Muslims' gender normalcy, distancing herself from them. Mounira's minor success in this awkward interfaith encounter, then, points to the way unequal multiculturalism shapes gendered debates about Islam in public space.

Migrant Modesty and the Saving Slot

The common liberation narrative cast Muslim migrant women as improperly gendered subjects in a different way than converts. They were placed into what might be called the *saving slot*. This category of savable third-world victims in need of feminist rescue often carries with it benevolence but also disciplining expectations that "victims" comply with benefactors' ideas about how they should feel and behave (Mahdavi 2010; Ticktin 2011; Volpp 2011). This is one gendered extension of the way performances of particular kinds of victimhood are demanded of migrants, and in particular of refugees, seeking humanitarian aid or rights and political recognition from European and American audiences more broadly (Besteman 2016; Malkki 1996; Cabot 2014). As Lila Abu-Lughod has made clear in a sustained critique of the idea that Muslim women need saving (2002, 2013), the saving narrative for Muslim women presupposes a world of static, bounded cultures; ignores the way global history and politics make life in Europe, the United States, and Muslim-majority regions always interconnected; and above all, does violence to the complexity of meanings and desires that animate the vastly diverse array of Muslim women's lives around the world, replacing real engagement with the messiness of human difference with neat political categories.

In Granada, while convert women were expected to explain, apologize for, or defend their new, seemingly strange practices and departures from Western feminist norms, migrant women were expected to change, to fit into and accept the role of Arab, Muslim, third-world women (*mujeres del tercer mundo*) who must desire liberation from enforced modesty. The recent production of this category in Andalusian feminist imaginaries likely stems in part from the global circulation of gender and human rights discourse since the end of the Cold War that frames gender and women's rights primarily in terms of rescue from patriarchy, gender violence, and trafficking (Hemment 2007). The emergence of this global discourse has set the parameters for NGO and activist funding and programming for women's rights and gender-based politics around the world. But Andalusians' perception of Muslim migrant women through this lens also reflects local cultural intimacy around the intersections of gendered and Moorish difference, described earlier. Interpreting migrant

Muslims in the saving slot helps solidify Andalusians as Europeans with proper gender norms.

The power of the saving slot to frame Moroccan women as in need of rescue was so strong that when Belén was charged with training and orienting me when I joined the antiracism NGO where she worked, she did so by telling me the story of helping a Spanish family "rescue" a Moroccan woman from marital abuse during their holiday trip to Morocco. She described how this family from Granada vacationed in the same Moroccan town each year and had become friendly with a waitress (who was never given a name in the story) at a local restaurant. At some point, they learned that the woman's husband was violent, and they decided to, as Belén put it, "smuggle her to Spain" in their car. She exclaimed, "You know, there, it's a totally different world than ours!" She explained that in Morocco, women's safety is ignored, even by the police, so the best option for this woman was to come to Granada. According to Belén, the woman was now employed in Granada as a live-in domestic worker.

It is of course quite possible that her relationship with the vacationing Spaniards presented this woman with a much-needed opportunity to leave behind an abusive relationship in Morocco. But what interests me about this case is how even Belén, a Muslim woman who spent much time and energy countering stereotypes about gender inequality in Islam, nevertheless offered this particularly dire case as "typical" of her nonprofit's work with Moroccans. She saw the woman's plight as emblematic of Moroccan women's experience and offered it as a sharp contrast to the gender equality of Spain, which figured as a land of salvation for the Moroccan woman in her personal life (saving her from her husband) and her political life (saving her from the state police).

Through my extended field research at this NGO, I learned that this case was not at all typical. In fact, I never saw a similar case, and indeed much of our work involved campaigning for the rights of undocumented migrant domestic workers in Andalusia, women in exactly the position in which this rescued Moroccan woman had landed upon arrival in Granada. Our campaign brochures and other materials called for better oversight, minimum wage, and humane treatment of women in these jobs, and we had data detailing the systematic abuses and inequalities faced by domestic workers, including rampant mistreatment and sexual violence, perpetrated by employers with impunity. However, so strong was this racially, nationally, and religiously inflected imaginary of savable third-world women that in this conversation about Morocco, it was clear to Belén that Spain was automatically a safer, better place for Moroccan women, an obvious place of rescue.

As part of this rescue-mission attitude, in encounters with teachers, university professors, strangers in the street, NGO workers, government officials, and employers, migrant Muslims experienced pressure to give up bodily practices that were integral to their senses of piety and dignified selfhood. The stakes were often quite high—failure to comply with locals' expectations of how rescuable proto-feminists ought to act resulted in compromises to their education, employment, and sometimes, legal status or security.

Rana, the young Moroccan woman who doubted the possibility of *convivencia* in chapter 4, struggled with her employer's demands that she adopt a headscarf style that made her uncomfortable. Her experience reflects non-Muslims' tendency to assume that Muslim migrant women are waiting patiently to be saved from their enforced Muslim practices. Rana's story also reveals how difficult it is for some non-Muslim *Granadinos*, often people in positions of power over migrants, to hear and to make sense of migrants' careful deliberations about their pious practices. Rana is a petite, soft-spoken, yet self-assured Moroccan woman in her early twenties. She initially immigrated to France to study translation but eventually left school to seek work. While working in the domestic sector in France, she met a friend of her employer's who was visiting from Granada and happened to be looking for a domestic worker.

When I met her, Rana was working in Granada as an *interna* (a live-in domestic worker) with this woman's Andalusian family, for whom she cooked and cleaned. I asked her what the family she worked for was like, and she revealed a simmering conflict with her employer over her headscarf, which Rana wore in what many in Granada considered to be the "Moroccan style"—her scarf covered her hair, forehead, ears, and neck. She said, "Well, the family, they're good, they treat me well, except there is one thing that I Do. Not. Like. It's that she [Rana's boss] pressures me a lot because they don't like my veil. My boss says she doesn't want to see me wearing the veil anymore." Rana was especially vexed by her employers' continual assertions that she should defy her family's "obligation" to wear a headscarf now that she was in Spain. In fact, in Morocco, Rana had not worn a headscarf, only beginning to wear hijab when she emigrated to France. She was glad she did, saying, "I feel very good about it." Her parents, whom she described as semipracticing, secular Muslims, were against the decision and still wish she would not cover her head. Rana was vehement about this, emphasizing the irony of her Spanish employers' desire to "free" her from a nonexistent patriarchal obligation.

Rana was worried that the situation had reached a boiling point. She said, "My boss has had it up to her limit with my veil. She says the veil is an obstacle to my integration here. I don't wear it at home, because there aren't men around, but I put it on when I go out, and she tells me not to." Rana then said that eventually, her boss told her that if she must insist on covering herself, she should at least wear the kind of veil used by convert women in Granada so she would stand out less—a loosely wrapped scarf in the shape of a small turban that covers women's hair (usually done up in a bun) behind the head, leaving the front of the hairline, ears, and neck uncovered. Wanting to avoid conflict, Rana tried this for a week, before switching back to her previous style of scarf. She recalled her week with the convert-style headscarf regretfully, saying, "I couldn't bear it, I just couldn't take it. I felt so uncomfortable!"

Rana thus tried, but failed, to conform to her employer's use of the liberation narrative in which it was Rana's "veil" that was an "obstacle" to her "integration," rather than local embodied norms of Andalusianness that privilege—and demand—flouting modesty. By wearing a headscarf with drastically less coverage, Rana tried to acquiesce to the demands of local embodied social norms, wearing a scarf that many locals associate with a bohemian chic style rather than gendered modesty. But in doing so, she became so uncomfortable that she had to give up. Rana attempted to fit into the saving slot for her employer, who saw the headscarf as evidence of her father's far-away orders, but she ultimately could not fit herself into it.

After this failed experiment, Rana worked out a careful system in which she strategically avoided her boss whenever she had to leave the house and thus don her headscarf. For instance, Rana took Spanish-language classes three days a week, still working toward her goal of becoming a translator. She risked arriving late to her classes because she waited until her boss was napping, in the bathroom, or out with friends to leave the house in her Moroccan-style headscarf without being caught. When Rana told me about this, the stress of sneaking around was wearing on her. She admitted that she had considered giving up and allowing her employers to catch her wearing a headscarf, although she knew this would lead to her being fired, and that it would be nearly impossible to find another job in Granada's faltering economy. Rana conceded that if this happened, she might have to move to another city to avoid joblessness or even homelessness, a risk for migrant women if they lose interna jobs that had also provided them with housing.

The liberation narrative created difficulties for Rana because she was unable to live up to the expectations of the saving slot, ultimately refusing her employer's efforts to save her from imagined patriarchy. Rana's experiences were all too familiar to other women with whom I worked, who were made vulnerable by their roles as (sometimes undocumented) domestic workers. But the enforced victimhood of the saving slot also delegitimized Muslim migrant women who were highly educated and better off than Rana. Soukaina, president of Najma, who enjoyed an unusual degree of mobility across the city and sported an unyielding, can-do attitude with respect to migrant inclusion, struggled to be taken seriously as an intellectual and professional at the University of Granada, where she was an advanced doctoral candidate in the sciences. Because of the liberation narrative, Soukaina's headscarf made her unworthy of professional status in the public sphere, and she often complained that gender stereotypes were the one obstacle she really could not overcome. She spoke angrily about how peers and superiors treated her in her microbiology lab and about her struggles on the job market. Talking about prospective employers, she said,

> You can see it in their faces sometimes. In their tone of voice other times. Because I have a really strong CV. I was the first in my class for four years in a row. I had an "excellent" [the highest grade] in my two research years. And I have seven years of lab experience combined, in three kinds of labs. And as soon as they see you with the veil, just like that, they throw you out the door.

Soukaina sometimes imagined out loud an alternate universe in which she did not wear the hijab and could obtain career success. Continuing her complaint about job discrimination, she fumed, "It's like, 'Ask me an interview question. Give me a contract with no salary for two months and see how I work and *then* judge me, but don't judge me for a piece of cloth. I'm *sure* if I went without a veil, made up, and I changed my name to Cristina! . . . The thing is, underneath this hijab is a brain, a head that thinks!" In all of the time I spent with Soukaina, she faced many high-pressure situations, from altercations with Polígono neighbors at Najma to reining in her rowdy children, and I rarely heard her complain, let alone raise her voice. But by the time Soukaina reached the end of her sentence, she was yelling into my audio recorder.

For Soukaina, disrespect at work was painfully ironic. She sensed that the one thing that would win her public recognition as an intelligent, professional scientist to be taken seriously—removing her headscarf—was also the one thing that would make her feel less like a dignified and valuable member of society according to her own values. For Soukaina, the hijab was a precursor to good involvement in Andalusian public sociality. She said, "I want to go out in the street, and for me, going out with my veil is going out as a person, going out with the right religious consciousness, going out as a citizen. . . . If I try to make myself beautiful for others, then I belong to them. No way! I'm Soukaina and I want to belong to myself. . . . The hijab for me is a spiritual relationship with God." Soukaina wanted to join Andalusian public sociality "in the street" but with the pious practices that made up her sense of dignified personhood and moral citizenship. Thus, despite in many ways personifying the "model migrant" by engaging in all of the practices demanded of migrants by the public—being educated and working hard, becoming involved in local civic life—Soukaina was flummoxed by the way interpretations of her headscarf rendered her visible always and only as a migrant woman in the saving slot: unthinking and unqualified.

CONCLUSION

In the course of interfaith encounters in public space, Andalusians' own embodied norms of public sociality, consumption, and comportment create a culturally specific social space that is difficult for pious Muslims to enter. These embodied norms are deeply rooted in Granada and reflect how profoundly cultural ways of being become naturalized in urban public space (Rotenberg 1992). Socializing in public is especially important to many *Granadinos* because it has become a way of defensively valorizing the forms of sociality that have stigmatized Andalusia as "southern." Pork and wine consumption are rooted in long-standing, Catholic-inflected modes of sociality and in local pride about hospitality and *convivencia*. Public physical affection and sexualized dress are central to efforts to refashion Andalusia as a modern, European space in the wake of its reputation for unmodern, puritanical standards under Franco. As a result, Andalusian embodied norms of sociality are at once naturalized so as to seem normal and unremarkable, and deeply compulsory and heavily enforced when breached. Finally, because gender difference figures prominently in depictions of Andalusia as a semi-Moorish space external to Europe, local anxiety about regional marginalization fosters vigilance of Muslims' gendered practices. In this context, the responsibility for social difference is displaced onto Muslims through a gendered logic, with the liberation narrative casting Muslim women's piety as an obstacle to Muslim inclusion.

Public space thus becomes unwelcoming, even dangerous for Muslims. Along with casual racism, gendered critiques of Islam make public space unnerving for Muslim women in particular. In interfaith encounters framed by the liberation narrative, non-Muslims treat convert women like Yassmin and Clara as dupes or traitors to feminism, and they cast migrant women like Rana as victims expected to accept the saving efforts of employers, NGO workers, and strangers. In these encounters, there is precious little room for attention to Muslim women's diverse and complex engagements with beliefs and practices of Islamic piety and with Spanish and European concepts of freedom and liberty. I have referred to the interactions of Muslims and non-Muslims in this chapter as "embodied encounters" because they are shaped by Andalusians' gendered imaginaries of Islam that focus intently on Muslim women's bodies, and because they reflect the centrality of naturalized bodily practices in Andalusian norms of public social life. Ethnography of these embodied encounters across religious difference illustrates the pain caused by the inability of interfaith encounters to encompass Muslim women's beliefs, thoughts, experiences, and hopes.

In addition to revealing what is omitted by the framing of interfaith encounters, this chapter also highlights the way gendered stereotypes about Islam intersect with women's racial, migratory, and class status in Granada. While convert women are often cast as derelict feminists and migrant Muslims as proto-feminists to be saved, converts are also more able to appease Andalusian feminist sensibilities, and they navigate lower political economic stakes in encounters in which their gender equality is suspect. Migrant Muslim women maneuver within a more risk-filled field of interaction, often facing precarious legal or economic hardship when they do not acquiesce to the expectations and demands of those who wish to rescue them from gendered oppression. Embodied encounters thus reflect and sustain Granada's unequal multiculturalism.

NOTES

1. The politicization of veiling in particular, and Muslim gender norms more broadly, is by no means limited to Western European insistence on this mode of modern subjectivity. This is evident in twentieth-century Bolshevik attempts to eradicate veiling in Uzbekistan (Northrop 2004) and ongoing veiling debates within Muslim-majority, Middle Eastern societies, perhaps most notably Turkey (Secor 2002).

2. When I began the research for this book, I was determined not to write about head-scarves and the topic of Muslim women's gendered practices of piety more generally. At the time, I felt the topic had been well covered by others' scholarship from various angles (Abu-Lughod 1986; Asad 2005; Bowen 2008; Duits and van Zoonen 2006; Hessini 1994; Hoodfar 1997; Kiliç 2008; Mahmood 2005; Scott 2007; Saharso and Lettinga 2008), and since then, recent work has made further inroads on headscarves, Islam, and gender in Europe (e.g., Fernando 2014; Selby 2012). I was concerned that extending academic focus on headscarf controversies and other debates about Islam and gender might simply sustain public and political tendencies to focus on headscarves and gender inequality as emblematic of Muslims' difference, to the exclusion of a vast array of topics shaping Muslims' lives around the world. However, in the course of fieldwork I quickly realized that emergent debates about headscarves and Muslim women's gendered practices were deeply important to my research participants, who broached these topics with me constantly. Eventually, I concluded that to ignore the issue would be to disregard a key social problem motivating my interlocutors' understandings of Islam in Granada.

3. For a comparative analysis of the particularly gendered dimensions of migrant incorporation into northern Spanish urban public space, see Nash et al. (2005) on Barcelona.

4. Official efforts to eradicate gender inequality pay narrow attention to gender at the expense of other kinds of social marginalization, which facilitates thinking about gender as an isolatable dimension of experience. This encourages the construction of simplistic

articulations of "gender" in relation to "culture," which become cornerstones of projects aimed at saving minority women from "their cultures" (e.g., Okin 1999) rather than assessing how racial and religious discrimination intersect with gender discrimination.

5. Here again, scholarship of the region has contributed to its image as a society defined by a Mediterranean honor-shame complex and stark gender imbalances (Driessen 1983; Gilmore 1990; Marvin 1984; Murphy 1983; Pitt-Rivers 1961, 1966).

6. *Botellón* is the augmentative form of the word *botella* (bottle), and literally means a very large bottle.

7. There are cafés in Granada that are essentially coffee shops, and there are tapas bars and shots bars (*chupiterías*) that do not serve coffee, but these are far less common than mixed cafeterías that function as bar-cafés where people go to drink alcohol or to grab a morning coffee and breakfast with equal frequency.

8. Moroccans I worked with also exchange kisses (usually three), but not between men and women.

Conclusion

Granada Moored and Unmoored

Perhaps because I grew up on an island, I have always been unable to hear the words *moro* or *Moor* without thinking of moorings, the docks and buoys used to safely attach boats, preventing them from floating off to sea. An unmoored boat is dangerous—it can crash into things, or become caught in a current and float off indefinitely. Unmooring thus evokes a dangerous dislodging and lack of attachment. These are ideal idioms for thinking about southern Spain, where the growing Muslim population provokes long-standing anxieties about a reinvasion of the Moors that will further unmoor Andalusia from Spain and Europe. Shaped by the Black Legend that cast Spain (especially the south) as racially peripheral to Europe because of its Muslim history, Andalusians have engaged in a long historical process of un-Mooring—of ridding official history of the trappings and tarnish of the Moorish stain. This un-Mooring has been crucial to the project of anchoring the Andalusian region to Spain, and Spain to Europe, ensuring that it is not dangerously cast off into the Mediterranean.

But this is an ambivalent tradition, always accompanied by voices that would rather celebrate than purge the region's Moorish legacy. Movements to embrace Islam—through conversion or simply through political and social expressions of inclusion and support for Muslims and migrants—have become for many people a way of overcoming the Franco era and a much longer history of Castilian suppression of cultural difference, enabling Andalusians to emerge as new kinds of modern, tolerant citizens. These new Andalusians believe a historically rooted love of diversity demonstrates their cosmopolitan Europeanness, or they outright reject European belonging in favor of a Mediterranean-oriented revival of imagined Moorish pasts.

This ambiguity and ambivalence about the connections between historical Moors and contemporary Muslims, and their meanings for the civilizational moorings of Andalusia, Spain, and Europe, provide the slippery grounds on which this ethnography is located. Through ethnography of interfaith encounters and urban social life among Muslim migrants, converts to Islam, and non-Muslim Andalusians, this book has teased apart the kinds of social relations made possible—and constrained—by pervasive historical anxiety about Islam in southern Spain, anxiety that is rekindled and refashioned in the context of a growing Muslim minority in this crisis-stricken, newly democratic region.

Residents of Granada differently memorialize the Moorish past but agree that it provides a font of wisdom and a political reference point for navigating multiculturalism today. Non-Muslim *Granadinos'* expressions of pride in and embarrassment of this past reflect a basic recognition of Islam as integral to city and regional identities. But they also overwhelmingly associate Andalusianness and Spanishness with Catholicism to such an extent that it becomes difficult for converts to establish Muslim selfhoods and communities without losing their "status" as Spaniards or Europeans. The racial, antimigrant undertones of this national-religious identity nexus make it nearly impossible for Muslim migrants and their children to achieve real recognition as citizens of Spain. Unequal multiculturalism—the ways in which convert and migrant Muslims are differently incorporated as minority subjects according to their perceived racial, gender, class, national, and (non)migratory backgrounds—further complicates this picture. Converts are able to confront the challenges of being Muslim in Spain by aligning Islam and conversion with historical memory of medieval cosmopolitanism in a discourse that suits celebratory public remembrance of *al-Andalus*. In contrast, migrants' claims of belonging, articulated in terms of ancestry, prior presence on Andalusian territory, and material contributions to founding the city of Granada, are often taken up as threats to racial purity and sovereignty.

These conundrums of belonging spill into interfaith encounters in public space in the city, shaping the spatialization of racial and religious difference across neighborhoods like the *Albayzín* and the Polígono, each differently constructed as touristy or dangerous Muslim space. They also produce the racialized, religious, and political tensions that simmer among diverse Muslims, whose efforts at public representation become painful reminders of how Islamophobia, Islamophilia, and unequal multiculturalism condition one another. Historical and newer constructions of Muslims as Europe's ultimate other combine with local historical anxiety about Islam, culminating in the raced and gendered communicative breakdowns in which non-Muslims cast convert women as traitors to feminism and migrant Muslim women as savable victims, leaving invisible Andalusians' own embodied norms of public sociality and the exclusions they create. These processes all illuminate how urban practices of historical memory that combine nostalgia with fear help produce ambivalent, racialized, and spatialized inclusion and exclusion of Islam and Muslims. Ethnography that spans distinct city neighborhoods and examines social relations across supposedly distinct social groups has revealed the relationships between historical memory-making and place-making in configurations of Muslim difference in Andalusian urban space.

Ultimately, ambivalence about Andalusian Moorishness and the region's European moorings has dire social and political consequences for Muslims in Granada and beyond. Spain lacks legislation like France's notorious headscarf ban (Fernando 2014) or Germany's well-documented restrictions on refugees (Partridge 2012). Yet even in a context not shaped by legal proscriptions on Islam or strict regulation of migrants and refugees, Muslim life in Granada is as circumscribed as it is celebrated. And while this book has focused on urban social encounters rather than traditional, formal political arenas, the politics of difference produced in these encounters contributes to public perception, shaping fundamental questions about whose humanity is recognized and valued, with consequences for law and policy. One only has to look at Spanish officials' insufficient reactions to the continuous arrival of boatloads of Muslim migrants and refugees every spring and summer—in boats that often capsize and never reach their moorings, leaving thousands dead in the Mediterranean—to see how ambivalence about Islam and migration shapes policy decisions.

Celebration of Islam in Spain has not halted these Mediterranean trage-
dies of migration, which now form part of a globalized drama of death at
the borders between wealthy and impoverished regions of the world (De
León 2015). Nor has it facilitated full inclusion for convert Muslims. Re-
dressing these seemingly intractable political problems requires bringing
ethical complexity to the often life-or-death stakes of Muslims' inclusion
and exclusion. Ethnography across various, overlapping "kinds" of social
difference in a heritage city where Islam is revered and reviled brings that
complexity to conversations about Europe.

CONVERTS, MIGRANTS, AND ANDALUSIANS

The starting point for this book was to move away from a traditional
ethnographic study of Muslim migrants or Muslim converts, to focus
instead on the interfaith encounters between migrants, converts, and
people who identify as Catholic and secular Andalusians, the so-called
host or mainstream society receiving Granada's new Muslims. This approach responds to the need for careful analyses of the social categories
currently in play in political discussions of Islam and migration in Europe. Europeans are by no means a homogeneous block and neither are
Muslims. Andalusia's Islamophilic traditions, Muslim migrants' claims
of rootedness and homecoming, and a growing community of European
convert Muslims suggest far more coincidence *between* the categories
"European" and "Muslim" than is usually assumed. At the same time,
non-Muslim Andalusians' unique preoccupation with (and disagreements
about) their Muslim history, and the pervasive tensions and inequalities
between Granada's Muslim converts and migrants, suggest far *less* coincidence of political identifications and subjectivities *within* the categories
of "European" and "Muslim."

Understanding how historical anxiety about Islam has produced experiences of political abjection and subjectivities of vulnerability among
all residents of Andalusia is crucial to bringing ethical complexity to the
politics of European multiculturalism. The question of Islam's place in
Spain is sometimes framed as a civilizational confrontation between a secular Europe and Islamic world. But examining Muslims' encounters with

Catholic and secular non-migrant Andalusians reveals long-standing, emphatically regional ideas about religious, racial, and ethnic difference. Historical constructions of Islam-as-other to Europe have cast Islam and Moorishness as non-European but also as constitutive of southern Europeans. This points at once to the internal nature of Islam to Europe (even to understandings of Europe as a Christian-secular space) and to the ways that Muslim difference extends to and constructs Andalusians' difference within Europe. The stakes of Muslim inclusion are relevant to Muslims and non-Muslims alike and are as central to the historical construction of different kinds of European as they are to the question of Muslims' place in Europe.

HISTORICAL ANXIETY, POSSIBLE FUTURES, AND IMMEDIATE TENSIONS

Thinking historically enables a new kind of Muslim politics in Europe. It allows converts and migrants to position themselves as always already belonging in southern Spain, as inheritors of Andalusia's former glory— either as sophisticated cosmopolitans in the case of converts, or as diasporic descendants rightly returning to a place their ancestors built in the case of migrants. Using discourses of old, long, slow histories of Mediterranean entanglement, then, allows Muslims in Granada to speed up the temporality of their claims of rootedness—they claim to belong immediately upon arrival from North Africa or to still belong as convert Muslims. This is a fairly unique stance, especially among recent Muslim migrants to Europe, where claims of cultural citizenship and belonging are more common from second- or third-generation migrants. Andalusia is peculiar in the sense that newly arriving Muslim migrants often feel that they are both migrating and coming home. Residents of Granada thus understand relationships between different religious and cultural groups to be temporal questions about the relationship between past and present as well.

In an essay called "Futures of al-Andalus," Gil Anidjar (2006) laments that in the vast scholarly literature, *al-Andalus* almost always figures as an exceptional, closed chapter of interfaith harmony that is unattainable now, its finite nature reified by its constant memorialization. Flipping the conversation, he asks, "What if bearing witness to al-Andalus meant to reconsider its being-past?" (226). In many ways, this book explores his rather philosophical question ethnographically. Anidjar clarifies that his goal is not to assess the facts of history but to "interrogate the meaning and consequences of the repeated affirmation" that *al-Andalus* is over (231). This book has uncovered precisely the "meaning and consequences" of Andalusians' "repeated affirmations" that *al-Andalus* is indeed *not* over at all. Through everyday historiography, my research participants imagine and enact various Muslim and Andalusian pasts, presents, and futures.

My interlocutors' mobilizations of historical memory lead them to new forms of politics, ethics, and possibilities for relationships across social difference. Everyday historiography has become a means to new ways of becoming pious individuals and communities and of constructing Andalusianness. Contemporary religious pluralism also precipitates new ways of cultivating relationships to medieval Iberia and new iterations of long-standing debates about Moorish history. In this sense, the Moorish legacy of Granada is not a historical straitjacket of determination for social life in the present. Rather, novel social relations today imbue historical anxiety with new urgency, meaning, and possibility, even as "the Moorish question" remains a long-standing and enduring frame for questions of Andalusian and Spanish identity and social life (Fuchs 2009). Within a social context structured by such long-term historical memory of Islam, my research participants are making significant changes to their lives, making their homes in a new country or remaking their lives by adopting a new religion.

My focus on historical anxiety thus brings attention not only to *longue-durée* narratives, but also to how people in Granada have begun to think differently about the future. Through their engagements with Moorish history, Muslim converts in Granada are actively creating new spiritual and ethical futures for themselves and their families. They are also constructing new political and cultural visions for the region of Andalusia, the Spanish nation-state, and the Mediterranean as a whole. Converts are moving from Catholicism or avowed atheism to lives shaped by Islamic piety and active engagement with an imagined tolerant, cosmopolitan Andalusian past. The newly Muslim woman Mounira, for instance, drew on her belief in Granada's Muslim past as inspiration for her ongoing project of spiritual renewal and her goal of achieving what she called "eternity with God." Belén saw embracing Islam as a religious path for herself and a political path toward a modern and tolerant Andalusia for her society at large. Migrants lead future-oriented lives as well. Women like Rana arrive in Spain hoping for better economic, educational, and political circumstances and enhanced quality of life for their children. They also want to rebuild Morocco and other countries of origin through remittances. Women like Soukaina actively work to improve the lives of fellow migrants and to reshape *Granadino* society to include Muslims in more city spaces.

Through everyday historiography of medieval Granada, non-Muslim Andalusians also construct engagement with Moorish history as a key determinant of their regional future. Andalusia's place in Europe and the Mediterranean remains (or has returned to being) uncertain today; democracy still feels unfinished for many people, and the economic crisis has upended recent decades' narratives of progress and modernity. The return of high unemployment and labor emigration revives questions of Andalusia's marginality and retraso (slowness), while at the same time the European Union increasingly calls on southern Spain and its Mediterranean neighbors to solve the constantly conflated "southern problems" of migration and terrorism. In this context, Andalusians ask what kind of region southern Spain will become, and where Islam and Muslims can and should fit in.

Thinking about Islam in Andalusia primarily as a question of historical narrative or projected futures, though, lends itself easily to the common scholarly approach of viewing *al-Andalus* as ephemera, as a ghostly dream, a hazy memory, an epistemological provocation, or a longed-for future. In contrast, this ethnography has demonstrated the real, palpable nature of *al-Andalus* and its serious, immediate political consequences. For my research participants, *al-Andalus* figures as a present-day conundrum, a defensive weapon in claims of cosmopolitanism and multiculturalism, or as a raw reminder of the rest of Spain's and Europe's disdain.

After Andalusian regional elections in March 2015 failed to bring together an obvious consensus government, an op-ed piece in the local newspaper *El Diario* bemoaned the rest of Spain's disparaging response to the Andalusian political process (2015). The author used the neologism

"Andaluzfobia" to describe Spanish national discussions of Andalusian elections, in a nod to Islamophobia that evokes the way perceptions of Moorishness color Spanish views of Andalusia. Responding to northern critiques of the southern election, including ever-present poking fun at Andalusian Spanish, the author retorted that those with racist views of southern Spain would do well to recognize the irony of critiquing Andalusian accents when much of the Castilian Spanish vocabulary is inherited from the Arabic of *al-Andalus*. Scores of readers contributed to the comments section of the article, and the online discussion devolved almost immediately from comments about contemporary Andalusian electoral politics to a discussion of the religious, cultural, and linguistic legacies of medieval Iberian Islam—the connections between these and recent elections taken for granted as obvious by participants. Some commentators accepted the idea of Andalusia's difference. They celebrated the Moorish legacy as Andalusia's unique cultural triumph, proudly refusing to be measured by the political standards of Madrid. Others denied the influence of Moorish heritage on Andalusian culture, language, or modern politics. The fact that a discussion of regional midterm elections could cede so easily to a fierce debate about Muslim history and its legacy in Andalusia reveals the tangible import of such questions for social and political life today.

CULTURAL INTIMACY AND MEDITERRANEAN SCALES OF BELONGING

This episode also speaks to the politicized role of cultural intimacy in Andalusian deliberations about Islam, which are linked to various scales of geographic and political belonging. My interlocutors saw the question of Islam in Granada as intensely local, sometimes even claiming city ownership over the Moorish legacy. Yet the local history that people turn to in discussions of Islam is also a regional one of movement across the Mediterranean. People living in Andalusia, a southern European periphery, orient their lives and politics in subnational directions (toward Andalusia rather than the Spanish nation-state) and in supranational directions that remain regional, rather than global (toward the Mediterranean, rather than global humanity). The Andalusian case thus shows how regional scales of belonging can crosscut the ever-assumed local-global dyad of social analysis. At the same time, globally circulating discourses about Islam *do* shape Andalusians' regional understanding of the place of Islam in society, and global economic structures propel the movement of people from all over the globe (including labor migrants and tourists from around the world) to Granada. My research participants—Muslim and non-Muslim alike—are hyperaware of outsiders looking in.

The contrasting ways Granada figures in locals' somewhat apocryphal stories about outsiders' interest in the city illustrates this dynamic. One day in the early 2000s, I took a guided tour of the *Albayzín* that began in the upper reaches of the neighborhood, near the construction lot that would later become the Mezquita Mayor, and wound downward to the Moorish-themed tourism center of the lower *Albayzín*. Along the way, we stopped periodically to hear brief lectures about the architectural, agricultural, and infrastructural innovations of the Moors—each medieval fountain, drainage ditch, and archway lauded as a sign of the civilizational achievements of *al-Andalus*. The highlight of our tour was a stop at the Mirador de San Nicolás, the public square and lookout point from which one can stand in the *Albayzín* and gaze at the Alhambra and the mountains behind it. When we got there, we were told by our proud tour guide that Bill Clinton had recently named this precise spot his favorite in all of Spain, and possibly Europe. The guide was visibly moved that a personality of the stature of Clinton had lavished praise on the city, particularly San Nicolás, which many locals see as the ultimate space for appreciating the city's Moorish legacy.

But Bill Clinton is not the only globally known public figure whose opinions about Granada circulate among locals. Waiting for a bus downtown one day, I chatted with two Catholic Andalusian friends, Lucía and Alma. We were facing away from the street, gazing uphill at the tip-tops of the *Albayzín's* Moorish-style houses visible from our bus stop near the border between the *Albayzín* and downtown. Lucía asked if we knew about the rumor that Granada was Osama bin Laden's favorite city in the world. I did not, but Alma said yes, that the way she'd heard it, Granada was his favorite place in Europe. Bin Laden had a weakness for a certain very expensive hotel next door to the Alhambra and would periodically rent out the entire hotel so that he could bring harems there, she said. Both women were certain this was true, and seemed equal parts horrified and titillated. I had previously lived in Granada shortly after the attacks of September 11, 2001, and rumors had swirled around the city that year that Granada, as an emblem of lost, former Muslim territory, "was next" on terrorists' minds. Lucía and Alma shuddered at the idea of bin Laden's possible presence in the city, even as they seemed proud that bin Laden's interest in Granada somehow confirmed its desirability as a site of Muslim opulence and authenticity.

In the *Albayzín* tour guide's Bill Clinton anecdote, the sophistication and civilizational glory of *al-Andalus* were enshrined in the contemporary neighborhood's materiality and given the stamp of approval by a man who symbolizes the power of the liberal Western world. Clinton's admiration for the *Albayzín* cemented the success of the legacy of *convivencia*—Granada's Moorish difference was desirable in the best possible way; its authenticity facilitated Islamophilia, a productive tourist economy, and approval from the tolerant, liberal West. In the second story, bin Laden's admiration for the *Albayzín* forewarned of the possible failure of *convivencia*. Here, Granada's Moorish difference was desirable but in the worst possible way, its authenticity providing grounds for terrorism, facilitating the specter of fundamentalist violence and territorial attack. Both urban legends reveal residents' understandings of Granada as a central node in global conversations about the relationship between a so-called Muslim world and an imagined non-Muslim "West." Both stories are about globally symbolic actors' appreciation of Granada, evoking its grand civilizational meaning and importance. In emphasizing outside figures' evaluations of the city, these stories reflect how pride and vigilance over outsiders' perceptions of Granada shape *Granadinos*' ambivalence about Islam.

Granadinos are quite correct in their belief that outsiders are paying attention to their city and to Islam in Spain more broadly, lending global stakes to questions of Muslim inclusion and exclusion there. For instance, Hisham Aídi (2003, 2014) has documented the global reach of *al-Andalus*, not just among emblematic figures like Clinton and bin Laden but also among Arab and Muslim poets, Latin American anticolonial heroes, contemporary Latino Muslim convert musicians, and Muslim

European youth, who all invoke in various ways the idea of Moorish heritage in their spiritual and artistic projects as well as in movements for racial and social justice. Jonathan Shannon (2015) and Jonathan Glasser (2016) have also described the widespread rhetorical deployment of the idea of *al-Andalus* in modern global discourses of difference and belonging among popular musicians across the Middle East and Mediterranean, with diverse political outcomes.

ISLAMOPHOBIA, ISLAMOPHILIA, AND AMBIVALENCE ABOUT DIFFERENCE

How are we to make sense of this global resonance of Islam in southern Spain? The historical anxiety and ambivalence about Islam that shape this book reflect powerful desires among local residents and global observers alike to see Andalusia as a harbinger of doom or a beacon of hope. These projections reflect a long history of philosophical and political thinking about the Mediterranean as a crossroads, a source of idealized multiculturalism ripe for emulation or a site of dangerous mixing, racial-cultural dilution, and impending conflict (Silverstein 2004). Like other areas on the periphery of Europe, southern Spain "appears either as a linking bridge or as a dividing fault line between civilizational complexes" (Ballinger 1999, 1).

These concerns have important ramifications beyond the world of scholarship and beyond Spain. Among scholars, politicians, activists, culture workers, minorities, and other citizens and residents who care about creating a more inclusive Europe, there exists a tremendous temptation to view interfaith relations in Spain, past and present, as a symbol of hope. Sparks of excitement about successful multiculturalism animate my conversations with interlocutors in academic and nonacademic circles in Europe and in the United States. During the Arab Spring, an Egyptian colleague exclaimed how "important" the topic of Islam in Spain was, for its ability to showcase the peaceful nature of Islam, so crucial today as North Africans and Middle Easterners struggle for democracy and face international skepticism about "Arab" and "Muslim" violence. American Jewish and Palestinian students are similarly excited to talk about interfaith peace in medieval Spain as a counterpoint to and relief from the sadness of the ongoing conflict in Israel-Palestine. Others take the opposite approach; assuming that an anthropologist researching Islam in Spain must have expertise in "fundamentalism," they ask questions about terrorism or medieval interfaith strife, revealing a prevalent tendency in public political discourse to equate Islam with violence and interfaith or intercultural interaction with inevitable conflict. In the face of such intense efforts to seize Andalusia as a comforting or cautionary metonym for interfaith connections, always overlain with grasping for *al-Andalus*, this ethnography reveals a more complex picture of the intertwined nature of inclusion and exclusion.

The idea of Andalusia as a bastion of tolerance is appealing. But many of my research participants experience the legacy of *al-Andalus* in Granada in terms of painful ostracism. Native-born Andalusians recall with stung pride how they were rebuffed in job interviews in Catalonia, sure their rejection was based on perceived regional or racial difference from northern Spain. Converts are cast out of their Catholic families or rejected by secular coworkers. Migrant Muslim women face financial hardship or even homelessness when they are refused jobs, service, or educational opportunities for wearing headscarves. They find themselves reeling from unanticipated conflict with convert women who question their "ethnic" practices of piety. Undocumented Moroccan men are fearful of local police, and the falafel shop owner Khadija, who struggled with illegality, eventually disappeared from the *Albayzín*.

Scholarly and pundit celebrations of the exceptionalism of Spain's legal provisions for Muslims and migrants also ignore the racialized workings of Spanish governance and NGOs, where legal provisions for health care, educational benefits, and housing are doled out asymmetrically according to hierarchies of race and religion, never living up to the inclusive goals of the laws themselves (Rogozen-Soltar 2012a). Muslim mothers express desperation at the exclusion of halal food options from public schools. Migrant Muslims marvel at the difficulty of obtaining or maintaining legal residence status and dignified working conditions. These frustrations reveal the shortcomings of claims of Spanish exceptionalism. Uncritical rejoicing about such exceptionalism easily becomes a liberal fantasy of inclusion that masks the pervasive inequalities revealed by detailed ethnography.

On the other hand, it is equally inadequate to depict Europe as a homogeneous, exclusionary region entirely inhospitable to Muslims, or only inclusive of Muslims as marginal migrant labor or as potential extremists to be carefully managed, regulated, or cunningly turned into profitable relics of heritage tourism. This ethnography has revealed genuine moves toward full inclusion of Muslims that take place on a daily basis. Despite their limitations, Catholic Andalusians spend countless hours volunteering in antiracism NGOs, certain that their great-grandparents' Moorish heritage was a blessing and an imperative to defend the rights of Muslims today. Moroccans insist that in spite of daily discrimination, they feel prideful ownership over the *Albayzín* and take comfort in the familiar Moorish architecture of Granada's urban landscape, which sometimes allows them to feel at home. Converts express deep gratitude for Islam, because finding the faith has brought them a long-desired spiritual path and a way of making sense of their place in the world.

This relationship between Islamophobia and Islamophilia, or Muslim inclusion and exclusion, is more than one of coexistence between two poles. I began this book by describing *Granadinos'* major idioms for discussing these processes, the tropes of Granada's *convivencia* and *malafollá*, the first referring to Granada as the world's most successful site of harmony across religious and cultural difference, and the second casting the city as habitually unfriendly, characterized by inhospitality. I asked why residents of Granada focused on interfaith and cross-cultural relationships in discussions of their city's ethos and identity, and why they spoke of approaches to Muslim and migrant difference in such contrasting ways. Ultimately, *convivencia* and *malafollá* in Granada are not dueling forces but rather are inherent to one another. Ambivalence, always shaped by historical memory and cultural intimacy, is etched into both inclusive and exclusionary social processes.

This mutuality is present in all of the urban social encounters that make up this book. Heritage tourism in the *Albayzín*, for example, facilitates an urban space for Muslim migrant men's sociality, carving out a small corner of the city where Muslims can enjoy the iftar meal of Ramadan in public. But the same tourism industry commodifies Islam and Arabness and contributes to Muslims' racialization and criminalization. Andalusians concerned with recuperating a tolerant politics and social ethic are often spiritually and aesthetically drawn to Islam through their interaction with the Moorish-built city of Granada. But while their enthusiasm for Islam successfully challenges binary divisions between "Europeans" and "Muslims," the broader societal rejection of Islam creates a context of fear and vulnerability in which converts sometimes shun their fellow Muslims, leaving migrants out of celebrations of Islam in Spain. Yet even in the midst of tensions wrought by unequal multiculturalism, convert and migrant Muslims enjoy moments in which a shared desire to support fellow Muslims around the world and make space for Islamic presence in Europe led them to set their differences aside. Several times during my fieldwork, converts and migrants joined one another and non-Muslim activists in the streets to march for justice for Palestinians, a popular public cause in Spain.

Both *convivencia* and *malafollá* exist in Granada, but more importantly, each infuses the other. Similar versions of this dynamic likely shape social life in regional peripheries around the world. It is easy to assume that political effectiveness or persuasive analytics require a blunt, forceful insistence on inclusion or exclusion as characteristic of social relationships. But a richer understanding of the politics of multiculturalism, the kind of understanding necessary for building a truly successful politics of peace that can support a real place for justice and belonging for Muslims, requires embracing the intellectual discomfort of carefully, ethnographically untangling the imbrication of *convivencia* and *malafollá* at the margins of Europe.

BIBLIOGRAPHY

20 Minutos. 2009. "Una Diputada del PP Afirma que el Acento de Magdalena Álvarez es 'de Chiste.'" 20 Minutos. January 12.

ABC (Sevilla). 2011. "Marruecos Pide a España la Mitad de los Ingresos de la Alhambra." ABC Sevilla. August 10, 2011.

———. 2014. "Los Alarmantes Datos de Paro Juvenil en Andalucía que Llamaron la Atención del Papa." May 28, 2014. ABC. http://sevilla.abc.es/economia/20140527 /sevi-datos-paro-andalucia-201405271320.html.

Abu-Lughod, Lila. 1986. *Veiled Sentiments: Honor and Poetry in a Bedouin Society*. Berkeley: University of California Press.

———. 2002. "Do Muslim Women Really Need Saving? Anthropological Reflections on Cultural Relativism and Its Others." *American Anthropologist* 104(3): 783–790.

———. 2013. *Do Muslim Women Need Saving?* Cambridge, MA: Harvard University Press.

Agencias. 2006. "El PSOE Critica la Actitud 'Irresponsible' de Aznar con sus Declaraciones Sobre el Islam." *El Pais*. September 23, 2006.

Aguilar, Paloma. 2002. *Memory and Amnesia: The Role of the Spanish Civil War in the Transition to Democracy*. London: Berghahn Books.

Ahmad, Attiya. 2010. "Explanation Is Not the Point: Domestic Work, Islamic Dawa and Becoming Muslim in Kuwait." *Asia Pacific Journal of Anthropology* 11: 293–310.

Ahmed, Leila. 1992. *Women and Gender in Islam: Historical Roots of a Modern Debate*. New Haven, CT: Yale University Press.

Aídi, Hisham. 2003. "Let Us Be Moors: Islam, Race, and 'Connected Histories.'" *Middle East Report*. 42–53.

———. 2014. *Rebel Music: Race, Empire, and the New Muslim Youth Culture*. New York: Pantheon Books.

Andersen, Bengt, and Heidi Biseth. 2013. "The Myth of Failed Integration: The Case of Eastern Oslo." *City and Society* 25(1): 5–24.

Andersson, Ruben. 2014. *Illegality, Inc.: Clandestine Migration and the Business of Bordering Europe*. Berkeley: University of California Press.

Anidjar, Gil. 2006. "Futures of al-Andalus." *Journal of Spanish Cultural Studies* 7(3): 225–239.

Arango, Joaquín. 2000. "Becoming a Country of Immigration at the End of the Twentieth Century: The Case of Spain." In *Eldorado or Fortress? Migration in Southern Europe*, edited by Russell King, Gabriella Lazaridis, and Charalambos Tsardanidis, 253–276. New York: Palgrave Macmillan.

Ardener, Edwin. 2012. "Remote Areas: Some Theoretical Considerations." *HAU: Journal of Ethnographic Theory* 2(1): 519–533. [Reprint].

Arendt, Hannah. 1991 [1951]. "The Decline of the Nation-State and the End of the Rights of Man." In *The Origins of Totalitarianism*, edited by Hannah Arendt. New York: Meridian Books.

Arigita, Elena. 2006. "Representing Islam in Spain: Muslim Identities and the Contestation of Leadership." *Muslim World* 96: 563–584.

———. 2009. "Spain: The Al-Andalus Legacy." In *The Borders of Islam: Exploring Samuel Huntington's Faultlines, from Al-Andalus to the Virtual Ummah*, edited by Stig Jarle Hansen, Atle Mesoy, and Tuncay Kardas, 223–234. New York: Columbia University Press.

Arkin, Kimberly. 2014. *Rhinestones, Religion, and the Republic: Fashioning Jewishness in France*. Stanford, CA: Stanford University Press.

Asad, Talal. 2003. *Formations of the Secular: Christianity, Islam, Modernity*. Stanford, CA: Stanford University Press.

———. 2005. "Reflections on Laïcité and the Public Sphere." *Social Science Research Council Items and Issues* 5(3): 1–11.

Astor, Avi. 2012. "Memory, Community, and Opposition to Mosques: The Case of Badalona." *Theory and Society* 41(4): 325–349.

Auslander, Leora. 2000. "Bavarian Crucifixes and French Headscarves: Religious Signs and the Postmodern European State." *Cultural Dynamics* 12(3): 283–309.

Baker, Catherine. 2008. "Wild Dances and Dying Wolves: Simulation, Essentialization, and National Identity at the Eurovision Song Contest." *Popular Communication* 6(3): 173–189.

Balibar, Étienne. 1991. "Is There a 'Neo-Racism'?" In *Race, Nation, Class: Ambiguous Identities*, edited by Étienne Balibar and Immanuel Wallerstein, 17–28. London: Verso Books.

Ballinger, Pamela. 1999. "Definitional Dilemmas: Southeastern Europe as 'Culture Area.'" *Balkanologie: Revue d'Études Pluridisciplinaires* 3(2). http://balkanologie.revues.org/745.

———. 2003. *History in Exile: Memory and Identity at the Borders of the Balkans*. Princeton, NJ: Princeton University Press.

Beck, Lauren. 2012. "Moros en la Costa: Islam in Spanish Visual and Media Culture." *Historia Actual Online* 29: 93–106.

Beckwith, Stacy, ed. 2000. *Charting Memory: Recalling Medieval Spain*. New York: Garland.

Behar, Ruth. 1991. *The Presence of the Past in a Spanish Village*. Princeton, NJ: Princeton University Press.

Ben-Yehoyada, Naor. 2011. "The Moral Perils of Mediterraneanism: Second-Generation Immigrants Practicing Personhood between Sicily and Tunisia." *Journal of Modern Italian Studies* 16(3): 386–403.

———. 2014. "Transnational Political Cosmology: A Central Mediterranean Example." *Comparative Studies in Society and History* 56(4): 870–901.

Berg, Mette. 2011. *Diasporic Generations: Memory, Politics, and Nation among Cubans in Spain*. New York: Berghahn Books.

Besteman, Catherine. 2016. *Making Refuge: Somali Bantu Refugees and Lewiston, Maine*. Durham, NC: Duke University Press.

Bledsoe, Caroline, and Papa Sow. 2011. "Family Reunification Ideals and the Practice of Transnational Reproductive Life among Africans in Europe." In *Reproduction, Globalization, and the State: New Theoretical and Ethnographic Perspectives*, edited by Carole Browner and Carolyn Sargent, 175–190. Durham, NC: Duke University Press.

Boehm, Deborah. 2012. *Intimate Migrations: Gender, Family, and Illegality among Transnational Mexicans*. New York: New York University Press.

———. 2016. *Returned: Going and Coming in an Age of Deportation*. Berkeley: University of California Press.

Borneman, John, and Nick Fowler. 1997. "Europeanization." *Annual Review of Anthropology* 26: 487–514.

Boum, Aomar. 2012. "The Performance of Convivencia: Communities of Tolerance and the Reification of Toleration." *Religion Compass* 6(3): 174–184.

Bourdieu, Pierre. 1977. *Outline of a Theory of Practice*. Cambridge: Cambridge University Press.

Bowen, John. 2008. *Why the French Don't Like Headscarves: Islam, the State, and Public Space*. Princeton, NJ: Princeton University Press.

———. 2010. *Can Islam Be French?: Pluralism and Pragmatism in a Secularist State*. Princeton, NJ: Princeton University Press.

Boym, Svetlana. 2001. *The Future of Nostalgia*. New York: Basic Books.

Brown, Jacqueline Nassy. 2005. *Dropping Anchor, Setting Sail: Geographies of Race in Black Liverpool*. Princeton, NJ: Princeton University Press.

Brown, Wendy. 2006. *Regulating Aversion: Tolerance in the Age of Identity and Empire*. Princeton, NJ: Princeton University Press.

Bubandt, Nils. 2009. "Gold for a Golden Age: Sacred Money and Islamic Freedom in a Global Sufi Order." *Social Analysis* 53(1): 103–122.

Buggenhagen, Beth. 2012. *Muslim Families in Global Senegal: Money Takes Care of Shame*. Bloomington: Indiana University Press.

Bunzl, Matti. 2005. "Between Anti-Semitism and Islamophobia: Some Thoughts on the New Europe." *American Ethnologist* 32(4): 499–508.

Bustelo, María, and Candice Ortbals. 2007. "The Evolution of Spanish State Feminism: A Fragmented Landscape." In *Changing State Feminism*, edited by Joyce Outshoorn and Johanna Kantola, 201–223. New York: Palgrave Macmillan.

Cabot, Heath. 2013. "The Social Aesthetics of Eligibility: NGO Aid and Indeterminacy in the Greek Asylum Process." *American Ethnologist* 40(3): 452–466.

———. 2014. *On the Doorsteps of Europe: Asylum and Citizenship in Greece*. Philadelphia: University of Pennsylvania Press.

Cagal, Ayse. 1997. "Hyphenated Identities and the Limits of 'Culture.'" In *The Politics of Multiculturalism in the New Europe*, edited by Tariq Modood and Pnina Werbner, 169–185. London: Zed Books.

Calavita, Kitty. 2003. "A 'Reserve Army of Delinquents': The Criminalization and Economic Punishment of Immigrants in Spain." *Punishment and Society* 5(4): 399–413.

———. 2005. *Immigrants at the Margins: Law, Race, and Exclusion in Southern Europe.* Cambridge: Cambridge University Press.

Calderwood, Eric. 2014. "The Invention of al-Andalus: Discovering the Past and Creating the Present in Granada's Islamic Tourism Sites." *Journal of North African Studies* 19(1): 27–55.

Calvo, Erena, and Reyes Gómez. 2011. "Marruecos Niega que Haya Reclamado los Ingresos de la Alhambra." *El Mundo.* August 10.

Calvo, Kerman, and Irene Mart. 2009. "Ungrateful Citizens? Women's Rights Policies in Zapatero's Spain." *South European Society and Politics* 4: 487–502.

Candea, Matei. 2006. "Resisting Victimhood in Corsica." *History and Anthropology* 17(4): 369–384.

———. 2010. *Corsican Fragments: Difference, Knowledge, and Fieldwork.* Bloomington: Indiana University Press.

Carr, Raymond, and Juan Pablo Fusi, eds. 1981. *Spain: Dictatorship to Democracy.* London: Allen and Unwin.

Carter, Donald. 1997. *States of Grace: Senegalese in Italy and the New European Immigration.* Minneapolis: University of Minnesota Press.

Castro, Américo. 1977 [1948]. *España en Su Historia: Cristianos, Moros y Judíos.* Buenos Aires: Editorial Losada.

Catlos, Brian. 2002. "Contexto y Conveniencia en la Corona de Aragón: Propuesta de un Modelo de Interacción entre Grupos Etno-religiosos Minoritarios y Mayoritarios." *Revista d'Història Medieval* 12: 259–268.

Chavez, Leo. 2008. *The Latino Threat Narrative: Constructing Immigrants, Citizens, and the Nation.* Stanford, CA: Stanford University Press.

Chua, Liana. 2012. *The Christianity of Culture: Conversion, Ethnic Citizenship, and the Matter of Religion in Malaysian Borneo.* New York: Palgrave Macmillan.

Chuse, Loren. 2003. *The Cantaoras: Music, Gender, and Identity in Flamenco Song.* New York: Routledge.

Cole, Jeffrey. 1997. *The New Racism in Europe: A Sicilian Ethnography.* Cambridge: Cambridge University Press.

Cole, Jennifer. 2014. "The Teléphone Malgache: Transnational Gossip and Social Transformation among Malagasy Marriage Migrants to France." *American Ethnologist* 41(2): 276–289.

Colectivo IOÉ. 1996. *La Educación Intercultural a Prueba: Hijos de Inmigrantes Marroquíes en la Escuela.* Laboratorio de Estudios Interculturales. Universidad de Granada.

———. 2012. *Impactos de la Crisis sobre la Población Inmigrante.* Madrid: Colectivo Ioé and Organización Internacional para las Migraciones.

Coleman, David. 2008. "The Persistence of the Past in the Albaicín: Granada's New Mosque and the Question of Historical Relevance." In *In the Light of Medieval Spain: Islam, the West, and the Relevance of the Past,* edited by Simon R. Doubleday and David Coleman, 157–188. New York: Palgrave Macmillan.

Coleman, Stephen. 2008. "Why Is the Eurovision Song Contest Ridiculous? Exploring a Spectacle of Embarrassment, Irony, and Identity." *Popular Communication* 6(3): 127–140.

Collier, Jane. 1997. *From Duty to Desire: Remaking Families in a Spanish Village.* Princeton, NJ: Princeton University Press.

Comaroff, Jean, and John L. Comaroff. 1991. *Of Revelation and Revolution, Volume I: Christi-anity, Colonialism, and Consciousness in South Africa.* Chicago: University of Chicago Press.
———. 2009. *Ethnicity, Inc.* Chicago: University of Chicago Press.
Cornelius, Wayne. 2004. "Spain: The Uneasy Transition from Labor Exporter to Labor Importer." In *Controlling Immigration: A Global Perspective,* 2nd ed., edited by Wayne Cornelius, Takeyuki Tsuda, and James Hollifield, 385–428. Stanford, CA: Stanford University Press.
Coutin, Susan. 2003. "Cultural Logics of Belonging and Movement: Transnationalism, Naturalization, and U.S. Immigration Politics." *American Ethnologist* 30(4): 508–526.
———. 2007. *Nations of Emigrants: Shifting Boundaries of Citizenship in El Salvador and the United States.* Ithaca, NY: Cornell University Press.
Crain, Mary. 1997. "The Remaking of an Andalusian Pilgrimage Tradition: Debates Re-garding Visual (Re)presentation and the Meanings of 'Locality' in a Global Era." In *Culture, Power, Place: Explorations in Critical Anthropology,* edited by Akhil Gupta and James Ferguson, 291–311. Durham, NC: Duke University Press.
Cruces-Roldán, Cristina. 2003. *El Flamenco y la Música Andalusí: Argumentos para un Encuentro.* Barcelona: Ediciones Carena.
Dávila, Arlene. 2001. *Latinos, Inc.: The Marketing and Making of a People.* Berkeley: Univer-sity of California Press.
Deeb, Lara. 2006. *An Enchanted Modern: Gender and Public Piety in Shi'i Islam.* Princeton, NJ: Princeton University Press.
De Genova, Nicholas. 2002. *Race, Space, and "Illegality" in Mexican Chicago.* Durham, NC: Duke University Press.
———. 2005. *Working the Boundaries: Race, Space, and "Illegality" in Mexican Chicago.* Durham, NC: Duke University Press.
DeGuzmán, María. 2005. *Spain's Long Shadow: The Black Legend, Off-Whiteness, and Anglo-American Empire.* Minneapolis: University of Minnesota Press.
De León, Jason. 2015. *The Land of Open Graves: Living and Dying on the Migrant Trail.* Berkeley: University of California Press.
Dietz, Gunther, ed. 2000. *El Desafío de la Interculturalidad: El Voluntariado y Las ONG ante el Reto de la Inmigración: El Caso de la Ciudad de Granada.* Granada, Spain: Fundación La Caixa.
Dietz, Gunther. 2004. "Frontier Hybridisation or Culture Clash? Transnational Migrant Communities and Sub-National Identity Politics in Andalusia, Spain." *Journal of Ethnic and Migration Studies* 30(6): 1087–1112.
Díez De Velasco, Francisco. 2010. "The Visibilization of Religious Minorities in Spain." *Social Compass* 57(2): 235–252.
Doubleday, Simon, and David Coleman, eds. 2008. *In the Light of Medieval Spain: Islam, the West, and the Relevance of the Past.* New York: Palgrave Macmillan.
Driessen, Henk. 1983. "Male Sociability and Rituals of Masculinity in Rural Andalusia." *Anthropological Quarterly* 56(3): 125–133.
Duits, Linda, and van Zoonen, Liesbet. 2006. "Headscarves and Porno-Chic: Disciplin-ing Girls' Bodies in the European Multicultural Society." *European Journal of Women's Studies* 13: 103–117.
Edles, Laura Desfor. 1998. *Symbol and Ritual in the New Spain: The Transition to Democracy after Franco.* Cambridge: Cambridge University Press.

Egea Jiménez, Carmen, et al. 2009. "Viejas y Nuevas Realidades Urbanas. Identificación de Zonas de Habitalidad Desfavorecida en la Ciudad de Granada." *Cuadernos Geográficos* 45: 83–105.

El Diario. 2015. "Andalucía Sólo Hay Una, y Menos Mal." Zona Crítica, May 3. http://www.eldiario.es/zonacritica/Barbijaputa-andaluzfobia_6_363323689.html.

El Hamel, Chouki. 2013. *Black Morocco: A History of Slavery, Race, and Islam*. Cambridge: Cambridge University Press.

Elinson, Alexander. 2009. *Looking Back at al-Andalus: The Poetics of Loss and Nostalgia in Medieval Arabic and Hebrew Literature*. Leiden, Netherlands: Brill.

Ellwood, Sheelagh. 1995. "The Extreme Right in Spain: A Dying Species." In *The Far Right in Western and Eastern Europe*, edited by Ronnie Ferguson, Luciano Cheles, and Michalina Vaughan. New York: Longman.

Encarnación, Omar. 2004. "The Politics of Immigration: Why Spain Is Different." *Mediterranean Quarterly* 15(4): 167–185.

Engelke, Matthew. 2004. "Discontinuity and the Discourse of Conversion." *Journal of Religion in Africa* 34(1/2): 82–109.

———. 2012. "Angels in Swindon: Public Religion and Ambient Faith in England." *American Ethnologist* 39(1): 155–170.

Ewing, Katherine. 2008. *Stolen Honor: Stigmatizing Muslim Men in Berlin*. Stanford, CA: Stanford University Press.

Feldman, Ilana. 2008. "Refusing Invisibility: Documentation and Memorialization in Palestinian Refugee Claims." *Journal of Refugee Studies* 21(4): 498–516.

Fernandez, James. 1988. "Andalusia on Our Minds: Two Contrasting Places in Spain as Seen in a Vernacular Poetic Duel of the Late 18th Century." *Cultural Anthropology* 3(1): 21–35.

Fernando, Mayanthi. 2010. "Reconfiguring Freedom: Muslim Piety and the Limits of Secular Law and Public Discourse in France." *American Ethnologist* 37(1): 19–35.

———. 2014. *The Republic Unsettled: Muslim French and the Contradictions of Secularism*. Durham, NC: Duke University Press.

Ferrándiz, Francisco. 2008. "Cries and Whispers: Exhuming and Narrating Defeat in Spain Today." *Journal of Spanish Cultural Studies* 9(2): 177–192.

Fikes, Kesha. 2009. *Managing African Portugal: The Citizen-Migrant Distinction*. Durham, NC: Duke University Press.

Flesler, Daniela. 2008a. "Contemporary Moroccan Immigration and Its Ghosts." In *In the Light of Medieval Spain: Islam, the West, and the Relevance of the Past*, edited by Simon Doubleday and David Coleman, 115–132. New York: Palgrave Macmillan.

———. 2008b. *The Return of the Moor: Spanish Responses to Contemporary Moroccan Immigration*. West Lafayette, IN: Purdue University Press.

Flesler, Daniela, and Adrián Pérez Melgosa. 2003. "Battles of Identity, or Playing 'Guest' and 'Host': The Festivals of Moors and Christians in the Context of Moroccan Immigration in Spain." *Journal of Spanish Cultural Studies* 4(2): 151–168.

Fletcher, Richard. 2006. *Moorish Spain*. Berkeley: University of California Press.

Frayer, Lauren. 2014. "Food for Thought: At Last, Muslims Can Savor a Halal Spin on Spain's Famous Jamón." *The Salt*. National Public Radio. December 16.

Frekko, Susan. 2009. "'Normal' in Catalonia: Standard Language, Enregisterment and the Imagination of a National Public." *Language in Society* 38(1): 71–93.

Fuchs, Barbara. 2002. "Virtual Spaniards: The Moriscos and the Fictions of Spanish Identity." *Journal of Spanish Cultural Studies* 4(2): 13–36.

———. 2009. *Exotic Nation: Maurophilia and the Construction of Early Modern Spain.* Philadelphia: University of Pennsylvania Press.

García-Cano Torrico, María. 2004. *Formación para el Trabajo en Contextos de Inmigración: El Caso de la Cidudad de Málaga.* Málaga, Spain: Ediciones Aljibe.

García Castaño, Francisco, ed. 2000. *Fiesta, Tradición, Cambio.* Granada: Proyecto Sur Ediciones.

García Sánchez, Inmaculada. 2014. *Language and Muslim Immigrant Childhoods: The Politics of Belonging.* Malden, MA: Wiley Blackwell.

Ghodsee, Kristen. 2009. *Muslim Lives in Eastern Europe: Gender, Ethnicity, and the Transformation of Islam in Postsocialist Bulgaria.* Princeton, NJ: Princeton University Press.

Gilmore, David. 1990. "Men and Women in Southern Spain: 'Domestic Power' Revisited." *American Anthropologist* 92(4): 953–970.

Gilroy, Paul. 1990. "The End of Anti-Racism." *New Community* 17(1): 71–83.

———. 1995. *The Black Atlantic: Modernity and Double Consciousness.* Cambridge, MA: Harvard University Press.

Glasser, Jonathan. 2016. "Andalusi Musical Origins at the Moroccan-Algerian Frontier: Beyond Charter Myth." *American Ethnologist* 42(4): 720–733.

Glick Schiller, Nina, Linda Basch, and Cristina Szanton Blanc, eds. 1995. "From Immigrant to Transmigrant: Theorizing Transnational Migration." *Anthropological Quarterly* 68(1): 48–63.

González Alcantud, José Antonio. 2005. *La Ciudad Vórtice: Lo Local, Lugar Fuerte de la Memoria en Tiempos de Errancia.* Barcelona: Anthropos Editorial.

———. 2011. "Social Memory of a World Heritage site: The Alhambra of Granada." *International Social Science Journal* 62(203–204): 179–197.

Goytisolo, Juan. 1981. *Crónicas Sarracinas.* La Coruña: Rueda Ibérico.

Granados, Antolin. 2004. "El Tratamiento de la Inmigración Marroquí en la Prensa Española." In *Atlas de la Inmigración Marroquí en España*, edited by Bárnabe López García and Mohamed Berriane, 438–439. Taller de Estudios Internacionales Mediterráneos. Madrid: Universidad Autónoma de Madrid Ediciones.

Gray, Lila Ellen. 2013. *Fado Resounding: Affective Politics and Urban Life.* Durham, NC: Duke University Press.

Guia, Aitana. 2014. *The Muslim Struggle for Civil Rights in Spain: Promoting Democracy Through Migrant Engagement, 1985–2010.* Brighton, UK: Sussex Academic Press.

Gutiérrez, Fernando Fernández, and Francisco Jiménez Bautista. 2000. "Preferencias, Conflictos y Usos Territoriales en la Ciudad de Granada." *Cuadernos Geográficos* 30: 263–279.

Harris, Max. 2000. *Aztecs, Moors, and Christians: Festivals of Reconquest in Mexico and Spain.* Austin: University of Texas Press.

Harvey, Leonard. 2005. *Muslims in Spain, 1500 to 1614.* Chicago: University of Chicago Press.

Hemment, Julie. 2007. *Empowering Women in Russia: Activism, Aid, and NGOs.* Bloomington: Indiana University Press.

Henkel, Heiko. 2006. "'The Journalists of Jylland-Posten Are a Bunch of Reactionary Provocateurs': The Danish Cartoon Controversy and the Self-Image of Europe." *Radical Philosophy* 137: 1–5.

Hessini, Leila. 1994. "Wearing Hijab in Contemporary Morocco: Choice and Identity." In *Reconstructing Gender in the Middle East*, edited by Fatima Gocek and Balaghi Shiva, 40–56. New York: Columbia University Press.

Herzfeld, Michael. 1987. "'As in Your Own House': Hospitality, Ethnography, and the Stereotype of Mediterranean Society." In *Honor and Shame and the Unity of the Mediterranean*, edited by David Gilmore, 75–89. Washington, DC: American Anthropological Association.

———. 2004. "Intimating Culture: Local Contexts and International Power." In *Off Stage/On Display: Intimacy and Ethnography in the Age of Public Culture*, edited by Andrew Shryock, 317–335. Stanford, CA: Stanford University Press.

———. 2005. *Cultural Intimacy: Social Poetics in the Nation-State*, 2nd ed. New York: Routledge.

———. 2009. *Evicted from Eternity: The Restructuring of Modern Rome*. Chicago: University of Chicago Press.

Hirschkind, Charles. 2006. *The Ethical Soundscape: Cassette Sermons and Islamic Counterpublics*. New York: Columbia University Press.

———. 2011. "Religious Difference and Democratic Pluralism: Some Recent Debates and Frameworks." *Temenos* 44(1): 123–138.

Hirschkind, Charles, and Saba Mahmood. 2002. "Feminism, the Taliban, and Politics of Counter-Insurgency." *Anthropological Quarterly* 75(2): 339–354.

Ho, Engseng. 2006. *The Graves of Tarim: Genealogy and Mobility across the Indian Ocean*. Berkeley: University of California Press.

Holmes, Seth. 2013. *Fresh Fruit, Broken Bodies: Migrant Farmworkers in the United States*. Berkeley: University of California Press.

Hondagneu-Sotelo, Pierrette. 2001. *Doméstica: Immigrant Workers Cleaning and Caring in the Shadows of Affluence*. Berkeley: University of California Press.

Hoodfar, Homa. 1997. "The Veil in Their Minds and on Our Heads: Veiling Practices and Muslim Women." In *The Politics of Culture in the Shadow of Capital*, edited by Lisa Lowe and David Lloyd, 248–279. Durham, NC: Duke University Press.

Howe, Marvine. 2012. *Al-Andalus Rediscovered: Iberia's New Muslims*. New York: Columbia University Press.

Howell, Sally, and Andrew Shryock. 2003. "Cracking Down on Diaspora: Arab Detroit and America's 'War on Terror.'" *Anthropological Quarterly* 76(3): 443–462.

Hunt, Lynn. 1996. *The French Revolution and Human Rights: A Brief Documentary History*. Boston: St. Martin's Press.

Huntington, Samuel. 1996. *Clash of Civilizations: Remaking of World Order*. New York: Touchstone.

Huyssen, Andreas. 2000. "Present Pasts: Media, Politics, Amnesia." *Public Culture* 12(1): 21–38.

———. 2003. *Present Pasts: Urban Palimpsests and the Politics of Memory*. Stanford, CA: Stanford University Press.

INE. 2008. *Instituto Nacional de Estadística*. Volume 2009. http://www.ine.es.

Inhorn, Marcia. 2011. "Globalization and Gametes: Reproductive 'Tourism,' Islamic Bioethics, and Middle Eastern Modernity." *Anthropology and Medicine* 18(1): 87–103.

———. 2012. *The New Arab Man: Emergent Masculinities, Technologies, and Islam in the Middle East*. Princeton, NJ: Princeton University Press.

Irving, Washington. 2007 [1851]. *The Alhambra*. Book Jungle. Victoria, Canada: Russel Books.

Jamal, Amaney, and Nadine Naber, eds. 2008. *Race and Arab Americans before and after 9/11: From Invisible Citizens to Visible Subjects*. Syracuse, NY: Syracuse University Press.

Jouili, Jeanette. 2015. *Pious Practice and Secular Constraints: Women in the Islamic Revival in Europe*. Stanford, CA: Stanford University Press.

Kamen, Henry. 1985. *Inquisition and Society in Spain*. London: Weidenfeld and Nicolson.

Khater, Akram. 2001. *Inventing Home: Emigration, Gender, and the Middle Class in Lebanon*. Berkeley: University of California Press.

Keane, Webb. 2007. *Christian Moderns: Freedom and Fetish in the Mission Encounter*. Berkeley: University of California Press.

Kelly, Dorothy. 2000. "Selling Spanish 'Otherness' since the 1960s." In *Contemporary Spanish Cultural Studies*, edited by Barry Jordan and Rikki Morgan-Tamosunas, 29–37. London: Arnold.

Kiliç, Sevgi. 2008. "The British Veil Wars." *Social Politics: International Studies in Gender, State and Society* 15: 433–454.

Kleinman, Julie. 2014. "Adventures in Infrastructure: Making an African Hub in Paris." *City and Society* 26(3): 286–307.

Labajo, Joaquina. 2003. "Body and Voice: The Construction of Gender in Flamenco." In *Music and Gender: Perspectives from the Mediterranean*, edited by Tullia Magrini, 67–86. Chicago: University of Chicago Press.

Labanyi, Jo. 2007. "Memory and Modernity in Democratic Spain: The Difficulty of Coming to Terms with the Spanish Civil War." *Poetics Today* 28(2): 89–116.

Lea, Henry. 1988. *A History of the Inquisition of Spain*. New York: Macmillan.

Leichtman, Mara. 2015. *Shi'i Cosmopolitanisms in Africa: Lebanese Migration and Religious Conversion in Senegal*. Bloomington: Indiana University Press.

Leinaweaver, Jessaca B. 2013. *Adoptive Migration: Raising Latinos in Spain*. Durham, NC: Duke University Press.

Leman, Johan, Christiane Stallaert, and Iman Lechkar. 2010. "Ethnic Dimensions in the Discourse and Identity Strategies of European Converts to Islam in Andalusia and Flanders." *Journal of Ethnic and Migration Studies* 36(9): 1483–1497.

Lemon, Alaina. 2000. *Between Two Fires: Gypsy Performance and Romani Memory from Pushkin to Postsocialism*. Durham, NC: Duke University Press.

———. 2002. "Without a 'Concept'"? Race as a Discursive Practice." *Slavic Review* 61(1): 54–61.

Libertad Digital. 2011. "Marruecos Exige a España que le Entregue la Mitad de los Beneficios de la Alhambra." Libertad Digital. August 9. http://www.libertaddigital .com/sociedad/2011-08-09/marruecos-exige-a-espana-que-le-entregue-la-mitad-de -los-beneficios-de-la-alhambra-1276432102/.

Liu, Morgan. 2012. *Under Solomon's Throne: Uzbek Visions of Renewal in Osh*. Pittsburgh, PA: University of Pittsburgh Press.

López García, Bernabé. 2006. "La Inmigración de Magrebíes y Africanos. Asumir la Vecindad." In *De la España que Emigra a la España que Acoge*, edited by Alicia Alted Vigil and Almudena Asenjo, 480–489. Madrid: Caja Duero-Fundación Largo Caballero.

Low, Setha. 2000. *On the Plaza: The Politics of Public Space and Culture*. Austin: University of Texas Press.

Lucht, Hans. 2012. *Darkness before Daybreak: African Migrants Living on the Margins in Southern Italy Today.* Berkeley: University of California Press.

Madariaga, María Rosa. 2006. *Los Moros que Trajo Franco: La Intervención de Tropas Coloniales en la Guerra Civil Española*, 2nd ed. Barcelona: Ediciones Martínez Roca.

Maddox, Richard. 2004a. *The Best of All Possible Islands: Seville's Universal Exposition, the New Spain, and the New Europe.* New York: SUNY Press.

———. 2004b. "Intimacy and Hegemony in the New Europe: The Politics of Culture at Seville's Universal Exposition." In *Off Stage/On Display: Intimacy and Ethnography in the Age of Public Culture*, edited by Andrew Shryock, 131–154. Stanford, CA: Stanford University Press.

Mahdavi, Pardis. 2010. "The 'Trafficking' of Persians: Labor, Migration, and Traffic in Dubayy." In *Comparative Studies of South Asia, Africa and the Middle East* 30(3): 533–546.

Mahmood, Saba. 2005. *Politics of Piety: The Islamic Revival and the Feminist Subject.* Princeton, NJ: Princeton University Press.

Malkki, Lisa. 1996. "Speechless Emissaries: Refugees, Humanitarianism, and Dehistoricization." *Cultural Anthropology* 11(3): 377–404.

Mandel, Ruth. 2008. *Cosmopolitan Anxieties: Turkish Challenges to Citizenship and Belonging in Germany.* Durham, NC: Duke University Press.

Marvin, Garry. 1984. "The Cockfight in Andalusia, Spain: Images of the Truly Male." *Anthropological Quarterly* 57(2): 60–70.

McDonald, Maryon. 1996. "'Unity in Diversity': Some Tensions in the Construction of Europe." *Social Anthropology* 4(1): 47–60.

McIntosh, Laurie. 2015. "Impossible Presence: Race, Nation, and the Cultural Politics of 'Being Norwegian.'" *Ethnic and Racial Studies* 38(2): 309–325.

McMurray, David. 2000. *In and Out of Morocco: Smuggling and Migration in a Frontier Boomtown.* Minneapolis: University of Minnesota Press.

Medina, Julio Cabrera, and Juan Carlos de Pablos. 2002. "Metamorfosis del Albaicín (Granada): Del Aislamiento a la Interdependencia." *Cuadernos Geográficos* 32: 73–96.

Meneley, Anne. 2007. "Fashions and Fundamentalisms in Fin-de-Siecle Yemen: Chador Barbie and Islamic Socks." *Cultural Anthropology* 22(2): 214–243.

Menócal, María Rosa. 1987. *The Arabic Role in Medieval Literary History: A Forgotten Heritage.* Philadelphia: University of Pennsylvania Press.

———. 2002. *The Ornament of the World: How Muslims, Jews, and Christians Created a Culture of Tolerance in Medieval Spain.* New York: Back Bay Books.

MESS. 2015. "Extranjeros Residentes en España a 31 de Diciembre de 2015. Principales Resultados." Ministerio de Empleo y Seguridad Social de España. http://extranjeros.empleo.gob.es/es/Estadisticas/operaciones/con-certificado/index.html.

Mintz, Jerome. 1997. *Carnival Song and Society: Gossip, Sexuality, and Creativity in Andalusia.* Oxford: Berg.

Mitchell, Timothy. 1990. *Passional Culture: Emotion, Religion, and Society in Southern Spain.* Philadelphia: University of Pennsylvania Press.

Modood, Tariq. 2005. *Multicultural Politics: Racism, Ethnicity, and Muslims in Britain.* Minneapolis: University of Minnesota Press.

Mozo González, Carmen, and Fernando Tena Díaz. 2003. *Antropología de los Géneros en Andalucía: De Viajeros, Antropólogos y Sexualidad.* Sevilla: Mergablum.

Muehlebach, Andrea. 2012. *The Moral Neoliberal: Welfare and Citizenship in Italy.* Chicago: University of Chicago Press.

Murphy, Michael. 1983. "Emotional Confrontations between Sevillano Fathers and Sons: Cultural Foundations and Social Consequences." *American Ethnologist* 10(4): 650–664.

Naficy, Hamid. 2001. *An Accented Cinema: Exilic and Diasporic Filmmaking.* Princeton, NJ: Princeton University Press.

Nair, Parvati. 2005. *Rumbo al Norte: Inmigración y Movimientos Culturales entre el Magreb y España.* Barcelona: Ediciones Bellaterra.

Nash, Mary, Rosa Tello, and Núria Benach, eds. 2005. *Inmigración, Género y Espacios Urbanos: Los Retos de la Diversidad.* Barcelona: Ediciones Bellaterra.

Newman, Andrew. 2015. *Landscape of Discontent: Urban Sustainability in Immigrant Paris.* Minneapolis: University of Minnesota Press.

Nirenberg, David. 2004. "Enmity and Assimilation: Jews, Christians, and Converts in Medieval Spain." *Common Knowledge* 9(1): 137–155.

Northrop, Douglas. 2004. *Veiled Empire: Gender and Power in Stalinist Central Asia.* Ithaca, NY: Cornell University Press.

Okin, Susan. 1999. *Is Multiculturalism Bad for Women?* Princeton, NJ: Princeton University Press.

Ong, Aihwa. 2003. *Buddha Is Hiding: Refugees, Citizenship, the New America.* Berkeley: University of California Press.

Ortbals, Candice. 2008. "Subnational Politics in Spain: New Avenues for Feminist Policy-making and Activism." *Politics and Gender* 4: 93–119.

———. 2009. "The Potential of Local Women's Associations in Andalusia: Pursuing Culture, Enriching Lives and Constructing Equality." *South European Society and Politics* 4: 203–223.

Ossman, Susan, and Susan Terrio. 2006. "The French Riots: Questioning Spaces of Surveillance and Sovereignty." *International Migration* 44(2): 5–21.

Özyürek, Esra. 2005. "The Politics of Cultural Unification, Secularism, and Islam in the New Europe." *American Ethnologist* 32(4): 509–512.

———. 2009. "Convert Alert: German Muslims and Turkish Christians as Threats to Security in the New Europe." *Comparative Studies in Society and History* 51(1): 91–116.

———. 2014. *Being German, Becoming Muslim: Race, Religion and Conversion in the New Europe.* Princeton, NJ: Princeton University Press.

Pack, Sasha. 2006. *Tourism and Dictatorship: Europe's Peaceful Invasion of Franco's Spain.* New York: Palgrave Macmillan.

Paetzold, Christopher. 2009. "Singing beneath the Alhambra: The North African and Arabic Past and Present in Contemporary Andalusian Music." *Journal of Spanish Cultural Studies* 10(2): 207–223.

Pardue, Derek. 2014. "Kriolu Scenes in Lisbon: Where Migration Experiences and Housing Policy Meet." *City and Society* 26(3): 308–330.

Partridge, Damani. 2012. *Hypersexuality and Headscarves: Race, Sex, and Citizenship in the New Germany.* Bloomington: Indiana University Press.

Pelkmans, Mathijs. 2010. "Religious Crossings and Conversions on the Muslim-Christian Frontier in Georgia and Kyrgyzstan." *Anthropological Journal of European Culture* 19(2): 109–128.

Peteet, Julie. 2005. *Landscapes of Hope and Despair: Palestinian Refugee Camps.* Philadelphia: University of Pennsylvania Press.

Pham, Theresa Thao. 2014. *Moroccan Immigrant Women in Spain.* Boulder, CO: Lexington Books.

Pitt-Rivers, Julian. 1961. *The People of the Sierra*. Chicago: University of Chicago Press.

———. 1966. "Honour and Social Status." In *Honour and Shame: The Values of Mediterranean Society*, edited by Jean Peristiany, 19–78. London: Weidenfeld and Nicolson.

Potuoğlu-Cook, Öykü. 2006. "Beyond the Glitter: Belly Dance and Neoliberal Gentrification in Istanbul." *Cultural Anthropology* 21(4): 633–660.

Povinelli, Elizabeth. 2002. *The Cunning of Recognition: Indigenous Alterities and the Making of Australian Multiculturalism*. Durham, NC: Duke University Press.

Puar, Jasbir. 2007. *Terrorist Assemblages: Homonationalism in Queer Times*. Durham, NC: Duke University Press.

Puar, Jasbir, and Amit Raj. 2002. "Monster, Terrorist, Fag: The War on Terrorism and the Production of Docile Patriots." *Social Text* 20(3): 117–148.

Raissiguier, Catherine. 2010. *Reinventing the Republic: Gender, Migration, and Citizenship in France*. Stanford, CA: Stanford University Press.

Ramadan, Tariq. 2004. *Western Muslims and the Future of Islam*. Oxford: Oxford University Press.

Ramírez, Ángela. 2004. "Las Mujeres Marroquíes en España a lo Largo de los Noventa." In *Atlas de la Inmigración Marroquí en España*, edited by Bárnabe López García and Mohamed Berriane, 223–224. Taller de Estudios Internacionales Mediterráneos. Madrid: Universidad Autónoma de Madrid Ediciones.

Ramos, Alberto. 2010. "Indolencia a los Andaluces." *Diario de Cádiz*. January 30. Online edition. http://www.diariodecadiz.es/article/opinion/618877/indolencia/los/andaluces.html.

Rivera, Augustín. 2009. "Griñán Crea un Plan para Desterrar los Tópicos de la Andalucía Subsidiada." *El Confidencial*. September 9. Online edition. http://www.elconfidencial.com/espana/2009-09-09/grinan-crea-un-plan-para-desterrar-los-topicos-de-la-andalucia-subsidiada_421205/.

Robbins, Joel. 2011. "Crypto-Religion and the Study of Cultural Mixtures: Anthropology, Value, and the Nature of Syncretism." *Journal of the American Academy of Religion* 79(2): 408–424.

Rogozen-Soltar, Mikaela. 2007. "Al-Andalus in Andalusia: Negotiating Moorish History and Regional Identity in Southern Spain." *Anthropological Quarterly* 80(3): 863–886.

———. 2012a. "Ambivalent Inclusion: Anti-Racism and Racist Gatekeeping in Andalusia's Immigrant NGOs." *Journal of the Royal Anthropological Institute* 18(3): 633–651.

———. 2012b. "Managing Muslim Visibility: Conversion, Immigration, and Spanish Imaginaries of Islam." *American Anthropologist* 114(4): 611–623.

———. 2016. "'We Suffered in Our Bones Just Like Them': Comparing Migrations at the Margins of Europe." *Comparative Studies in Society and History* 58(4): 880–907.

Rome, Adam. 2008. "Nature Wars, Culture Wars: Immigration and Environmental Reform in the Progressive Era." *Environmental History* 13(3): 432–53.

Root, Deborah. 1988. "Speaking Christian: Orthodoxy and Difference in Sixteenth-Century Spain." *Representations* 23: 118–134.

Rosello, Mireille. 2001. *Post-colonial Hospitality: The Immigrant as Guest*. Stanford, CA: Stanford University Press.

Roseman, Sharon. 1996. "How We Built the Road: The Politics of Memory in Rural Galicia." *American Ethnologist* 23(4): 836–860.

Roseman, Sharon, and Wayne Fife. 2008. "Souvenirs and Cultural Politics in Santiago de Compostela." *International Journal of Iberian Studies* 21(2): 109–130.

Roseman, Sharon, and Shawn Parkhurst. 2008. *Recasting Culture and Space in Iberian Contexts*. Albany: SUNY Press.

Rosón Lorente, Javier. 2008. *¿El Retorno de Tariq? Comunidades Etnorreligiosas en el Albayzín Granadino*. Granada: Universidad de Granada.

Rotenberg, Robert. 1992. *Time and Order in Metropolitan Vienna: A Seizure of Schedules*. Washington, DC: Smithsonian Institution Press.

Roy, Olivier. 2010. *Holy Ignorance: When Religion and Culture Part Ways*. New York: Columbia University Press.

Saharso, Sawatri, and Doutje Lettinga. 2008. "Contentious Citizenship: Policies and Debates on the Veil in the Netherlands." *Social Politics: International Studies in Gender, State and Society* 15: 455–480.

Said, Edward. 1978. *Orientalism*. New York: Vintage Books.

Salih, Ruba. 2003. *Gender in Transnationalism: Home, Longing and Belonging among Moroccan Migrant Women*. London: Routledge.

Sánchez-Albornoz, Claudio. 1976. *España: Un Enigma Histórico*. Barcelona: Editora y Distribuidora Hispanoamericana.

Sawalha, Aseel. 2010. *Reconstructing Beirut: Memory and Space in a Postwar Arab City*. Austin: University of Texas Press.

Scott, Joan W. 2007. *The Politics of the Veil*. Princeton, NJ: Princeton University Press.

Secor, Anna. 2002. "The Veil and Urban Space in Istanbul: Women's Dress, Mobility and Islamic Knowledge." *Gender, Place and Culture: A Journal of Feminist Geography* 9(1): 5–22.

Seizer, Susan. 2005. *Stigmas of the Tamil Stage: An Ethnography of Special Drama Artists in South India*. Durham, NC: Duke University Press.

Selby, Jennifer. 2012. *Questioning French Secularism: Gender Politics and Islam in a Parisian Suburb*. New York: Palgrave Macmillan.

Serra i Salame, Carles. 2004. "Rhetoric of Exclusion and Racist Violence in a Catalan Secondary School." *Anthropology and Education Quarterly* 35(4): 433–450.

Shannon, Jonathan. 2015. *Performing Al-Andalus: Music and Nostalgia across the Mediterranean*. Bloomington: Indiana University Press.

Shore, Cris. 2000. *Building Europe: The Cultural Politics of European Integration*. New York: Routledge.

Shryock, Andrew. 2004a. "The New Jordanian Hospitality: House, Host, and Guest in the Culture of Public Display." *Comparative Studies in Society and History* 46: 35–62.

———, ed. 2004b. *Off Stage/On Display: Intimacy and Ethnography in the Age of Public Culture*. Stanford, CA: Stanford University Press.

———, ed. 2010. *Islamophobia/Islamophilia: Beyond the Politics of Enemy and Friend*. Bloomington: Indiana University Press.Shryock, Andrew, Sally Howell, and Nabeel Abraham, eds. 2011. *Arab Detroit 9/11: Life in the Terror Decade*. Detroit, MI: Wayne State University Press.

Sieg, Katrin. 2010. "Cosmopolitan Empire: Central and Eastern Europeans at the Eurovision Song Contest." *European Journal of Cultural Studies* 16: 244–263.

Silverstein, Paul. 2000. "Sporting Faith: Islam, Soccer, and the French Nation-State." *Social Text* 18(4): 25–53.

———. 2004. *Algeria in France: Transpolitics, Race, and Nation.* Bloomington: Indiana University Press.

———. 2005. "Immigrant Racialization and the New Savage Slot: Race, Migration, and Immigration in the New Europe." *Annual Reviews in Anthropology* (34): 363–384.

———. 2011. "Masquerade Politics: Race, Islam and the Scale of Amazigh Activism in Southeastern Morocco." *Nations and Nationalism* 17(1): 65–84.

———. 2013. "The Pitfalls of Transnational Consciousness: Amazigh Activism as a Scalar Dilemma." *Journal of North African Studies* 18(5): 768–778.

Slyomovics, Susan. 1998. *The Object of Memory: Arab and Jew Narrate the Palestinian Village.* Philadelphia: University of Pennsylvania Press.

Soifer, Maya. 2009. "Beyond Convivencia: Critical Reflections on the Historiography of Interfaith Relations in Christian Spain." *Journal of Medieval Iberian Studies* 1(1): 19–35.

Soto Bermant, Laia. 2007. *The Myth of Al Andalus: A Study of Spanish Identity.* Anthropology Department, Oxford University.

Sotomayor Blázquez, Carmen. 2005. "El Moro Traidor, El Moro Engañado: Variantes del Estereotipo en el Romancero Republicano." *Anaquel de Estudios Árabes* 16: 233–249.

Spivak, Gayatri. 1994. "Can the Subaltern Speak?" In *Colonial Discourse and Postcolonial Theory,* edited by Patrick Williams and Laura Chrisman, 66–111. New York: Columbia University Press.

Stolcke, Verena. 1995. "Talking Culture: New Boundaries, New Rhetorics of Exclusion in Europe." *Cultural Anthropology* 36(1): 1–24.

Stoler, Ann Laura. 1995. *Race and the Education of Desire: Foucault's History of Sexuality and the Colonial Order of Things.* Durham, NC: Duke University Press.

Suárez-Navaz, Liliana. 2004. *Rebordering the Mediterranean: Boundaries and Citizenship in Southern Europe.* New York: Berghahn Books.

———. 2006. "Un Nuevo Actor Migratorio: Jóvenes, Rutas y Ritos Juveniles Transnacionales." In *Menores Tras la Frontera: Otra Inmigración que Aguarda,* edited by Ángeles Arjona Garrido et al., 17–50. Barcelona: Icaria Editorial.

Sundberg, Juanita. 2008. "'Trash-Talk' and the Production of Quotidian Geopolitical Boundaries in the USA-Mexico Borderlands." *Social and Cultural Geography* 9 (8): 871–890.

Tarlo, Emma, and Annelies Moors, eds. 2015. *Islamic Fashion and Anti-Fashion: New Perspectives from Europe and North America.* London: Bloomsbury.

Terrio, Susan. 2009. *Judging Mohammed: Juvenile Delinquency, Immigration, and Exclusion at the Paris Palace of Justice.* Stanford, CA: Stanford University Press.

Threlfall, Monica. 1998. "State Feminism or Party Feminism?: Feminist Politics and the Spanish Institute of Women." *European Journal of Women's Studies* 5: 63–93.

———. 2007. "Explaining Gender Parity Representation in Spain: The Internal Dynamics of Parties." *Journal of West European Politics* 30(5): 1068–1095.

Ticktin, Miriam. 2011. *Casualties of Care: Immigration and the Politics of Humanitarianism in France.* Berkeley: University of California Press.

Tilly, Charles. 1994. "Afterword: Political Memories in Space and Time." In *Remapping Memory: The Politics of Timespace,* edited by Jonathan Boyarin, 241–256. Minneapolis: University of Minnesota Press.

Tofiño-Quesada, Ignacio. 2003. "Spanish Orientalism: Uses of the Past in Spain's Colonization in Africa." *Comparative Studies of South Asia, Africa and the Middle East* 23(1/2): 141–148.

Tremlett, Giles. 2008. "Foreword: 'Welcome to Moorishland.'" In *In the Light of Medieval Spain: Islam, the West, and the Relevance of the Past*, edited by Simon Doubleday and David Coleman, xi–xx. New York: Palgrave Macmillan.

Tsing, Anna. 2005. *Friction: An Ethnography of Global Connection*. Princeton, NJ: Princeton University Press.

Tucker, Joshua. 2014. "Sounding the Latin Transatlantic: Music, Integration, and Ambivalent Ethnogenesis in Spain." *Comparative Studies in Society and History* 56(4): 902–933.

UCIDE. 2012. "Estudio Demográfico de la Población Musulmana." *Unión de Comunidades Islámicas de España*. http://oban.multiplexor.es/estademograf.pdf.

Urla, Jacqueline. 2012. *Reclaiming Basque: Language, Nation, and Cultural Activism*. Reno: University of Nevada Press.

Vale Music Spain S.L. 2002. "Corazón Latino." David Bisbal. Released August 20, 2002.

Vallejo, Mar. 2009. "Vecinos del Albaicín Avisan con Carteles del Peligro de Atracos." *El Ideal*, March 27. Online edition. http://www.ideal.es/granada/20090327/granada/vecinos-albaicin-avisan-carteles-20090327.html.

Vallejo, S. 2011. "Una Noticia Falsa Sobre la Alhambra Abre un Conflicto Sentimental con Marruecos." *Granada Hoy*. August 11. Online edition. http://www.granadahoy.com/article/granada/1040359/una/noticia/falsa/sobre/la/alhambra/abre/conflicto/sentimental/con/marruecos.html.

Van der Veer, Peter. 2006. "Pim Fortuyn, Theo van Gogh, and the Politics of Tolerance in the Netherlands." *Public Culture* 18(1): 111–124.

Van Nieuwkerk, Karin, ed. 2006. *Women Embracing Islam: Gender and Conversion in the West*. Austin: University of Texas Press.

VNN Forums. 2007. "Al-Murabitun: Concealed [White] Racialism and Eugenics through Islam (Incl. Video)." May 15. http://vnnforum.com/showthread.php?t=48459.

Volpp, Leti. 2011. "Framing Cultural Difference: Immigrant Women and Discourses of Tradition." *Differences* 22(1): 90–110.

Washabaugh, William. 2012. *Flamenco Music and National Identity in Spain*. Burlington, VT: Ashgate.

Werbner, Pnina. 2002. *Imagined Diasporas among Manchester Muslims: The Public Performance of Pakistani Transnational Identity Politics*. Santa Fe, NM: School of American Research Press.

Woolard, Kathryn. 2013. "The Seventeenth-Century Debate over the Origins of Spanish: Links of Language Ideology to the Morisco Question." In *A Political History of Spanish: The Making of a Language*, edited by José del Valle, 61–76. Cambridge: Cambridge University Press.

Zapata-Barrero, Ricard. 2006. "Immigration to Spain: The Case of Moroccans." In *Metropolis Network and Foundation for Population Report, Migration and Environment* 1–30.

Zontini, Elisabetta. 2004. "Immigrant Women in Barcelona: Coping with the Consequences of Transnational Lives." *Journal of Ethnic and Migration Studies* 30(6): 1113–1144.

INDEX

inclusion/exclusion (*continued*)
and, xiv–xvii; margins of Europe and,
28; migrants and, 3–4, 5, 23, 77, 81,
227–228; migration policies and, 228;
Moroccans and, 143, 147, 148–149; multiculturalism and, 23; Muslims and, 3–4,
23–24, 76–78, 186, 227, 228, 229, 237;
Polígono and, 143, 147, 156; public sociality and, 227; racialization and, 117; social
encounters and, 237; Spain and, 81; tourism and, 136; unequal multiculturalism
and, 3–4; urban landscape and, 227;
women and, 38; zones of encounter and,
36. *See also* belonging/nonbelonging;
rootedness/remoteness
Infante, Blas, 25–26, 30, 96
Inquisition: Arabs and the, 114n6; arraigo
(rootedness) and the, 80; conversion
and the, 83; costumes and the, 74n5, 94;
Jews and the, 51–52, 206; Moroccans
and the, 45, 119; Muslims and the, 24–25,
51–52, 93, 206–207; pork/alcohol and
the, 206–207; racism and the, 55, 56
interfaith encounters, 196, 222–223, 226,
227, 228, 235–236. *See also convivencia*
(interfaith harmony)
Irving, Washington, 25, 26, 30
Islam, 1–38; *al-Andalus* (medieval Muslim
Spain) and, 168, 183, 226; *Albayzín* and, 1,
115–117, 131–132, 155; Andalusia and, xvii,
23, 28–29, 36, 37, 42–43, 54–55, 71, 72, 76,
82, 96–97, 112, 169, 222, 225–226, 228, 231,
232–233, 237–238; Andalusian identity
and, 37, 96–97; Arabs and, 184–185; arraigo (rootedness) and, 80; Bulgaria and,
183, 210; Catholicism and, 14–15, 39n3, 55,
88; Christianity and, 13–16; conversion
and, 83–84; converts and, 5, 6, 7–8, 76, 82,
83–84, 107, 156, 159, 160, 166–167, 178, 187,
226, 230, 237; *convivencia* (interfaith harmony) and, xv–xvi; cultural authenticity
and, 183; culture-free Islam, 38, 159, 179–
180, 181–186; democratic transition and,
126; Europe and, xvii, 7, 18, 23–24, 38, 56,
73, 182, 183, 184–185, 228–229, 238; extremism and, 178; feminism and, 212–213,
214–215; flamenco and, 96–97; gender

and, 32–33, 38, 86–88, 166, 185, 186, 187,
192–193, 200, 201, 215, 222; Granada and,
xvi–xvii, 3, 5, 6, 8, 16–21, 23–24, 28–31,
33, 37–38, 42, 44, 46, 47, 92, 112, 170, 181,
232–233; *Granadinos* and, 12, 29, 46, 88,
226, 234; headscarves/hijabs and, 19–20,
212, 213–214, 223n2; hybridity and, 18;
inclusion/exclusion and, xvi–xvii, 227;
Martínez, Belén and, 84–89, 231; Maurophilia and, 131; media bias and, 161–162,
162–163; Mediterranean and, 28–29, 73;
migrants and, 16, 156, 159, 160, 164–167,
187, 226; migration and, 12, 16, 156n2, 186,
227–228; Moroccans and, 180, 181, 184–
186; Murabitun converts and, 89–98;
Muslims and, 90–91, 158–167, 182–183;
North Africa and, xvii; Polígono and,
150; public discourse and, 162–163; racialization and, 20–21, 116–124, 169; representation and, 159–167; secularism and,
13–16; Spain and, 16, 24, 34, 50, 52–53, 73,
79, 80, 82, 88, 92, 93, 98, 101, 117, 173–174,
183, 226, 228, 235–236; stereotypes and,
223; terrorism and, 184, 236; tourism and,
23–24, 30, 237; United States and, 183; *Yama'a Islámica de al-Andalus* (al-Andalus
Muslim Community), 31. *See also* Islamophilia; Islamophobia
Islam, Catholicism, and secularism nexus,
13–15, 39n3
Islamic Commission of Spain, 80
Islamic terrorism, 161–162. *See also* global
war on terror; terrorism
Islamic tourism. *See* tourism
Islamophilia, 21–28, 235–238; *Albayzín* and,
37, 115, 125, 128, 131, 155, 234; Andalusia
and, 228; everyday historiography and,
44; Granada and, 3, 30, 116–117, 186;
inclusion/exclusion and, 50–51; Islamophobia and, 237; Muslims and, 22, 187;
representation and, 227; unequal multiculturalism and, 227. *See also* belonging/
nonbelonging; rootedness/remoteness
Islamophobia, 21–28, 235–238; *Albayzín* and, 125; Andalusia and, 232;
Europe and, 186, 187; everyday historiography and, 44; Granada and, 3, 21, 28, 30,